How to Do
Everything™

Kindle Fire

About the Author

Jason R. Rich (www.JasonRich.com) is the bestselling author of 52 books, covering a wide range of topics. Some of his recently published books include *How to Do Everything: Digital Photography* (McGraw-Hill, 2011), *How to Do Everything: iCloud* (McGraw-Hill, 2012), *Your iPad 2 at Work* (Que, 2011), *Using iPhone: iOS 5 Edition* (Que, 2012), and *iPad and iPhone Tips and Tricks* (Que, 2011).

To read more than 60 feature-length how-to articles about the iPhone and iPad, visit www.iOSArticles.com. Jason's work also appears in a wide range of other national magazines, major daily newspaper, and popular websites. You can follow Jason on Twitter (@JasonRich7).

About the Technical Editor

Guy Hart-Davis is the author of *How to Do Everything: iPhone 4S, How to Do Everything: Samsung Galaxy Tab, iPhone Geekery,* and about 70 other books. His website is at www.ghdbooks.com.

How to Do Everything™

Kindle Fire

Jason R. Rich

New York Chicago San Francisco Lisbon
London Madrid Mexico City Milan New Delhi
San Juan Seoul Singapore Sydney Toronto

The McGraw·Hill Companies

Cataloging-in-Publication Data is on file with the Library of Congress

McGraw-Hill books are available at special quantity discounts to use as premiums and sales promotions, or for use in corporate training programs. To contact a representative, please e-mail us at bulksales@mcgraw-hill.com.

How to Do Everything™: Kindle Fire

Cover image courtesy of Jason R. Rich

1234567890   QFR QFR   1098765432

ISBN   978-0-07-179360-5
MHID   0-07-179360-7

Sponsoring Editor	**Technical Editor**	**Composition**
Megg Morin	Guy Hart-Davis	Cenveo Publisher Services
Editorial Supervisor	**Copy Editor**	**Illustration**
Jody McKenzie	Lisa McCoy	Cenveo Publisher Services
Project Manager	**Proofreader**	**Art Director, Cover**
Vastavikta Sharma, Cenveo Publisher Services	Claire Splan	Jeff Weeks
	Indexer	**Cover Designer**
Acquisitions Coordinator	Claire Splan	Jeff Weeks
Stephanie Evans		
	Production Supervisor	
	George Anderson	

This book is dedicated to my niece, Natalie Shay Emsley Skehan, who was born on December 6, 2011, as I was putting the finishing touches on the manuscript for this book. Congratulations to Melissa and Rob!

Contents at a Glance

Contents

Acknowledgments

Thanks to Megg Morin at McGraw-Hill for inviting me to work on this book. Thanks also to Stephanie Evans, Guy Hart-Davis, Vastavikta Sharma, Claire Splan, Lisa McCoy, and everyone else who contributed their talents and publishing know-how as this book was being created.

I am also grateful for the assistance of Patrick Miltner, the founder and managing editor of Tabletorials.com, for his assistance in capturing the screen shots you see featured in this book. If you're interested in learning more about the technical aspects of your Kindle Fire, Tabetorials.com is worth checking out.

Thanks also to my friends and family for their endless support and encouragement.

The Publisher would like to thank Nicole Nagorsky at Amazon for her help with the cover.

Introduction

Tablets have been around for several years now. However, what's kept them from becoming massively popular has been their price tags, lack of easy accessibility to content, and that the devices have difficult-to-use user interfaces or operating systems. Recently, that's all changed. Apple released the original iPad and later the iPad 2, which made tablets easy to use and made a massive amount of content available, but the price of even the most basic iPad 2 continues to be high.

With the release of the Kindle Fire from Amazon, consumers now have easy access to an inexpensive, easy-to-use tablet that is supported by an incredible amount of content in the form of eBooks, digital editions of newspapers and magazines, apps, music, TV shows, movies, audiobooks, games, and more.

With its built-in, seven-inch touch screen display and Wi-Fi Internet connectivity, the Kindle Fire tablet also offers easy access to the Internet, allowing users to surf the Web, manage multiple e-mail accounts, and access online social networking sites (like Facebook and Twitter) directly from their tablet.

Beyond all of the apps that come preinstalled on the Amazon Kindle Fire, the functionality of this highly portable, handheld device increases dramatically when you begin adding third-party apps acquired from the Amazon App Store. For example, between the preinstalled and optional third-party apps available for the Kindle Fire, you can access, view, edit, and share Microsoft Office files; view PDF files; edit, view, and share digital photos; manage your schedule; maintain a detailed contacts database; enjoy multimedia content; read eBooks and digital publications; listen to music; keep track of personal or work-related expenses; shop online for virtually any product and save money; and play hundreds of exciting, challenging, and fun games.

How to Do Everything: Kindle Fire offers an easy-to-understand introduction to your new Kindle Fire and will help you set up, customize, and begin using your device very quickly, even if you do not consider yourself to be a technologically savvy person. You'll then discover how to use all of the apps that come preinstalled on your tablet, plus learn about some of the more popular third-party apps you can install on the Kindle Fire to enhance its capabilities.

First and foremost, the Kindle Fire was designed to be a powerful eBook reader. From this book, you'll discover how to find, acquire, and read eBooks as well as digital publications using your tablet. However, when you utilize the tablet with its Wi-Fi Internet capabilities, you can also use it for a wide range of other useful tasks, which you'll learn all about from this book. The $199.00 that you've invested in your Kindle Fire provides you with a powerful, highly functional, and versatile tablet, plus it offers you an entre into the future of tablet computing.

Every day, new apps are being published for the Kindle Fire and made available from Amazon's App Store, while additional content (eBooks, digital editions of newspapers and magazines, apps, music, TV shows, movies, audiobooks, and games) is being made available directly from Amazon and other sources for use with your tablet. Meanwhile, the programmers at Amazon are constantly working to update and improve the Kindle Fire operating system, which is based on the popular Android OS. As new updates are released and automatically installed on your Internet-connected tablet, you'll continue to discover new features and functionality being added to your Kindle Fire in the near future.

In no time at all, from this book, you'll discover how to best access and utilize the functionality of your tablet, as well as the content available for it—anytime, and from virtually anywhere. In its traditionally printed form, *How to Do Everything: Kindle Fire* is the ideal how-to guide for learning how to use your tablet. However, if you acquire this book in eBook form from Amazon.com, it can also serve as the perfect reference tool as you begin utilizing your Kindle Fire while on the go.

What Does This Book Cover?

This book covers all you need to know to get the most out of your Amazon Kindle Fire. The book contains 15 chapters, broken up into two parts.

Part I, Introduction to the Kindle Fire

- Chapter 1, "See What Your Kindle Fire Is and What It Does," introduces you to your new tablet and offers an overview of what it's capable of.
- Chapter 2, "Get Started Using Your Kindle Fire," shows you how to initially set up and begin using your new tablet.
- Chapter 3, "Customize Your Kindle Fire Using the Settings Menu" explains how to personalize the various settings of your tablet in order to fully customize your Kindle Fire.
- Chapter 4, "Optional Kindle Fire Accessories," provides an overview of the optional accessories you can use with your tablet to further enhance its functionality.

Part II, Your First Week Using a Kindle Fire

- Chapter 5, "See What the Kindle Fire's Built-in Apps Are All About," will introduce you to the apps that come preinstalled on your tablet and explain how to get started using them.
- Chapter 6, "Use Amazon Silk to Surf the Web with Your Kindle Fire," explains how to utilize your tablet's Wi-Fi Internet connectivity and preinstalled Amazon Silk web browser in order to surf the Web.

- Chapter 7, "Send and Receive E-mail on Your Kindle Fire" shows you how to manage one or more, preexisting e-mail accounts from your tablet.
- Chapter 8, "Access, View, and Edit Microsoft Office Files on the Kindle Fire," introduces you to several apps that can be used to view, edit, and share Microsoft Office files and documents, as well as PDF documents.
- Chapter 9, "Experience the Kindle Fire's Multimedia Capabilities," explains how to enjoy watching TV shows, movies, and other video-based content on your tablet.
- Chapter 10, "Use Your Kindle Fire as a Powerful eBook Reader," shows you how to acquire and read eBooks from Amazon.com and enjoy reading them on your tablet.
- Chapter 11, "Read Your Favorite Newspapers and Magazines Using Newsstand," will teach you how to acquire and read the latest issues of your favorite publications on your Kindle Fire.
- Chapter 12, "Download and Listen to Music on Your Kindle Fire," offers a detailed explanation about how to transform your tablet into a powerful digital music player that gives you access to your entire digital music collection.
- Chapter 13, "Transfer Data Between Your Kindle Fire and Computer," explains the different methods for easily transferring data, documents, files, photos, music, content, and apps between your computer and tablet.
- Chapter 14, "Find and Download Apps to Your Kindle Fire," provides detailed instructions for finding, purchasing (or acquiring), installing, and using optional, third-party apps.
- Chapter 15, "Explore a Sampling of Apps for Your Kindle Fire," showcases 24 popular and highly useful apps that you can acquire from the Amazon App Store to expand the capabilities of your tablet.
- Appendix A, "What to Do If Something Goes Wrong with Your Kindle Fire," provides easy steps that can help you fix the most common problems you may encounter while using your Kindle Fire.

Conventions Used in This Book

To help you better understand some of the more complex or technical aspects of using your Kindle Fire, plus to help focus your attention on particularly useful features and functions offered by the tablet, throughout this book, you'll discover Note, Tip, and Caution paragraphs that highlight specific tidbits of useful information.

Plus, throughout this book, you'll discover How To... and Did You Know? sidebars that provide additional, topic-related information and advice that pertains to what's being covered within the chapter you're reading.

PART I

Introduction to the Kindle Fire

1

See What Your Kindle Fire Is and What It Does

HOW TO...

- Get acquainted with what the Kindle Fire is capable of
- How Kindle Fire is different from other eBook readers
- Determine if a Kindle Fire is the right tablet for you
- Discover similarities and differences between Kindle Fire, Nook Tablet, and Apple's iPads

Since it was first introduced in 2007, Amazon's Kindle eBook readers have changed the way people enjoy reading full-length books, magazines, newspapers, and a wide range of text-based content (including PDF documents). Instead of holding a physical book or publication in your hands, an eBook reader displays text on its built-in screen. A typical eBook reader, including the various Amazon Kindle models, can simultaneously hold at least 1,000 full-length books in its internal memory.

To make browsing and shopping for eBooks easy, Amazon.com created what has ultimately become the world's largest and most successful eBookstore, which you can access from any computer or directly from any Kindle eBook reader model (either through a Wi-Fi or 3G Internet connection, depending on the model).

 Note An eBook can simply be a traditionally published book that has been adapted into digital form, so it can be read on an eBook reader. When you look at the page of a printed book versus the page of a book displayed on an eBook reader's screen, what you'll see can be virtually identical. Or you can customize the look of the eBook on your tablet or eBook reader's screen. There is a vast collection of available eBooks, however, that are no longer available in printed form, or that were originally created as eBook-only editions.

FIGURE 1-1 You can access Amazon's eBook store from your computer (shown here) or directly from your Kindle.

From Amazon's eBook store (shown in Figure 1-1), millions of full-length books are available, including the latest fiction and nonfiction bestsellers from popular authors. You'll also discover eBooks from up-and-coming authors, self-published authors, and books that are considered true classics, not to mention eBooks that fall into more than two dozen different categories or genres. In addition to offering literally millions of eBooks for sale, Amazon.com offers a collection of more than two million free eBooks, including out-of-copyright titles.

More recently released eBook reader models offer a full-color screen, which has allowed book publishers and authors to begin offering children's books, cookbooks, photography books, and graphic novels in digital format. Plus, newspaper and magazine publishers have been more easily able to adapt the content of their printed publications into digital form. As a result, hundreds of popular magazines (shown in Figure 1-2) and major daily newspapers are now available on the various Kindle eBook readers.

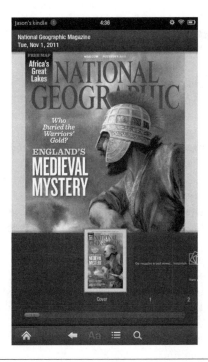

FIGURE 1-2   Read current or past issues of many popular magazines, in full color, on your Kindle Fire's screen.

So, What's an eBook Reader Anyway?

An eBook reader is a handheld device designed specifically for reading digital eBooks. While dedicated eBook readers (like the various Amazon Kindle models, except for the Kindle Fire) have been introduced by a handful of companies, the two pioneers in this product category that have achieved the most success are Amazon.com with its Kindle eBook readers and Barnes & Noble with its Nook eBook readers.

Currently, Amazon offers several different eBook reader models, as well as the Amazon Kindle Fire (shown in Figure 1-3). Each of Amazon's eBook readers has a built-in display. Each is also compact, lightweight, and designed to be carried anywhere. The Kindle eBook readers also have a rechargeable battery built in, and enough internal storage to hold at least 1,000 full-length books.

Most eBook Reader Manufacturers Have Their Own eBook File Format

Most eBook reader manufacturers have a proprietary format for their eBooks. Thus, while the content within an eBook may be identical when downloaded and read on

How to... Purchase an eBook from Amazon.com from Your Kindle

When you purchase your Kindle eBook reader or tablet directly from Amazon .com, it arrives at your door pre-registered to the Amazon.com account you used to make the Kindle purchase. If you purchased the Kindle from a retail store, when you activate it, you'll need to enter your Amazon.com account information, or set up a free Amazon.com account at that time.

Then, as you're shopping for eBooks, when you find a title you want to purchase and download, simply tap the appropriate icon, and the purchase price of that eBook title will automatically be billed to the credit or debit card associated with your Amazon.com account, and the Kindle-formatted eBook content will automatically be downloaded and installed on your Kindle device. Depending on the length of the eBook, this process typically takes between 15 and 30 seconds.

When you shop for Kindle-formatted eBooks on Amazon.com, the majority of current bestsellers in eBook format are priced at $9.99 or less. However, you'll find thousands of eBook titles priced between $0.99 and $3.99, as well as a vast selection of free eBook titles. In fact, when you utilize your Amazon Prime membership, an even greater selection of free eBook titles is available from Amazon.com.

FIGURE 1-3 The Kindle Fire is both an eBook reader and full-featured tablet device that can run apps and surf the Web, for example.

a Kindle, Nook, or iPad's screen, for example, the file format will be different. Books for the Kindle Fire use a proprietary Kindle format; however, the tablet also allows you to view Portable Document Format (PDF) files.

Kindle-formatted eBooks can only be read on a Kindle eBook reader, or used with a free Kindle app on a compatible smartphone, tablet, or computer. As you build up a personal Kindle eBook library, books from your collection can be read on any Kindle-compatible eBook reader or device, and be transferred easily between Kindle devices without incurring additional charges.

You can download the free Kindle app for your iPad 2, for example, to read Kindle-formatted eBooks on that tablet device. However, you cannot shop for Kindle-formatted eBooks from Apple's iBookstore. eBooks sold through iBookstore are formatted to work with the iBooks app on the iPad, while eBooks sold online from Barnes & Noble (www.bn.com) are formatted exclusively to work on the Nook eBook readers (or using a compatible Nook app on a computer, smartphone, or tablet).

Some eBook readers have other capabilities. For example, because the Kindle eBook readers can connect to the Internet, these readers come with web browser software preinstalled. They also serve as a digital audio player, so you can enjoy listening to audiobooks on your eBook reader. And, like full-featured tablets, some eBook readers can run optional apps.

If you opt to spend between $79 and $149 for the Amazon Kindle, Amazon Kindle Touch, or Amazon Kindle Touch 3G, for example, what you get is a dedicated handheld device designed primarily for reading eBooks, but that can handle a few other tasks.

Discover What a Tablet Is ... And Isn't

The concept behind a tablet is to offer users a handheld computing device that is larger than a smartphone, and that can handle many of the same tasks as a traditional desktop, laptop, or netbook computer, but without a keyboard or mouse. Instead, a flat, interactive touch screen, in conjunction with the user utilizing a series of finger taps, swipes, and other gestures, is used.

These days, if you shop for a tablet, you'll typically find them with anywhere from a 6-inch to a 12-inch, full-color, high-definition, touch screen display. Instead of using a traditional keyboard, a virtual keyboard appears on the tablet's screen only when it's needed.

Some tablets offer an optional external keyboard that can be connected using a physical cable or a wireless Bluetooth connection. Adding an external keyboard to a tablet temporarily takes away from its portability and handheld functionality, allowing it to work more like a netbook than a tablet.

Like a regular computer, a tablet has an operating system, and it runs programs (which are referred to as apps) to add functionality to the device. Depending on the tablet manufacturer and model, some offer built-in cameras,

(Continued)

as well as a microphone, speaker, headphone jack, memory card slot, Bluetooth functionality, and one or more standard or proprietary ports used for connecting the tablet to other computers or peripherals.

Tablet-based computers have been around for many years. However, it wasn't until Apple released the iPad that these devices became popular, and began to be a preferred device, instead of a laptop computer or netbook, among people on the go.

… And Then Came Amazon's Kindle Fire

In October 2011, Amazon broadened the eBook reader product category a bit when it introduced the Kindle Fire ($199). Offered at less than half the price of the popular Apple iPad 2 tablet, the Kindle Fire is a full-featured eBook reader, with a seven-inch, full-color screen, 8GB of internal memory, and Wi-Fi Internet connection capabilities. It weighs 14.6 ounces and measures 7.5 inches by 4.7 inches by 0.45 inches, so it fits nicely in your hands.

Unlike the Kindle eBook readers, however, the Kindle Fire runs a proprietary version of the popular Android operating system (developed by Google), so it is compatible with an ever-growing library of third-party apps. Plus, the Kindle Fire can be used for watching TV show episodes or movies, and listening to music (or audiobooks) that are transferred to and stored on the device or that are streamed from the Internet.

Thanks to the Kindle Fire's web browser, called Amazon Silk, users have the ability to surf the Web as long as a Wi-Fi Internet connection is available. Or, with the addition of an app, it's easily possible to manage one or more e-mail accounts and participate on online social networking services, like Facebook, Twitter, and Google +.

 Using an optional app, the Kindle Fire can also store, edit, display, and share vibrant digital photos transferred into the tablet.

Dozens of well-known companies, like Acer, Dell, HP, Motorola, and RIM (Blackberry) have released tablets, although none have come close to achieving the success of Apple's iPad 2. However, when Amazon announced the Kindle Fire, for a variety of reasons, it immediately captured the attention of avid readers and people interested in acquiring a tablet. Most notably, while the least expensive Apple iPad 2 model is priced at $499.99, the Amazon Kindle Fire is priced at just $199. We'll compare the two devices shortly.

 While the Kindle Fire is powerful, it's designed to be an eBook reader and entertainment device that also surfs the Web, can send/receive e-mail, and perform a range of other functions, but it wasn't designed to be a business or productivity tool. Think of the Kindle Fire as an extremely advanced eBook reader that also offers tablet functionality.

FIGURE 1-4 Download and watch (or stream and watch) TV shows, movies, music videos, and other content on your Kindle Fire that's obtained directly from Amazon.com.

Beyond having a very attractive and affordable price, the Kindle Fire offers one other important thing that its competition doesn't: easily accessible music, video (TV shows and movies), audiobooks, apps, and other content via Amazon.com.

Amazon.com offers a vast selection of eBook, audio, video, and app content. Using apps and functionality built into the Kindle Fire, you can access Amazon.com to acquire and watch more than 100,000 movies and TV shows (shown in Figure 1-4), not to mention 18 million songs, hundreds of thousands of audiobooks, and millions of eBook titles. Plus, you can use the Amazon Silk browser to surf the Web, or take advantage of a handful of optional apps to stream additional multimedia content, including TV shows, movies, and audio, directly from the Web.

Use Your Kindle Fire for Many Tasks ... Not Just Reading eBooks

Ultimately, if you're planning to use the Kindle Fire for one of the many tasks it was designed for, you're going to be extremely pleased with your tablet purchase and get a lot of use from the mobile device, whether at home or while you're on the

FIGURE 1-5 Purchase and download hundreds of game apps, such as the wildly popular Angry Birds games for your Kindle Fire, and keep yourself entertained for hours on end.

go (and perhaps on the job as well). Some of the tasks you can use your Kindle Fire for include

- Accessing and reading e-mails and composing short outgoing e-mails
- Listening to music downloaded from the Amazon MP3 store or streamed from other sources
- Participating on Facebook, Twitter, Google +, and other online social networking sites
- Playing games (shown in Figure 1-5)
- Reading digital editions of major daily newspapers and popular magazines
- Reading eBooks
- Surfing the Web
- Viewing and annotating documents, such as Microsoft Word files or PDF documents, created on a computer
- Watching TV shows, movies, and videos downloaded from Amazon.com or streamed from other sources

The Kindle Fire Measures up Well When Compared to Its Competition

Feature for feature, the Kindle Fire compares most closely to the Nook Tablet, which was introduced by Barnes and Noble for $249, about two weeks after the Kindle Fire was released. However, the Kindle Fire is vastly superior to the other Kindle and Nook eBook readers on the market for a variety of reasons.

In addition to offering a vibrant, full-color touch screen and having considerably more internal memory than a typical eBook reader, the Kindle Fire utilizes a faster processor and runs a proprietary version of the Android operating system, which gives it more functionality than just displaying eBooks.

Beyond offering a full-color screen, the resolution of the screen is also vastly superior to other eBook readers. This allows you to enjoy the digital editions of newspapers and magazines on your Kindle Fire and view that content (and the photos embedded within that content) in a way that closely resembles the printed pages of the publications. The Kindle Fire and Nook Tablet's screen resolution are both 1024 × 600 pixels at 169 dots per inch, with the capability of showcasing 16 million colors. Not only does this make text, graphics, photos, video, and other multimedia content look amazing, it's also easy on the eyes as you're viewing it in a wide range of lighting situations.

The Kindle Fire also utilizes Amazon's proprietary Kindle app for shopping for and then reading eBooks. Not only does this make reading eBooks an easy and intuitive experience, even if you're not a technologically oriented person, it's also a highly customizable experience. As you'll discover when reading an eBook on your Kindle Fire's screen, you have a lot of control over the appearance of the text when reading almost any book or document.

However, when you're done reading, if you want to listen to music, watch a TV show episode, watch a movie, play a game, check your e-mail, or surf the Web, for example, this functionality is also readily accessible to you with a few taps on the screen.

If your goal is simply to read text-based eBooks, any of Amazon's other Kindle eBook readers, like the $79 Kindle, will meet your needs. However, if you want to enjoy reading newspapers and magazines in full color, plus experience and utilize the other capabilities of a tablet device and have access to a vast and ever-growing collection of free and paid apps and content, the Kindle Fire will be an ideal digital companion.

 If you've owned an older Kindle eBook reader in the past or the Kindle app on your computer or smartphone, for example, any eBooks you've acquired from Amazon .com will automatically become available to you on your Kindle Fire, without your having to repurchase those books. Likewise, any music or video content acquired in the past using your Amazon.com account will also be available right away on your new Kindle Fire, via your free, cloud-based Amazon Cloud Drive account, which will be explained shortly.

Plenty of Content for Your Kindle Fire Is Just a Few Screen Taps Away

Like a desktop computer or laptop computer, a tablet device operates using a microprocessor and an operating system. To add functionality to the device, software (or, in this case, apps) are used. Many tablets on the market come with a handful of apps preinstalled on the device, and then offer a collection of optional third-party apps.

The most successful tablets on the market are supported by thousands or even hundreds of thousands of third-party apps. However, because tablets are also used as mobile multimedia entertainment centers, it's essential that the device you choose also have easy access to digital content that can be downloaded into and/or streamed to the device via the Internet.

The Apple iPads are popular because they are supported by more than 500,000 third-party apps, in addition to providing millions of songs, TV show episodes, movies, music videos, eBooks, and audiobooks that can be purchased and acquired through Apple's iTunes Store, App Store, and/or iBookstore, directly from the device.

Like Apple's iPads, Amazon's Kindle Fire quickly gained popularity and sold upwards of five million units within its first few months of availability, because of the vast array of (and the easy access to) digital content that Amazon.com, and its subsidiaries, like Audible.com, make available for it.

Your Content and Data Can Also Be Stored on a Cloud

Amazon has incorporated seamless integration of Amazon's Cloud Drive, an online-based file sharing service, into the Kindle Fire's operating system. This makes transferring and syncing content, app-specific data, documents, photos, and files very easy.

For example, anytime you purchase digital content from Amazon, whether you make the purchase from a computer, Kindle Fire, another Kindle eBook reader, or any other device, that content is stored within a free Amazon Cloud Drive account that's established in conjunction with your Amazon.com account.

Once content you own is stored online within your cloud-based account, you can easily download or stream it to your Kindle Fire. Plus, you can wirelessly share, sync, or transfer documents, files, photos, and app-related data via Amazon Cloud Drive between your Kindle Fire and primary computer, for example.

By integrating cutting-edge, but easy-to-use, cloud-based computing technology with the Kindle Fire's operating system and certain apps, it's dramatically broadened what the tablet's capabilities are, especially when it comes to sharing, syncing, or transferring data and content. This is a no-cost feature that the Kindle Fire offers but that most other competing tablet devices (with the exception of Apple's iPad) do not.

 As you'll discover, the Kindle Fire can handle some of the tasks that a full-featured laptop computer or netbook can be used for, especially while you're on the go. However, if you're a businessperson or entrepreneur who uses your laptop computer to compose documents, create and give presentations, manage complex spreadsheets or databases, and/or to edit photos, for example, realistically, the Kindle Fire will not replace the need for your laptop computer or netbook. Likewise, because it lacks the ability to make or receive calls, it can't replace your cell phone or smartphone either.

The Kindle Fire Is a Mobile Entertainment System ... and More!

As you're about to discover from this book, the Kindle Fire packs of lot of power into a handheld tablet that allows it to serve as a feature-packed mobile entertainment system and more, based on what apps you install on it.

While the Apple iPad 2 offers some additional features and functions, such as 3G Internet connectivity and two built-in cameras, its base price is between $499 and $829, depending on the system configuration, which is obviously considerably more than the Kindle Fire's $199 price tag.

 In 2012, Amazon is expected to release a Kindle Fire with a larger size, full-color touch screen. This new model could offer a built-in camera and microphone, which would allow for real-time video conferencing, for example, as well as 3G or 4G Internet connectivity in addition to Wi-Fi, a memory card slot, and other functionality found in competing tablets.

The Amazon Kindle Fire Is an eBook Reader with Powerful Tablet Functionality

The Kindle Fire is a well-designed eBook reader with tablet functionality that is greatly enhanced when you begin utilizing some of the third-party apps being released specifically for it. Plus, if you add peripherals and/or accessories to the Kindle Fire via the built-in Micro-B USB port, you can further enhance its capabilities.

So, for a mere $199, the Kindle Fire offers a powerful tablet that can be used as a mobile entertainment system, eBook reader, and web surfer. And, because it's tied so closely to Amazon.com, it can be used for price comparison shopping and/or for making online purchases.

 Using the Kindle Fire, as a savvy online shopper, you can quickly find the best deals on virtually anything you're shopping for, and over time, save hundreds or thousands of dollars.

Throughout this book, you'll learn all about what the Kindle Fire can do and how to use it for a wide range of reading, web surfing, entertainment-related, and even some work-related tasks.

2

Get Started Using Your Kindle Fire

HOW TO...

- Unpack your Kindle Fire
- Register your Kindle Fire
- Set up your Amazon.com 1-Click account
- Charge the battery
- Start using your new Kindle Fire

If the Amazon Kindle Fire is the first tablet device you've ever used, you're in for an exciting experience. In your hands is not just a powerful eBook reader, but a powerful tool that can surf the Web, run apps, allow you to watch movies and television shows, serve as a digital music player, and so much more. Among the tablets that have earned a high level of popularity among consumers and business people, until Amazon released the Kindle Fire for $199.00, this much power was only available in tablets that cost considerably more money.

As soon as you take your new Kindle out of the box, you'll probably notice one very obvious thing—there's no keyboard. And, if you examine the tablet closely, you'll discover just one button on its bottom. This is the power button, and it's used to turn the device on and off (shown in Figure 2-1).

All of your other interaction with the Kindle Fire will be through the device's sensitive touch screen. When appropriate, an on-screen virtual keyboard will appear that allows you to input information. Otherwise, you'll be able to navigate your way around the device's various menus, and ultimately use your favorite apps, by utilizing a series of finger taps, swipes, and other finger gestures directly on the Kindle Fire's full-color touch screen. You'll learn all about how to use the touch screen to control your tablet shortly.

FIGURE 2-1 On the bottom of the Kindle Fire is the power button, Micro-B USB port (also used for charging the device), and the headphone jack.

 Your Kindle Fire's touch screen is very sensitive. There's never a need to press down too hard on the screen in order to tap on icons or perform a finger gesture, for example. Be gentle. Ultimately, to reduce finger smudges and to protect your tablet's screen, you'll probably want to apply an optional, ultra-thin protective film over the screen. These are available from many companies. For example, there's the InvisibleShield from Zagg.com ($24.99, www.zagg.com). You'll learn more about this and other Kindle Fire accessories in Chapter 4.

Located to the immediate left of the tiny power button on the bottom of the device is the Kindle Fire's Micro-B USB/power port. The AC power adapter for the tablet was the only other thing that was included in the tablet's packaging. Initially, the rechargeable battery that's built into your Kindle is probably about halfway charged. It's a good idea to plug it in and fully charge the battery as you get started using it. Located next to the Micro-B USB/power port is the headphone input jack. You'll learn more about its various uses later.

Turning on Your Kindle Fire for the First Time

Okay, so you're probably pretty excited to start using your new tablet. Once you unwrap the device from the clear plastic that it came wrapped in, gently press the power button once on the bottom of the device. It will light up and turn green.

Within about five seconds, the Kindle Fire logo will appear on the tablet's screen. This appears when the tablet initially boots up. A few seconds later, the Lock screen

FIGURE 2-2   The Lock screen appears whenever the Kindle Fire is turned on or awoken from Sleep mode.

will appear. Displayed near the center of the Lock screen is the time and date. To the right, you'll see an orange, arrow-shaped icon.

Gently place your finger on this arrow-shaped icon, and swipe it from right to left, across the center of the Lock screen (shown in Figure 2-2). This will unlock the tablet. You'll need to do this every time you power on your device or wake it up from Sleep mode.

Congratulations! You're on your way to becoming an experienced tablet user. Before you get started downloading and reading eBooks; downloading, installing, and using apps; listening to music; streaming web content; surfing the Web; playing games; and seeing all that your new tablet is capable of, you'll first need to activate the device and register it with Amazon.

By registering your device, you'll set up an Amazon.com account (or link your existing Amazon.com account to your new Kindle). This will allow you to instantly make purchases from your tablet and acquire a wide range of digital content (or any other products) from Amazon.com. As a result of setting up an Amazon.com account, a free Amazon Cloud Drive account will also be set up for you. But more on that later.

To register your Kindle Fire, it will need access to the Internet via a Wi-Fi connection. Before proceeding, make sure you're within the radius of a Wi-Fi hotspot or wireless network. If the network or hotspot you're accessing is locked (password protected), you'll need to know the appropriate password to obtain access to it. Anytime your tablet requires Internet access, you'll need to be within the radius of a Wi-Fi hotspot or wireless network. However, to use apps or to access content that's already stored on your tablet, an Internet connection is not necessarily needed. So, to purchase an eBook from Amazon.com, you will need Wi-Fi Internet access. However, once the eBook is installed on your tablet, you can begin reading it anywhere and anytime, whether or not a wireless Internet connection is available.

Connect Your Kindle Fire to the Internet and Activate It

In order to activate your Kindle Fire for the first time, you'll need to establish an Internet connection. Thus, you'll need to be within a Wi-Fi hotspot, or within the radius of a wireless network.

Begin by pressing the power button to turn on the tablet. Then, swipe your finger across the Lock screen to unlock the device. The Welcome To Kindle Fire screen will appear. From this screen, you'll begin registering your new Kindle.

 The initial activation process only needs to be done once, the first time you begin using your new Kindle Fire. In the future, this process will only need to be repeated if, for some reason, you needed to use the Reset To Factory Defaults option from the Settings menu, but this is seldom necessary.

Below the Connect To A Network heading on the screen is a listing of available Wi-Fi networks you can connect to (shown in Figure 2-3). This listing will change based on your location and what networks are available.

 If you're at home, the strongest Wi-Fi signal will probably emanate from your own wireless router (i.e., your wireless network). However, your device may pick up other Wi-Fi networks from your neighbors, for example.

Tap the listing for the Wi-Fi network of your choice. If the network is password protected, you will be prompted to enter the appropriate password to access the wireless network from your tablet. If this is the case, a small lock-shaped icon will appear to the left of the network's name (as part of the signal strength indicator) on the Wireless Networking screen. When you tap a locked (password-protected) network's listing, a pop-up window will appear asking for the appropriate password. Upon entering the password, the "Connecting..." message will appear on your Kindle's screen. If no password is required, upon tapping a network's listing, your tablet will connect to that network.

FIGURE 2-3   Below the Connect To A Network heading, tap the Wi-Fi hotspot or wireless network that you want your tablet to connect to.

Next, you'll be prompted to select your time zone. On the screen will be a handful of options, including Pacific Time, Mountain Time, Central Time, Eastern Time, Hawaii, Alaska, Arizona, and an option to Select Another Time Zone. Using your finger, tap your time zone selection. An orange dot will appear to the right of your selection. Tap the Continue icon that's displayed near the bottom-right corner of the screen to continue the activation process.

If you purchased your Kindle Fire directly from Amazon.com using your Amazon account, it will arrive at your door pre-registered with your Amazon account information, including your Amazon user name and password preinstalled. At the top of the screen, your Kindle Fire will welcome you by name, and inform you that it's automatically checking for an updated version of the Kindle operating system (a proprietary version of the popular Android OS from Google).

 If you purchased your Kindle Fire from a retail store, you'll need to enter your pre-existing Amazon account information (if you've previously been an Amazon .com customer, or you've owned a different Kindle eBook reader). Or you'll need to create an Amazon account from scratch. Doing this takes just a minute or two. Be prepared to provide information about yourself, including your name, address, phone number, e-mail address, and credit card information (so 1-Click online purchases can later be made directly from your Kindle Fire and be billed to your credit or debit card.)

The next step of the activation process involves your Kindle Fire automatically downloading and installing the most current version of the Kindle operating system software (also known as the Android OS). For this process, make sure your device is plugged into an external power source. It will take several minutes for the software to download and install itself, so be patient.

After the operating system software is downloaded, your Kindle will reset. It will turn itself off and then back on, and reboot. This is perfectly normal. Just kick back and watch the process happen. There's no need for you to do anything.

 As your Kindle activates itself, you'll receive an e-mail welcoming you to your free trial month of Amazon Prime. You'll learn more about this premium service later and the benefits it offers to you as a Kindle Fire user.

Within three to five minutes, your Kindle Fire's Lock screen will once again appear. Swipe your finger from right to left to unlock the device. Since this is your first time using the tablet, a Welcome Tutorial will automatically run, which offers a brief overview of how your tablet functions.

For example, you'll be introduced to the Navigation bar at the top of the Home screen. It's from here that you can access the features, functions, and apps that are available from your tablet. To continue with the tutorial, tap the arrow-shaped Next icon that's displayed near the bottom-right corner of the screen.

You'll now learn about the Carousel, which allows you to quickly search through recent books, music, videos, websites, documents, content, and apps you've used on your tablet. The tutorial will also teach you about the Favorites bar. It's displayed near the bottom of the tablet's Home screen. Again, tap the Next icon to continue.

Located near the upper-right corner of the tablet's Home screen is a gear-shaped icon, called the Quick Settings icon. It's used to customize some of the basic functions of your Kindle, such as adjusting the volume or screen brightness. If you look near the bottom-left corner of the screen, you'll discover the Home icon. No matter what you're doing on your Kindle, at anytime, you can tap this Home icon to return to the tablet's Home screen.

Once your mini tutorial comes to an end, you'll find yourself viewing your Kindle's Home screen. The following section will help you become acquainted with everything you need to know in order to navigate your way around the Home screen like a pro, and ultimately begin using your Kindle Fire.

Navigating Your Way Around the Kindle Fire's Home Screen

The Home screen of your Kindle Fire is divided into four main sections (shown in Figure 2-4). At the very top of the screen (displayed near the upper-left corner) is your name. For example, it will say "Jason's Kindle." To the immediate right of your user name, if a circular icon with a number within it appears, this means one or more notifications are waiting to be viewed. Notifications are messages, alerts, or alarms that are generated by your tablet or the apps installed on it. Tap your user name or the number icon to reveal the notification message(s).

FIGURE 2-4   This is the Kindle Fire's Home screen just after it's initially activated.

 As you're looking at the Notification screen, tap the Clear All icon to delete the notification messages. Or tap any message listing to access the appropriate app or data that the notification relates to. For example, if you're not currently connected to a Wi-Fi network, but your tablet's Wireless Networking feature is turned on and it detects an available network, you'll receive a notification that says, "Wi-Fi Network Available." In this case, tap the notification listing to access the Wireless Network settings menu of your tablet.

To the right of your user name on the Home screen is the time. It's displayed near the top-center area of the screen. Located near the upper-right corner of the screen is the Quick Settings icon and battery life indicator. If you're connected to the Internet, a Wi-Fi signal indicator also appears between the Quick Settings icon and battery life indicator.

Directly below this information is the Search field. It's used to quickly find data, files, or content on your tablet or the Web. When you tap the Search field with your finger, the Kindle's virtual keyboard appears near the bottom of the screen. Directly below the Search field, however, you'll see two command icons, labeled Library and Web (shown in Figure 2-5).

After entering a keyword or search phrase in the Search field, if you tap Library, the contents of your tablet will be searched. If you tap Web, you'll be able to perform a web search for what you're looking for, assuming your Kindle is connected to the Internet. We'll take a closer look at how to use the Kindle's virtual keyboard shortly.

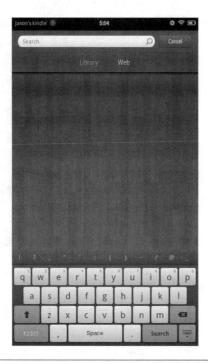

FIGURE 2-5   The Search option is accessible from the Kindle Fire's Home screen.

 After tapping the Search field, if you tap the Cancel icon, you'll quickly return to the Home screen. Or, if you perform a search, your search results will be displayed in the center area of the screen, between the Search field and the virtual keyboard. Tap any of your search results to access that content or data, or to visit the appropriate website.

Get Acquainted with the Navigation Bar

Located directly below the Search field is the Navigation bar. On your tablet, it's from here that you can access any content or data stored on your device, launch and use any app, or begin surfing the Web. You'll discover seven main command tabs associated with the Navigation bar (refer back to Figure 2-2). They're labeled as follows:

- **Newsstand**   This built-in app has two purposes. It gives you access to the Amazon Store in order to browse, purchase (or subscribe to), and download digital editions of newspapers and magazines. Once the newspaper or magazine content is acquired and stored on your tablet, the Newsstand app is used to access and read that content. You'll discover hundreds of newspapers and magazines available from Newsstand. In many cases, you can purchase individual issues of your favorite publications, or sign up for a subscription. Chapter 10 offers more information about how to use Newsstand on your Kindle Fire.

To select Newsstand, Books, Music, Video, Docs, Apps, or Web from the Navigation bar, simply tap the appropriate command icon that's displayed on the Home screen. Then, at anytime, tap the Home icon (displayed in the lower-left corner of the screen) to exit out of that application and return to the Home screen.

- **Books**   The Kindle Fire's technological heritage includes a long line of powerful eBook readers. Meanwhile, Amazon.com has evolved into the largest digital bookstore on the Internet. Thus, it makes perfect sense that not only does your Kindle Fire have a powerful eBook Reader app, but it also gives you easy access to Amazon's eBookstore, as long as the tablet has a web connection.

  Tap the Books icon to launch the Kindle eBook Reader app. On the virtual bookshelf (the Library screen), you'll see all of the eBook titles currently stored on your tablet. To browse, purchase, and download additional eBooks (or acquire free eBooks), tap the Store icon that's displayed near the upper-right corner of the screen to access Amazon's Kindle eBookstore.

 You can also shop for eBooks (or acquire free eBooks), and pay for them with your Amazon account, by visiting www.amazon.com/Kindle-eBooks using the web browser on your primary computer. You can then transfer your eBook purchases from your online-based Amazon Cloud Drive account (which will be explained later) directly to your Kindle.

Amazon's Kindle eBookstore offers a selection of more than one million book titles, with new titles being published every day. This includes more than 800,000 eBooks that are priced at $9.99 or less each, and more than 1,000 illustrated children's books. You'll also find several million additional free eBooks available for download, including out-of-copyright titles.

- **Music**   In addition to being a powerful eBook reader, as well as a fully functional tablet device, your Kindle Fire can be used as a digital music player. You can purchase or acquire music from the Amazon MP3 online-based music store, where you'll find a collection of more than 18 million songs.

  All of your Amazon MP3 music purchases, past and present, are now automatically stored within your Amazon Cloud Drive account, so that music is readily accessible from your computer or Kindle, regardless of where the music was first purchased. By tapping the Music icon from the Kindle's Navigation bar, you can access digital music that's stored on your tablet, or access music stored within your Amazon Cloud Drive account. You can also shop for or acquire free music from the Amazon MP3 store, or transfer music acquired from other sources into your tablet.

 How to use your Kindle Fire as a digital music player is the topic of Chapter 11.

Your Amazon.com Content Purchases Also Get Stored in the Cloud

Whenever you make a content purchase for your Kindle, whether it's from the tablet itself, from your primary computer, or from any other computer or device, that eBook, digital publication, music, TV show, movie, or app automatically gets stored on Amazon's cloud-based file sharing service. It then becomes instantly accessible to you from your Kindle at anytime, as long as you've purchased or acquired that content using the same Amazon account that was used to register your Kindle Fire (and it has Internet access).

This free feature means you can purchase music, for example, from Amazon MP3 on your computer and enjoy listening to it there, but at anytime, you can also download that music to your Kindle Fire, without having to repurchase that music. This applies to any type of purchasable digital content from Amazon.

When you first registered your Kindle, your free Amazon Cloud Drive account was set up automatically. You'll learn more about how to access and use it in Chapter 12.

- **Video**   As you'll discover, your Kindle Fire is capable of playing video on its high-definition screen and using its built-in speakers to transform the tablet into a portable multimedia entertainment center. For a more intense listening experience, you can also plug stereo headphones into your tablet, or connect the device to external speakers as you watch TV shows, movies, or other video content; play games; or listen to music.

  Video content can be purchased and downloaded to your Kindle directly from Amazon.com. Or, using a variety of apps, such as Hulu Plus or Netflix, for example, you can stream video content (including TV shows and movies) from the Internet to your tablet, as long as it's connected to the Internet.

  By tapping the Video tab from the Navigation bar, you can access video content that's been purchased from Amazon (including TV shows, movies, and music videos), and then watch that content. You can also acquire new video content. You'll need to utilize a third-party app to stream content from the Web, via Hulu Plus or Netflix, for example.

You'll learn all about using your Kindle Fire as a portable entertainment center for watching TV shows, movies, music videos, and other content in Chapter 9. You'll also discover the difference between buying and downloading content, and streaming content from the Web. Chapter 9 also explains how to enjoy audio content (such as audiobooks, podcasts, or Internet-based radio stations) from your tablet.

- **Docs**   While it may not be ideal for word processing, spreadsheet management, or creating digital slide presentations, your Kindle Fire can be used to access and read document files created using popular software packages on your PC or Mac. As you'll discover, when you tap the Docs tab that's displayed on the Navigation bar, you have access to document files stored on your tablet.

  The Docs feature of your Kindle automatically links to Amazon's Cloud Drive file sharing service and allows you to easily transfer document files, including Microsoft Word and PDF files, to your device via this cloud service by sending files or documents from any computer or mobile device to a personal (password-protected) e-mail address that Amazon assigns to you.

Your free Amazon Cloud Drive account includes 5GB worth of online storage space. Any content purchases you make from Amazon (such as music, TV shows, movies, eBooks, or apps) that are automatically stored within your Cloud account do not utilize your 5GB of allocated storage space. As much additional online storage space as you need to store your purchased content from Amazon.com within your cloud-based account is provided for free.

In Chapter 8, you'll learn how to access, view, and edit documents on your Kindle Fire using the Docs app that's built into your device, as well as third-party apps, like Quickoffice or Adobe PDF Reader.

- **Apps**   You've probably figured out by now that your Kindle Fire is capable of handling a wide range of tasks right out of the box, thanks to its powerful operating system and the apps that come preinstalled on the device.

  When you tap the Apps tab from the Navigation bar, you'll see a Library screen, which displays icons representing all of the apps currently installed on your tablet.

  However, by tapping the Store icon that's displayed near the upper-right corner of the screen, you're given access to Amazon's App Store. From here, you can purchase, download, and install an ever-growing collection of third-party apps to greatly enhance the capabilities of your tablet.

You'll learn all about how to find, download, and install apps on your Kindle Fire in Chapter 14. The focus of Chapter 5, however, is on the apps that come preinstalled on your tablet or that are readily accessible from your Cloud account. These 15 apps include Gallery, The Weather Channel, Audible, Pulse, Contacts, Email, Facebook, Quickoffice, and Amazon Shop.

Whether you're looking for exciting games, to enhance your productivity, to transform your tablet into a powerful organizational tool, or to use your tablet to help you communicate more efficiently on the Web and participate on the various online social networking sites like Twitter and Facebook, you'll find apps for all this and more. Some third-party apps are offered for free. Others cost money. The majority of top-quality apps for your Kindle Fire are priced between $0.99 and $4.99.

How to...   Transfer Apps from the Cloud to Your Tablet

Once you purchase an app from Amazon's Appstore, or if you acquire a free app, if you're making the purchase directly from your tablet, it will be immediately downloaded and installed on your device, as well as stored within your Amazon Cloud account.

However, if you acquire an app using your personal computer, the purchased (or acquired free app) will also automatically be stored within your Amazon Cloud account. From your tablet, to access and install apps that are stored within your Amazon Cloud account, launch Apps from the Navigation bar. At the top of the screen, tap the Cloud command icon. Apps that are stored on the cloud, but not on your tablet, will have a small downward-pointing arrow icon displayed in the lower-right corner of the app icon that's displayed on the Library screen.

Tap the icon that represents the app you want to transfer from your Cloud account to your tablet. It will automatically be downloaded and installed. Once you purchase an app, you own it. You will not be charged again to download and install it from your Cloud account onto your tablet.

If you use your PC or Mac to browse and shop for apps from Amazon's Appstore, you can take advantage of Amazon's Test Drive Now feature, which allows you to run demo versions of many apps on your computer's screen before purchasing them.

- **Web**   Built into your Kindle Fire is a full-featured web browser, called Amazon Silk, that enables you to surf the Internet, as long as your tablet is connected to the Web via a Wi-Fi connection (shown in Figure 2-6). The web browser that's built into your tablet offers tab-based browsing, so you can instantly switch between multiple open webpages or browser windows. You can also create and maintain a list of bookmarks for frequently visited websites. From your Kindle Fire, you can easily access almost any website on the Internet with ease.

Note   Chapter 6 focuses on how to use the web browser that comes preinstalled on your Kindle Fire to surf the Web. In Chapter 7, you'll discover how to manage one or more e-mail accounts from your web-connected tablet using an e-mail app.

Take the Carousel for a Quick Spin

As you begin using your Kindle Fire, the device itself keeps track of what you use it for. All of your most recent activities are displayed in the main area of the Home screen in the form of icons displayed within a rotating Carousel.

Using your finger, swipe from right to left (or from left to right) to scroll through your recent activities using your tablet. This includes apps you've used, websites

FIGURE 2-6   Use the Amazon Silk web browser to easily surf the Web.

you've visited, music you've listened to, TV shows or movies you've watched, documents you've viewed, and eBooks you're reading.

You can instantly return to any of those activities and pick up exactly where you left off by double-tapping the icon that represents the activity. The appropriate app and content will launch and be displayed on your tablet's screen.

 Double-tapping an icon or area of the screen is one of the finger gestures you'll use often when navigating your way around your Kindle Fire and using it. A double-tap involves quickly tapping the same icon or area of the screen twice in quick succession. It typically serves the same purpose as double-clicking a mouse when you're using a computer.

Access Your Most Frequented Apps and Content Using the Favorites Bar

Constantly displayed at the bottom of the Home screen is the Favorites bar. Here, icons that represent apps that you most frequently use are displayed. The Favorites bar is customizable. You can add an eBook, digital publication, app, photo album, video, or frequently visited website to this listing. To add an item to your Favorites bar, from the Carousel, for example, press and hold down its icon for about two seconds. An Add To Favorites tab will appear. Tap this tab.

Each shelf of the Favorites bar can display up to four icons. When one shelf becomes full, another shelf will automatically be created below the previous one. So, once your Favorites bar is composed of multiple shelves (shown in Figure 2-7), you'll need to use your finger to swipe upward, from the bottom of the screen toward the top, to reveal the additional Favorites bar shelves. To return the Home screen to its original appearance, swipe your finger in a downward direction.

 Once an app, website, eBook, or another piece of content is added to your Favorites bar, you can launch and access it with a single tap. To remove an item from your Favorites bar, press and hold your finger on the appropriate icon that you want removed for about two seconds. When the Remove From Favorites command tab appears, tap it. This will not delete the content or app from your device. It will only delete the shortcut icon from your Favorites bar.

 To rearrange the order of icons within your Favorites bar, press and hold your finger on the icon you want to move, and then slowly drag it to another location within the Favorites bar. When you release your finger from the screen, the location where the icon has been moved to will be saved.

FIGURE 2-7 The Favorites bar can have multiple shelves, with each shelf displaying icons for up to four apps, websites, eBooks, or other frequently used content.

Adjust Your Kindle's Settings by Tapping the Quick Settings Icon

Many of the core features of your Kindle Fire are customizable. To make adjustments to various settings, tap the small, gear-shaped icon that's displayed near the top-right corner of the Home screen.

At the top of the screen, a series of six command icons will be displayed (shown in Figure 2-8). They're labeled Unlocked, Volume, Brightness, Wi-Fi, Sync, and More. Here's a short summary of what each settings command icon is used for:

- **Unlocked**   This feature is used to turn on or off the auto-screen rotation feature of your tablet. When you tap this icon, the Unlocked icon will transform into a Locked icon. In the Unlocked state, if you rotate your tablet from portrait to landscape mode by changing the way you hold it, the screen will automatically rotate accordingly. However, when locked, if you rotate the device, the screen will remain in whichever mode it's currently in, and will not automatically rotate.

FIGURE 2-8   The Kindle Fire's Quick Settings icons displayed on the Home screen. Here, the Brightness option is selected, so the Brightness slider is shown.

- **Volume** Tap this icon to adjust the volume of the audio that's being generated by your tablet or whichever app is running. This includes sound effects, music, or the audio from content you're listening to or watching. As soon as you tap the Volume command icon, just below the command icons, a slider will appear. Place your finger on the white dot displayed within the slider, and drag it to the right to increase the volume (make it louder), or drag it to the left to decrease the volume (make it quieter).

  The volume control impacts the tablet's built-in speakers, but will also control the volume of headphones or external speakers that are connected to the device using the headphones jack. Some headphones or external speakers have their own volume controls, which can be used to control the volume level as well.

 Dragging the Volume slider to the extreme left is equivalent to placing your tablet in Mute mode, so no sound will be generated by the device.

- **Brightness** Use this command icon to change the brightness of your Kindle Fire's display. When you're using it in the dark, for example, you may want to turn down the brightness. When using the tablet in bright light, however, it may be necessary to boost the screen's brightness to improve its clarity.

  When you tap the Brightness command icon, a slider will appear below the command icons near the top of the screen. Place your finger on the white dot that appears within the slider and drag it to the right to increase the screen's brightness level. Or drag the white dot within the slider to the left in order to decrease the brightness level of the tablet's screen.

 Operating the Kindle Fire at a lower brightness level will slightly increase the battery life of your tablet.

 In most lighting conditions, the default location of the Brightness slider should be suitable. You'll notice this default setting is just to the right of the slider's midway point.

- **Wi-Fi** Tap the Wi-Fi icon to connect to a Wi-Fi hotspot or wireless network (so your device can access the Internet), or to change wireless networks if you're moving around and go outside of a hotspot or network's wireless signal radius. When you tap the Wi-Fi command icon, a listing of available networks is displayed below the Connect To A Network heading. Tap the network of your choice to make the connection.

  To the left of each network listing is its signal strength indicator. The more signal bars that are displayed in dark grey, the stronger the Wi-Fi Internet signal is.

To increase the signal strength, try moving closer to the wireless router that's generating the Wi-Fi signal.

If the signal strength indicator displays a tiny lock in the lower-right corner, this means the wireless network is password protected. Upon choosing a locked network, a password field will be displayed. Enter the appropriate password to gain access to that network.

Located between the command icons and the Connect To A Network heading when you tap the Wi-Fi command icon is a virtual Wireless Networking switch. When turned on, your Kindle Fire will actively search for a wireless network to connect to. When turned off, your tablet will not be able to send or receive data from the Web or connect to a wireless network.

 When you're traveling on an airplane, or you're in an area where there's no Wi-Fi hotspot or wireless network, turn off the Wireless Networking option. This will keep your device from attempting to transit wirelessly, which is prohibited aboard an aircraft, unless that aircraft is equipped with Wi-Fi access. It will also conserve battery life. Otherwise, your tablet will continue to actively search for a Wi-Fi signal until it finds one when the Wireless Networking feature is turned on.

- **Sync**   This feature is used to sync app-specific data or content between your tablet and the Internet, or to establish a wireless connection with another device or computer via the Internet or a wireless network. Chapter 12 focuses on syncing data.
- **More**   When you tap this command icon, a dozen different settings categories are displayed within the Settings menu. These options include Help & Feedback, My Account, Sounds, Display, Security, Applications, Date & Time, Wireless Network, Kindle Keyboard, Device, Legal Notices, and Terms of Use. Many of these settings options have submenus associated with them. Everything you need to know about each of these options is explained within Chapter 3. To exit out of the Settings menu, tap the Home icon that's displayed in the lower-left corner of the screen.

You Can Always Find Your Way Home by Tapping the Home Icon

No matter what app you're running on your Kindle Fire, you can return to the Home screen at any time by tapping the Home icon that's almost always displayed near the lower-left corner of the screen (except for when the Home screen itself is being displayed).

 In order to make full use of the screen, some third-party apps hide the Home button, or require you to tap a Menu icon first in order to access it. However, regardless of what app you're using, there is always a Home button that's accessible.

When you tap the Home icon, whatever you were previously doing on your tablet will typically be saved. For example, if you're reading an eBook, a virtual bookmark will be created and the page you last read will be stored. So, when you return to reading that eBook, you can pick up exactly where you left off.

Using the Kindle's Virtual Keyboard

Much of your interaction with the Kindle Fire will be through a series of taps and swipes on the device's touch screen. However, you'll periodically need to enter information into the device. When this becomes necessary, your Kindle Fire will display its virtual keyboard on the screen.

The virtual keyboard always appears along the bottom of the tablet's screen (shown in Figure 2-9). It's a qwerty-style keyboard that's configured very much like a traditional computer keyboard, but with a few minor differences.

Along the top row of keys on the virtual keyboard, in the upper-right corner of each key, is a tiny number. For example, the "q" key also displays the number "1," and the "w" key also displays the number "2," and so on. To enter numbers using the Kindle's virtual keyboard, first press the Numbers key that's displayed in the lower-left

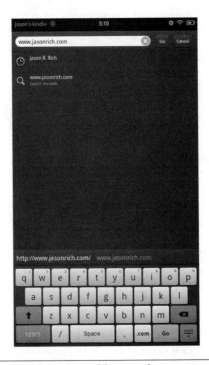

FIGURE 2-9 This is the virtual keyboard layout that appears when you launch the Amazon Silk web browser and tap the webpage address field.

FIGURE 2-10 Tap the "123!?" key to make the number keys and commonly used symbols and punctuation mark keys appear.

corner of the keyboard. The Numbers key says "123!?". When you tap it, the top row of letters on the virtual keyboard becomes numbers (one through nine, followed by zero). The other letter keys are transformed into symbol or punctuation mark keys (shown in Figure 2-10).

To return the keyboard to its normal appearance, tap the "ABC" key, which replaced the Numbers key in the lower-left corner of the screen. Or, while looking at the Numbers screen, tap the "* + =" key that's displayed directly above the "ABC" key to once again transform the keyboard and display a different selection of commonly used symbols and punctuation marks (shown in Figure 2-11).

As you're looking at the default virtual keyboard screen, all of the letters are displayed in lowercase. To switch to uppercase, tap the upward-pointing arrow key that's displayed on the left side of the screen, just above the "123!?" key. This serves as your SHIFT key.

Tip Double-tap the SHIFT key (which displays an upward-pointing arrow) to switch to CAPS LOCK. As a result, until you tap the key again, all of the text you type will be displayed in uppercase letters.

Located in the lower-right corner of the virtual keyboard is the REMOVE KEYBOARD key. Tap it to make the virtual keyboard disappear from the screen. You can always make the keyboard reappear by tapping any empty text field, for example, that requires you to manually input text, numbers or data.

Directly above the REMOVE KEYBOARD key is the BACKSPACE key. Tap it to delete the last character you typed, or hold it down to delete multiple characters quickly. You'll find the SPACEBAR key displayed near the bottom-center area of the virtual keyboard.

FIGURE 2-11 Tap the "* + =" key to transform the keyboard so a new selection of popular symbols and punctuation marks becomes accessible.

As you'd expect, it has the word "Space" displayed within it, and it's more than twice the length of the other keys.

Depending on what app you're using, the Kindle Fire's virtual keyboard will change, based on the type of information you'll be entering. For example, when you use the built-in web browser app, at the bottom of the screen, to the right of the SPACEBAR, you'll see a ".com" and an orange-colored "Go" key. As you're entering a website URL into the address field near the top of the screen, you can quickly add the ".com" portion of the website's address by tapping the ".com" key.

Then, when the website address you want to visit is fully entered, you can tap the GO key that's displayed as part of the virtual keyboard, or at the top of the screen, to the right of the website address field.

If you use the Search option found at the top of the Home screen, the virtual keyboard will display commonly used punctuation marks and symbols in a separate row directly above the keyboard. The ".com" and "Go" key that was displayed when using the web browser app, for example, will be replaced by a single, oversized "Search" key. While the location and layout of special keys will change, the basic position of the letter keys ("a" through "z") will remain constant and be consistent with a qwerty keyboard layout.

Control Your Tablet with a Finger

As you use your Kindle Fire, you'll primarily use your index finger to tap or double-tap command icons, links, and other aspects of the touch screen. However, as you interact with your tablet, several other finger gestures will also be used.

Here's a quick summary of the finger movements and gestures you'll utilize when using your tablet:

- **Tap** This involves using your index finger to quickly tap once on a specific icon, link, field, or area of the touch screen.
- **Touch and hold** Instead of quickly tapping an icon, for example, you'll place your finger on an icon, link, field, or area of the touch screen and hold it there for a few seconds, until something specific happens. Or, you may need to touch and hold an icon in order to drag it around the screen.
- **Double-tap** Tap an icon, link, field, or area of the touch screen twice in quick succession. This is similar to using a double-click motion with a mouse as you use your computer.
- **Swipe** This finger motion can be from left to right, from right to left, from the top of the screen to the bottom, or from the bottom of the screen to the top. It involves brushing your finger along the screen in a specific direction to turn the page of an eBook, or scroll up, down, left, or right on the screen.
- **Reverse pinch** Start with your thumb and index finger touching each other and the touch screen, and then quickly move them apart. This finger gesture is used to zoom in on an area of the screen or on a photo, for example. It works in some, but not all apps.

- **Pinch gesture**   Start with your thumb and index finger slightly separated and then drag them together, using a pinch motion as they're touching the tablet's screen. This is used to zoom out after you've zoomed in on a screen, photo, or graphic, for example.

Turning the Kindle Off

Whenever you're done using the Kindle Fire, you can press and hold down the Power button on the bottom on the device until a message appears confirming that you want to shut down the device. When it's powered off, the tablet cannot send or receive data, and no apps will continue running in the background. When you turn the device back on, the operating system will need to relaunch, which takes a minute or so.

 In general, it's much more efficient and faster to simply place the tablet into Sleep mode rather than turning it off altogether and then having to boot up the device each time you want to use it.

Alternatively, you have the option to place the Kindle into Sleep mode. To do this, press and release the power button quickly. This turns off the tablet's screen, but allows the device to continue running in the background. While in Sleep mode, the tablet can automatically wake up and alert you of an appointment or an incoming e-mail, for example, and it can communicate as needed with the Internet.

 If you have music playing using the Music or Pandora app, for example, it will continue playing in the background, even when you place your tablet in Sleep mode, or if you switch to using another app. To stop the music from playing, return to the Music or Pandora app, and press the Pause button. (More information about the Pandora app can be found in Chapter 9, while details about how to use the Music app can be found in Chapter 12.) However, if you're playing a video using the Video or Netflix app, for example, it will automatically pause if you press the tablet's power button to place it into Sleep mode.

If you leave your tablet unattended for a predefined time interval, between 30 seconds and one hour (depending on how you have it set), the device will automatically transition into Screen Timeout (aka Sleep mode). When this occurs, the tablet will continue being fully operational; however, the touch screen will turn itself off to conserve battery life.

To modify how long the tablet can be left unattended before entering into Screen Timeout mode, follow these steps:

1. Tap the Quick Settings icon that's displayed on the Home screen.
2. Tap the More command icon that's displayed near the top of the screen.
3. When the Settings menu appears, tap the Display menu option.
4. From the Display menu screen, tap the Screen Timeout option. The default setting for this feature is 5 minutes.

5. From the Screen Timeout menu screen, tap the option for 30 seconds, 1 minute, 5 minutes, 15 minutes, 30 minutes, 45 minutes, 1 hour, or Never to determine how quickly the tablet will transition into Screen Timeout mode.

6. Tap the Home button to save your changes and return to the Home screen.

 If your Kindle Fire freezes or hangs, press and hold down the power button for 20 seconds to reset the device. The tablet will turn itself off and then reboot, but no content that's stored on your device will be erased. You may, however, lose any unsaved data that you were working on right when the device crashed or froze.

Caring for Your Kindle

Your Kindle Fire is pretty durable and has an internal chargeable battery that lasts for a long time, depending on how the device is being used. However, the device is not indestructible, and you will need to regularly recharge its battery to keep it operational.

There are several things you can do to protect your Kindle during everyday use and when it's being stored or transported. For example, you can

- Apply an ultra-thin and crystal-clear screen protector over the Kindle Fire's display to help protect it from smudges or from getting cracked or damaged.
- You can keep the device within an optional cover, which can either be opened when the tablet is in use or removed altogether.
- Instead of using a cover, when transporting your tablet, you can insert it into an optional padded case. This will help protect the Kindle if it accidently gets dropped.
- While you're sitting at your desk, lounging on a couch, or comfortably propped up in bed using your Kindle, you can use a tabletop stand or pillow-like lap desk to keep your hands free but keep your tablet positioned at the perfect angle for reading or using it.

 Information about optional protective screen films, covers, cases, stands, and lap desks that can be used with your Kindle Fire is showcased in Chapter 4.

 Do not expose your tablet to extremely hot or cold temperatures or any liquid whatsoever. It's not waterproof! For example, don't keep it on the dashboard of your car, leaving it exposed to direct sunlight, or leave it in your car overnight when the temperature drops below freezing or gets extremely hot. Using common sense, and keeping it away from your infant or dog, will go a long way toward extending the life of your Kindle Fire.

Charging Your Kindle's Battery and Keeping It Charged

Your Kindle Fire came with an AC charger for plugging the tablet into an electrical outlet in order to recharge the battery. When the device is plugged in and recharging, it can still be used. You'll notice that in the upper-right corner of the screen, the battery indicator icon will flash with a green color as the tablet is charging. When it's fully charged, the battery indicator will remain a solid green color.

Once it's unplugged and being used, as the battery gets depleted, the battery life indicator will transition from solid green to grey. The more gray that appears within the battery life indicator, the less battery life you have remaining.

 To fully charge your Kindle when it's plugged into an electrical outlet and left unattended could take up to four hours. If you continue using the Kindle while it's recharging, the recharge process will take longer.

 In Chapter 4, you'll learn about optional external battery packs, car chargers, USB chargers, and other charging options available that allow you to recharge the tablet's internal battery and/or keep it operational when an AC electrical outlet is not available.

According to Amazon, your Kindle Fire's battery should last between 7.5 and 8 hours per charge, depending on how it's being used. Excessive use of Wi-Fi, the tablet's built-in speakers, the use of the mini-USB port for a task other than charging the device, or keeping the screen on an extra-bright setting will drain the battery slightly faster.

Protecting and Cleaning the Touch Screen

One of the most annoying things about using any tablet device, not just the Kindle Fire, is that when you start using the touch screen, fingerprints, dirt, and smudges start to appear on the screen. Not only does this look unattractive, but it can detract from the screen's clarity.

Using a dry microfiber cleaning cloth—not a tissue, paper towel, or your shirt sleeve—you can easily wipe off the fingerprints, dirt, and smudges that begin to build up on the touch screen. It's essential that you use a microfiber cleaning cloth, like you'd use when cleaning your eyeglasses or a camera's lens. Using a tissue, paper towel, or another type of cloth could result in tiny scratches appearing on the screen.

In general, you never want to use any liquid or harsh chemicals to clean your touch screen or tablet. This includes window cleaner or just plain water. However, if a microfiber cleaning cloth doesn't remove all of the fingerprints, dirt, or smudges, you can apply a few drops of water directly to the microfiber cleaning cloth, and then use it to wipe down your tablet's screen. Only a few drops of water will be needed. The cloth should not be soaked. When cleaning your tablet's screen, there's never a need to press down too firmly on the display as you wipe it down.

You can purchase a microfiber cleaning cloth for between $4.00 and $7.00 wherever eyeglasses or sunglasses are sold, as well as from most pharmacies or camera shops. For example, within most shopping malls, you'll find a LensCrafters, Pearl Vision Center, or Sunglass Hut International. Any of these optical shops will offer a selection of microfiber cleaning cloths. You can keep the cloth in your pocket or in a pocket that's built into your Kindle Fire's carrying case.

While it typically is not needed, you can use a very small amount of liquid-based screen cleaner that's designed specifically for computer screens, LCD displays, and monitors. Specialty liquid cleaner, like Monster ScreenClean (www.monstercable .com/screenclean), is available from office supply stores and computer stores. It comes in a spray bottle and should be applied to your microfiber cleaning cloth in order to clean your tablet's screen. Generally, a liquid screen cleaner will not be necessary, however.

To make cleaning your screen easier, while protecting it, seriously consider applying an ultra-thin protective film over the touch screen, from a company like Zagg, 3M, or Marware. They come precut specifically for the Kindle Fire's screen, and they're designed to be kept on permanently, but can be removed in seconds with no sticky residue. See Chapter 4 for details.

Investing in Insurance or Amazon's Two-Year Protection Plan

Your tablet is not designed to be dropped, crushed, sat on, submerged in liquid, or thrown. However, accidents do happen. To protect your device against damage you accidently inflict (or against manufacturer defects), consider investing in insurance.

Amazon includes a one-year manufacturer's warranty with your Kindle Fire. However, this does not protect the device against user-inflicted damage or accidents. For this type of coverage, you'll need to purchase optional third-party insurance.

For example, Amazon has teamed up with SquareTrade (www.squaretrade.com) to offer comprehensive tablet coverage for two years. Available to U.S. residents only, this optional two-year protection plan for the Kindle Fire is currently priced at $44.99. It includes accidental damage coverage, with no deductible, for two years from the tablet's purchase date. During the warrantee period, you can make up to three repair or replacement claims. Each repair or replacement includes two-day shipping both ways, so you won't be without a working device for more than a few business days.

You can purchase the optional SquareTrade insurance coverage from Amazon (www.amazon.com/SquareTrade-Warranty-Accident-Protection-customers/dp/ B0058WELD2/) or directly from the SquareTrade website.

The manufacturer's warranty that comes with your Kindle Fire lasts for one year, but does not include accidental damage. The optional insurance plan from SquareTrade does cover accidental damage for two years, but does not cover the unit if it gets lost or stolen.

Worth Ave Group (www.worthavegroup.com) is another third-party insurance company that offers coverage to Amazon Kindle Fire users. Their coverage includes accidental damage, as well as loss or theft of the unit for one, two, or three years. However, a deductible will be charged for each claim, and other conditions apply. See the company's website for details.

How to Reach Amazon's Technical Support

The Kindle Fire comes with the *Kindle Fire User's Guide* preinstalled as an eBook on your device. Plus, many of the questions or problems you may encounter in regard to the Kindle Fire will be addressed within this book. However, if you need to obtain technical support from Amazon, whether in reference to the Kindle Fire itself, the use of Amazon's cloud-based file sharing services, or digital content you purchase from Amazon, you can contact the company's technical support team directly by e-mail, online chat, or telephone.

To obtain free technical support for your Kindle, begin by visiting Amazon's website (www.Amazon.com) and seeing if your question or problem is addressed within the free support or discussion forums. If not, you can make contact with Amazon's technical support by entering your phone number into the appropriate field and having a support specialist call you instantly.

To reach Amazon's free technical support for the Kindle Fire, follow these steps:

1. From your computer or your tablet's web browser, visit www.Amazon.com.
2. On the left side of the Amazon.com screen, click the Kindle menu option.
3. Select the Manage Your Kindle option from the submenu that appears.
4. Sign into your Amazon.com account using your user name and password.
5. Located in the upper-right corner of the screen, click the Kindle Support option.
6. On the right side of the screen, under the Self-Service heading, click the Contact Us icon.
7. From the Customer Service screen that appears, make sure the I Need Assistance With Kindle option is selected, and then click the icon representing your Kindle Fire. Then, in steps 2 and 3 on the Customer Service screen, using the pull-down menus, choose the options that best describe your question or problem.
8. At the bottom of the Customer Service screen, click the Email, Phone, or Chat option to determine how you want to communicate with Amazon's Technical Support department. If you select Phone, you'll be prompted to enter your phone number. Amazon will then call you immediately or at the time you specify. If you select Email, you can send an e-mail message outlining your question or problem. Or if you select Chat, you can chat in real time with a Kindle Technical Support specialist using instant text messaging via the Web.

 Many frequently asked questions and problems people have with their Kindle are addressed within the Kindle Forum on Amazon's website. To access this forum, follow steps 1 through 4 that are outlined in the steps above. From the Manage Your Kindle screen, however, click the Discussions option that's displayed near the top-center area of the screen below the Search field.

You're Now Ready to Use Your Kindle Fire

This chapter provided an introduction to the core information you need to begin using your Amazon Kindle Fire and protect the device during everyday use. In the next chapter, you'll learn how to customize the tablet's functions by adjusting options within the Settings menu. Then, in Chapter 4, you'll discover how to enhance your Kindle Fire experience by adding optional accessories to your tablet.

Starting in Part II of this book, you'll learn how to use the various apps that come preinstalled in your device, so you'll have no trouble surfing the Web, managing your e-mail, participating in the popular online social networking sites, reading eBooks, viewing documents and files, watching TV shows and movies, listening to music, and/or syncing data between your tablet and computer.

Part III of this book focuses on how to find, download, install, and use specific apps on your Kindle Fire. You'll get a comprehensive overview of the types of apps available and exactly how to find information about the newest apps being released for your tablet.

Unlike other tablets on the market, the Kindle Fire is designed primarily as a device for utilizing content supplied by Amazon.com and other online services in order to read eBooks and digital publications; watch TV shows, movies, and videos; listen to music and audio; surf the Web; and manage e-mail. You can also easily view work-related documents, such as Microsoft Word files or PDF files, on your Kindle Fire too, and you'll find some great apps that expand the capabilities of your Kindle Fire.

As you begin using your Kindle Fire, make sure your expectations are realistic in terms of its capabilities and what computing tasks simply are not practical to do on the device's seven-inch screen. The Kindle Fire is not meant to replace a laptop computer or netbook, for example. This book, particularly what's covered within Part III, will help you get the most out of using your tablet in conjunction with third-party apps that expand its core functionality.

The Kindle Fire is an extremely powerful tablet, and there's a definite reason why one million devices sold per week in the closing weeks of December 2011. Industry analysts expect that five million of these devices would sell within the first two to three months of the Kindle Fire becoming available from Amazon, and the sales are right on track with these estimates.

3

Customize Your Kindle Fire Using the Settings Menu

HOW TO...

- Access and customize the various features and functions of the Kindle Fire from the main Settings menu.
- Discover what each Settings menu option is used for.

From the previous chapter, you learned that you can quickly customize five of the most commonly used settings within your Kindle Fire by tapping the gear-shaped Quick Settings icon that's displayed near the upper-right corner of the Home screen. Doing this reveals six command icons (shown in Figure 3-1) that allow you to turn the screen rotation lock of the tablet on and off, adjust the volume, change the screen brightness, connect to a Wi-Fi network, and sync your Kindle Fire to a computer.

If you tap the More icon, however, which appears near the upper-right corner of the Fire's Home screen when you tap the Quick Settings icon, the complete Settings menu for the tablet is revealed. From this menu, you can customize a wide range of features and options related to the operation of your Kindle Fire and apps.

This chapter focuses on the Settings menu, what's available from it, and how each menu option can be used to personalize or customize how your tablet operates.

 While you should understand how to adjust the Quick Settings options right away, some of the other Settings menu options are less important, so you can wait to learn more about them until they're actually needed. You can always refer back to this chapter later and use it for reference. Right now, use the information within this chapter to familiarize yourself with what's possible in terms of the customization of your Kindle Fire.

FIGURE 3-1 The Kindle Fire's Quick Settings command icon

The Main Settings Menu Options

When you access the main Settings menu, the Settings screen (shown in Figure 3-2) replaces the Home screen. Here, a dozen main menu options are displayed. As you're about to discover, many of these main menu options grant you access to submenus.

 When you're viewing a submenu accessed from the main Settings menu, to return to the main Settings menu or the Home screen, tap the left-pointing arrow icon that's displayed at the bottom-center area of the submenu screen, or tap the Home icon that's displayed near the lower-left corner of the screen, respectively.

Access the Help & Feedback Option

This interactive help menu offers a handful of topics you can get instant help with as you use your Kindle Fire. The submenu screen displays three command tabs near the top of the screen, just below the Help & Feedback heading. They're labeled FAQ & Troubleshooting, Contact Customer Service, and Feedback.

Tap the FAQ & Troubleshooting command tab to see a menu of 15 topics under the Get Help With heading. Tapping any of these topic headings will reveal on-screen information pertaining to that topic, such as Home Screen and Navigation, Apps, Docs, Web, and E-Mail. Some of the text-based content within these help files are preinstalled on your tablet and can be accessed at any time. Others are web-based, and require that your Kindle Fire be connected to the Internet to access them.

If the topic you need help with is not listed under the Get Help With heading, and you can't find the answer you're looking for within this book, tap the blue More

FIGURE 3-2 The Kindle Fire's main Settings menu screen

Online Help option that's displayed near the bottom of the screen to access additional online-based help topics.

 Tip You'll also find free discussion forums related to the Kindle Fire at the Kindle Fire Forum (www.kfforum.com) and Fireblog (www.thefireblog.com), both of which are free, independent, online resources.

To reach Amazon's Customer Service and Technical Support department by phone, e-mail, or online chat, tap the Contact Customer Service command tab that's displayed near the top of the screen when viewing the Help & Feedback menu. To utilize these features, your Kindle Fire must be connected to the Web via a Wi-Fi connection. From the What Can We Help You With pull-down menu, select a topic that most closely resembles your question or problem. Next, choose how you want to contact Customer Service: by e-mail or telephone. Follow the on-screen prompts to obtain the help you need.

If you have a comment or suggestion in regard to your Kindle Fire that you want to share with Amazon, any time your device is connected to the Internet, tap the Feedback command tab and follow the on-screen prompts.

Manage Your Amazon.com Account Using the My Account Option

As a Kindle Fire owner, you must have an active Amazon.com account set up and have a credit or debit card connected to that account so you can make 1-Click purchases directly from your tablet. To be able to make online purchases of eBooks, apps, magazines, newspapers, music, TV show episodes, or movies from Amazon.com, you'll need to have a credit or debit card associated with the Kindle Payment Settings option of the Manage My Kindle webpage found at Amazon.com.

By tapping the My Account menu option on the main Settings screen, you can register or unregister your Kindle Fire, plus discover the free e-mail address that has been assigned to you as part of your free Amazon Cloud Drive account.

Customize Sound-Related Features Using the Sounds Menu Option

Your Kindle Fire has built-in speakers. However, the built-in volume controls can also increase or decrease the volume of audio, sound effects, or music generated by your tablet that you hear through headphones or external speakers that are connected to the device.

By tapping the Quick Settings icon from the Home screen, the second command icon from the left is labeled Volume. It's associated with a volume control slider that allows you to increase or decrease the volume of all sounds and music generated by your tablet. Move the slider to the right to increase the volume; move it to the left to decrease the volume.

How to... **Quickly Send Documents from Any Computer to Your Kindle Fire**

When you tap the My Account option displayed within the main Settings menu, you will discover your personal Send-To-Kindle e-mail address that has been assigned to you in conjunction with your Amazon Cloud Drive account.

From any computer or mobile device, you can e-mail yourself documents, files, or photos, for example, using this Send-To-Kindle e-mail address. Once these files have been sent to the supplied e-mail address, they can be downloaded directly from your online-based Amazon Cloud Drive account to your tablet via the Web. How to do this is fully explained within Chapter 8.

To edit the supplied Send-To-Kindle e-mail address, or to add preapproved addresses that can be given the ability to send files to your tablet, visit www.amazon.com/myk.

Once you sign in to your Amazon.com account, click the Manage My Kindle option (displayed on the left side of the webpage's screen), and then click the Personal Document Settings option.

FIGURE 3-3   The Sounds menu screen

When you tap the Sounds option from the Settings menu, in addition to seeing the volume slider displayed near the top of the screen, just below it, you'll see a menu option labeled Notification Sounds (shown in Figure 3-3).

Tap the Notification Sounds option to select the default alert sound that you'll hear when your Kindle Fire requires your prompt attention. You'll discover 11 sound effects to choose from. Tap a selection to preview the sound. It will be highlighted in orange. When you exit out of this menu screen by tapping the left-pointing arrow icon (displayed at the bottom-center area of the screen) or the Home icon, your highlighted selection will be saved automatically.

Modify the Kindle Fire's Display Using the Display Submenu

By tapping the Quick Settings icon from the Home screen, the third command icon from the left is labeled Brightness. It's associated with a screen brightness slider that allows you to increase or decrease the brightness of the Kindle Fire's screen. Move the slider to the right to increase the screen's brightness; move it to the left to decrease the screen's brightness.

 When you're in a brightly lit room or area, you might want to increase the screen's brightness to make it easier to view. Or if you're in a low-light area, you may opt to decrease the screen's brightness to make it easier to read.

If you access the Brightness slider by selecting the Display option from the main Settings menu, just below it you'll find the Screen Timeout option. Tapping this option allows you to decide how long your Kindle Fire can remain inactive before automatically entering into Sleep mode. Your options are 30 seconds, 1 minute, 5 minutes (the default), 15 minutes, 30 minutes, 45 minutes, 1 hour, or never. When the tablet is not being used, this option will help you conserve battery life, even if you forget to press the power button to place the Kindle Fire into Sleep mode manually.

As with the other Settings options, when you tap your selection, it will be highlighted in orange. You can then exit the Settings submenu screen by tapping the left-pointing arrow icon that's displayed near the bottom-center area of the screen, or the Home icon, to save your changes.

Password-Protect Your Kindle Fire by Adjusting the Security Settings

The Kindle Fire has several built-in security features that you can customize and activate by tapping the Security option that's part of the main Settings menu. The Security menu screen is composed of three options (shown in Figure 3-4), each of which reveals a separate submenu. The options are labeled Lock Screen Password, Credential Storage, and Device Administrators.

Lock Screen Password

The Lock Screen Password option is accompanied by a virtual on/off switch. The default setting is off. This means that anyone can turn on your Kindle Fire, swipe their finger across the Lock screen, and freely begin using your tablet.

By turning on the Lock Screen Password feature (switch the virtual on/off switch to the On position), the Lock Screen Password submenu screen is replaced by a blank Enter Password field with the virtual keyboard displayed at the bottom of the screen. Within this blank field, enter your own custom password that's composed of at least four alphanumeric characters (shown in Figure 3-5).

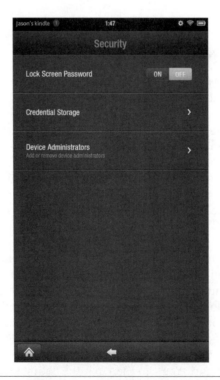

FIGURE 3-4   The Security submenu screen

FIGURE 3-5   You can password-protect your Kindle Fire and prevent unauthorized people from gaining access to your private data or using the device.

After entering your password once, re-enter the exact same password within the Confirm Password field. Then, tap the Finish icon. Assuming the passwords you entered into both fields match, this will become your tablet's new password. From this point forward, anytime you power on the Kindle Fire or awaken it from Sleep mode, when the Lock Screen appears, you'll first be required to enter your password to unlock the device before using it.

 After setting a password, once the Kindle Fire is unlocked, you can return to the Lock Screen Password screen from the main Settings menu to turn off the Lock Screen Password feature. Tap the Lock Screen Password switch that's associated with this option, and turn it to the Off position. Upon doing this, a password will no longer be needed to access your Kindle Fire.

Credential Storage

In the first two chapters of this book, the concept of using your free Amazon Cloud Drive account to transfer documents, data, and files to your device has been alluded to. There are several ways to do this, including e-mailing the documents or files as attachments to the personal Send-To-Kindle e-mail address that's been assigned to you by Amazon.com in conjunction with your Amazon Cloud Drive account.

This method of transferring files to your tablet was designed for personal use. However, it's also possible to create guest accounts so other people whom you preauthorize can also send documents and files to your tablet. From the Credential Storage option that's listed on the Security screen, you have the option to create guest accounts and establish an additional layer of password protection to prevent unauthorized people from sending content to your tablet.

 How to use these Credential Storage security features and the process of transferring, syncing, and copying data, files, documents, photos, and other content to your Kindle Fire is covered in Chapter 8.

Device Administrators

In the future, this feature will most likely be used to "childproof" your Kindle Fire before handing it over to your kids so they can read children's books, watch movies, or play games, for example. Or, it could ultimately be used to provide enterprise solutions to the device, allowing employers to easily manage a fleet of Kindle Fires that have been distributed to employees.

At the time the Kindle Fire was launched, however, the Device Administrators functionality had not yet been implemented. At least initially, when using version 6.1 of the Kindle Fire operating system, if you tap this menu option from the Security submenu, a message that says "No available device administrators" is displayed, with no further user-adjustable options.

 In the future, if you want to "childproof" your device or perform a remote reset of your device (erasing its content), this is the feature that will be used. For example, you could potentially block your kids from purchasing content when using the tablet, or from accessing the Web. Or you could make it so they can only watch preapproved video content, or read only the eBooks you preselect. They would theoretically be locked out of all other tablet functionality. It may also be used to delete all content from the tablet via the Web if your Kindle Fire is lost or stolen.

When this feature does become active, make sure you remember the password you use that's associated with the Device Administrators option(s), or you could wind up getting locked out of your own device, and ultimately have to delete everything on it and manually reinstall your apps and data.

Manage the Apps Stored on Your Kindle Fire Using the Applications Menu Option

One of the features that makes your Kindle Fire highly customizable and that allows it to perform many tasks beyond what a typical eBook reader is capable of is the tablet's ability to run third-party apps. Your Kindle Fire's operating system is a proprietary version of Google's Android OS, which is used by a wide range of smartphones and tablets. As a result, thousands of third-party apps are compatible with this operating system.

However, Amazon has put limits on which third-party apps can be used with your Kindle Fire, as well as where those apps are to be acquired from. As you'll discover later, there are ways to bypass these limitations (at least somewhat). You'll learn more about finding, downloading, and installing third-party apps to your tablet in Chapter 14.

By tapping the Applications menu option from the main Settings menu, you can adjust specific settings for the apps that are installed on your device. When the Applications menu screen is displayed (shown in Figure 3-6), what you'll initially see is a listing of applications installed on your device that have user-adjustable settings available.

One at a time, tap each app listing to adjust its user-adjustable settings and features. Keep in mind that once you tap each app listing separately, the selection of features you can adjust will vary. However, at the top of each app's menu screen will be a Force Stop and potentially an Uninstall icon.

If an app is running but crashes, or for whatever reason stops functioning properly but does not shut itself down, you can use the Force Stop command to manually shut down the app. Or, if the app is one that you installed yourself on the device (not a preinstalled app), you can uninstall and delete it from your tablet by tapping the Uninstall icon (shown in Figure 3-7).

FIGURE 3-6   Listed on the Applications menu screen are icons for all preinstalled and third-party apps that have user-adjustable options.

FIGURE 3-7 Tap the Uninstall icon related to a third-party app to delete it from your device. You can always reinstall it later.

Even if you uninstall an app from your Kindle Fire, it remains stored online within your Amazon Cloud Drive account. So, as long as your tablet has access to the Internet, you can always reinstall that app, for free, at any time in the future. Keep in mind that apps that came preinstalled on your tablet cannot be deleted from it.

As you look at the app-specific menu screen for each of your Kindle Fire's preinstalled and third-party apps, if that app is utilizing file storage space on your tablet (which depletes some of the available 8GB of storage space built into the Kindle Fire), this information will be displayed. For example, how much storage space the app itself utilizes, as well as how much additional storage space is being utilized by app-specific data, is displayed.

If a specific app stores its own app-specific data on your tablet, from that app's Settings submenu, there will most likely be a Clear Data icon displayed as well. Tapping this icon will keep the app itself installed on your tablet, but erase all data associated with it. For example, if you tap the Browser option from the Applications menu, you'll have the option to tap a Clear Data icon to delete browser-related data stored on your device. There's also a Clear Cache icon, which allows you to delete website-related data from sites you've visited, which is also stored on your tablet.

As you install new third-party apps onto your Kindle Fire, new options will become available to you from the Applications submenu, so check it periodically to determine if there are new user-adjustable settings you can alter to make using your favorite third-party apps more efficient.

Adjust the Date & Time Formatting Options

By default, when your Kindle Fire is connected to the Web, it will automatically determine the exact time and date, and then display and utilize this information. However, the ability to automatically set the time and date is a user-adjustable option. From the main Settings menu, if you tap the Date & Time option and then you tap the virtual on/off switch that's associated with the Automatic option to turn this feature off, you will then be able to manually set the date and time information your tablet will utilize.

From the Date & Time submenu screen, you can also manually select your time zone, which is something you initially selected when you first activated your tablet. If you travel and change time zones, you can manually change this option.

Connect to or Change Wireless Networks

The options available when you select Wireless Networks from the main Settings menu are identical to the options available when you tap the Wi-Fi command icon from the Quick Settings menu. From the Wireless Network screen, manually select which available Wi-Fi network your Kindle Fire will connect to.

The listing of available wireless networks will change, depending on what networks are available at your current location. If you visit a bookstore, café, or hotel, for example, that offers free Wi-Fi, a listing for that wireless network or hotspot will be displayed when you access the Wireless Networks menu. However, if you leave the signal radius of a specific wireless network, its listing will disappear from the screen, since it will no longer be available to connect to.

 If you're given a selection of wireless networks or Wi-Fi hotspots to connect to from the Wireless Networks screen, select the network that's giving off the strongest signal. This will ensure the best Internet connection possible. If any of the listed networks are locked, however, a password will be required to connect to them.

Change How the Virtual Keyboard Performs Using the Kindle Keyboard Submenu

Like many other features built into your Kindle Fire, the virtual keyboard also has a few user-adjustable settings. When you tap the Kindle Keyboard option from the main Settings menu, three menu options are displayed on the Kindle Keyboard menu screen (shown in Figure 3-8). They're labeled Sound On Keypress, Auto-Capitalization, and Quick Fixes. Each has a virtual on/off switch associated with it.

FIGURE 3-8 You can turn on or off user-adjustable features associated with the Kindle Fire's virtual keyboard.

Sound On Keypress

When the Sound On Keypress feature is turned on, every time you tap one of the virtual keyboard's keys, you'll hear a click sound. As you'll discover, the sound changes slightly, based on which keys you press as you're typing. If you don't want to hear these key clicking sounds as you type, turn off the Sound On Keypress submenu option.

 To increase the size of the virtual keyboard (and the individual keys) as you're typing, consider rotating the tablet to landscape mode. Also, practice using just your thumbs to "touch type" as opposed to all of your fingers. This may help to increase your typing speed and accuracy.

How to... **Turn Your Kindle Fire's Wireless Communications Capabilities On and Off**

In situations when no Wi-Fi network is available, or you're not allowed to use your tablet to send/receive wireless data (on an airplane, for example), tap the virtual switch associated with the Wireless Network option to turn off Internet connectivity altogether.

By doing this, your tablet will still function, but it will not be able to access the Internet or send/receive data wirelessly. When Internet connectivity is not being used, turning off the Wireless Network feature will also help to extend your Kindle Fire's battery life.

When the virtual on/off switch associated with the Wireless Network option is left on, the tablet will constantly search for a wireless network to connect to until it finds one. This constant activity drains your tablet's battery.

Auto-Capitalization

As you're typing, your Kindle Fire can often automatically determine when a letter should be capitalized—for example, when you begin a new sentence. While this feature is not always 100 percent accurate, it does do a good job, and can help speed up your touch-typing speed when using the Kindle Fire's virtual keyboard. To turn off this feature, tap the virtual on/off switch associated with the Auto-Capitalization submenu option.

Quick Fixes

When you begin trying to "touch type" on the small virtual keyboard that's built into the Kindle Fire, you'll discover typos are common. As you're typing, however, your Kindle Fire will pay attention to what you're typing and can automatically fix typos. To utilize this feature, turn on the virtual switch that's associated with the Quick Fixes option on the Kindle Keyboard submenu screen.

 Sometimes, your Kindle Fire will insert the wrong word when it implements a "quick fix," and this could lead to sending an embarrassing e-mail that has a meaning you didn't intend. Be sure to proofread all text you generate on your tablet prior to sending or sharing it with others. To see embarrassing situations caused by the Quick Fix feature (or a similar Auto Correct feature on other smartphone and tablet models), visit http://damnyouautocorrect.com.

Access Details About Your Tablet or Reset It Using the Device Menu Option

When you access the Device menu option from the main Settings menu, you're given seven submenu options that are displayed on the Device screen (shown in Figure 3-9). These include Storage, Battery Remaining, System Version, Serial Number, Wi-Fi MAC Address, Allow Installation Of Applications From Unknown Sources, and Reset To Factory Defaults.

Storage

Displayed at the top of the Device menu screen is how much of your tablet's 8GB of internal storage space is being utilized. This is a noninteractive feature, but it does allow you to see how much storage space is available and how much is being used up by apps, content, files, documents, and data, for example.

Battery Remaining

Almost constantly displayed near the upper-right corner of your Kindle Fire's screen is a graphic battery indicator, which shows how much of a charge your tablet's internal battery has remaining. However, the Battery Remaining indicator that's displayed on the Device screen offers more detailed battery-related information, including the percentage of battery life that's remaining.

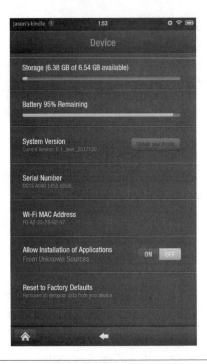

FIGURE 3-9 The Device menu offers further customization options.

System Version

This menu option displays what version number of the proprietary edition of the Android OS is currently running on your tablet. If your tablet is connected to the Internet, a command icon that's labeled Update Your Kindle will also be available. Tap this icon to determine if a newer edition of the operating system is available from Amazon. If so, you can automatically (and wirelessly) download and install it on your tablet.

 Making sure your Kindle Fire is utilizing the latest version of its operating system will help to ensure a bug-free experience using your tablet, plus help to ensure it is fully compatible with the latest third-party apps being released. At least once per month, get into the habit of checking to see if an update to the Kindle Fire's operating system has been released.

The Serial Number and Wi-Fi MAC Address Options

Like most computers, tablets, smartphones, and other devices, your Kindle Fire has a unique serial number, which is registered with Amazon.com when you activate the device. To determine your device's serial number, look under the Serial Number heading on the Device submenu screen. Your device's serial number is composed of 16 numbers and letters.

Below the device's serial number is the Wi-Fi MAC Address, which relates to the Wi-Fi network (or Wi-Fi hotspot) it's connected to. If you're having trouble accessing the Internet from your tablet, contact Amazon's Technical Support department to receive help adjusting the Wi-Fi MAC address information.

Allow Installation of Applications from Unknown Sources

By default, your Kindle Fire is permitted to download and install third-party apps only from Amazon's own Kindle Fire App Store. However, when you turn off the virtual on/off switch associated with the Allow Installation Of Applications From Unknown Sources feature, you can theoretically acquire Android OS–compatible apps from other sources as well. We'll focus more on how to do this later in the book.

Reset To Factory Defaults

If you select this menu option, you will be given the opportunity to delete everything on your Kindle Fire and restore all of the settings to factory defaults. In other words, it will be as if you first purchased the Kindle Fire. All of your personal data, settings, and any files or third-party apps stored on the device will be erased.

After you activate the Reset To Factory Defaults option (shown in Figure 3-10), you will need to reactivate your tablet and re-enter your Amazon.com account settings. Should something go very wrong with your tablet, or if you opt to give it away or sell it to someone else, use this option to erase everything.

FIGURE 3-10   Be sure to back up your data before using the Reset To Factory Defaults option.

Know Your Rights … Read the Kindle Fire–Related Legal Notices

Blah, blah, blah, blah … blah. Okay, that's not exactly what you'll see when you access the Legal Notices option from the main Settings screen, but what will be displayed is an extremely long document filled with legal jargon related to your use of the Kindle Fire. If you're a lawyer, you may find this content fascinating, but for the average person, it's information that you'll have little or no use for whatsoever. In a nutshell, don't do anything illegal with your Kindle Fire, like pirate copyrighted content, and you'll be all set.

More Fine-Print: Read the Terms of Use Text

Just in case you weren't totally bored out of your mind reading the Legal Notices fine-print, just wait until you access the terms of use legal jargon that's displayed when you tap the Terms Of Use option from the main Settings menu. It's a real snooze-fest, and to access it, your tablet will need to be connected to the Internet.

Again, as long as you don't plan to do anything illegal in connection with using your Kindle Fire, chances are the mysterious men in black from the government won't be showing up at your door anytime soon to throw you in jail, or make you and your tablet disappear.

4

Optional Kindle Fire Accessories

HOW TO...

- Learn what optional accessories are available for your Kindle Fire
- Choose which accessories are ideal for you
- Save money when shopping for accessories

As you begin using your new Kindle Fire and considering the various types of optional accessories available for it, ask yourself two questions:

1. What types of accessories do I need to protect my Kindle Fire while it's in use, as well as when it's being transported?
2. What types of accessories do I want for my Kindle Fire that will enhance its functionality based on how I use it?

In addition to the accessories that Amazon offers for the Kindle Fire, a growing number of third-party companies have begun offering their own accessories specifically for the Kindle Fire, or that can be used in conjunction with it.

 As you know, a handful of Kindle eBook readers are available. As you shop for accessories, make sure you select products designed specifically for the Kindle Fire or that are compatible with it. The size and shape of the other Kindle eBook readers are all different, so cases, covers, or screen protectors designed for a Kindle eBook reader or Apple iPad 2, for example, will typically not work with a Kindle Fire.

Accessories That Will Protect Your Kindle Fire

When it comes to protecting your Kindle Fire, you can use any or all three options: a case, a cover, and/or a screen protector film. A padded case is ideal for transporting your tablet when it's not in use, while a cover or protection film will mainly protect the Kindle Fire's screen.

Cases for Your Kindle Fire

Some cases are well padded and completely protect the tablet from all sides. The Kindle Fire is inserted into the case, which can then be inserted into a purse, briefcase, backpack, or messenger bag, for example, to keep your tablet safe while it's being transported. Some cases have handles and are designed to provide stand-alone protection while on the go, or can be used while your tablet is being stored.

You'll also find messenger bags and other types of cases that have a padded pocket designed specifically for holding the Kindle Fire, but the case itself can be used to hold other items as well.

Slipcovers are another type of case. These are typically padded and enclosed on three sides, almost like an envelope. The tablet is inserted into the slipcover for a snug fit when it's not in use and can be transported safely.

Tip   Using a case when transporting your Kindle Fire will protect the screen from getting scratched or cracked, keep the tablet clean, and help to protect it from getting crushed or otherwise damaged.

Covers for Your Kindle Fire

Unlike a case that completely encloses your tablet, a cover is designed primarily to protect the touch screen when it's not in use. Many covers have a portfolio design. The tablet itself attaches to or fits into the right side of the cover, while the left side folds over the screen for protection.

Some covers also serve as a tabletop stand when the tablet is in use. If this is the case, ideally you want a cover that will allow you to position the Kindle Fire in portrait or landscape mode. Even when closed, a cover will protect the tablet's screen and back, but typically not its sides, top, or bottom, and covers are not typically well padded.

You can shop for covers for your Kindle Fire directly from Amazon.com (shown in Figure 4-1), from retailers that sell the Kindle Fire, or from companies that sell covers, cases or protective films on the Internet (some of which are listed within this chapter). The price typically ranges between $9.99 and $39.99.

Tip   On the left side of the Amazon.com home page, under the Shop All Departments heading, hold your mouse over the Kindle option. Then, select the Accessories submenu option. In the main part of the screen, click the Covers option under the Kindle Fire heading.

Where to Shop for Covers and Cases

While retailers that sell the Kindle Fire, like Best Buy, will typically stock two or three cover or case options, for the broadest selection in terms of design, quality, and price,

FIGURE 4-1   You can shop for Kindle Fire accessories, including cases and covers, directly from Amazon.com.

you'll definitely want to shop for a case or cover online. Some of the many companies offering cases and/or covers for the Kindle Fire include

- **Belkin** (www.belkin.com)   Belkin offers the Verve Tab Folio for the Kindle Fire ($29.99) in several colors. Shown in Figure 4-2, it's a portfolio-style cover with a faux leather exterior and soft inner lining. The company also offers a selection of cases for the Kindle Fire, including several that also serve as tabletop stands.
- **Boxwave** (www.boxwave.com)   More than a dozen different styles of cases and covers are offered by Boxwave, including a padded leather envelope-style slipcover ($22.95) that comes in manila or black. The BodySuit ($14.50) fits over the entire tablet, and is designed to be kept on the Kindle Fire at all times. It's available in several colors, and made from thermoplastic polyurethane, which is thin, but offers durable protection.
- **Case Mate** (www.case-mate.com)   The two styles of Kindle Fire covers this company offers also serve as multiposition tabletop stands. The ultra-thin Amazon Kindle Fire Tuxedo Cases ($40.00), for example, resemble the Smart Covers that Apple created for the iPad 2, and also feature smart magnet technology. These cases are made from what the company refers to as "Italian leather–inspired" material. They look business-like and conservative.

FIGURE 4-2 The Belkin Verve Tab Folio comes in a variety of colors and is a stylish cover for your Kindle Fire.

- **Incipio** (www.myincipio.com) These cases are made from Ripstop nylon and surround the tablet with a Sport Zip enclosure. These cases not only offer padding to protect the tablet itself, but some have several external pockets for holding the charger, cables, and other accessories. Priced at $24.99, the Sport Zip Case (shown in Figure 4-3) is designed to keep your tablet safe when placed within a purse, briefcase, backpack, or messenger bag.

FIGURE 4-3 The Incipio Sport Zip Case offers padded protection for your tablet while on the go.

- **Lightwedge** (www.lightwedge.com)   Available in more than a dozen designs, these covers re-create the look of a classic, leather-bound, hardcover book. The company also offers several covers in its *New York Times*–inspired series, which features iconic black-and-white images of New York City. These covers are priced at $39.99. Figure 4-4 shows the Lightwedge Prologue cover.
- **Marware** (www.marware.com)   This company offers a handful of contemporary-style Kindle Fire cover designs, each available in black or gray. Most are made from padded leather on the outside and soft microsuede on the inside. Prices range from $29.99 to $44.99.
- **Pad & Quill** (www.padandquill.com)   These designer tablet covers are handmade in America using fine Italian leather, Baltic birch wood, and book bindery cloth. The elegant Fire Keeper covers ($59.99) come in five colors.
- **Timbuk2** (www.timbuk2.com)   This company is known for its customizable, extremely durable, and somewhat trendy (made-in-America) messenger bags, including several messenger bags with internal pockets designed to hold an eBook reader. Among the Kindle Fire accessory products Timbuk2 offers are cases and slipcovers. Like the messenger bags, these padded cases are made from ballistic nylon, come in a wide range of colors, and offer Velcro closures.
- **Waterfield** (www.sfbags.com)   With more than eight Kindle Fire cases, covers, and bags to choose from (each of which is available in a variety of colors), you'll easily find a way to protect and show off your tablet in a way that perfectly fits your lifestyle. The majority of the company's products are priced under $60.00. While the Kindle Fire Ultimate SleeveCase ($55.00), for example, is ideal for transporting your tablet in a briefcase or purse, the stylish Muzetto is a

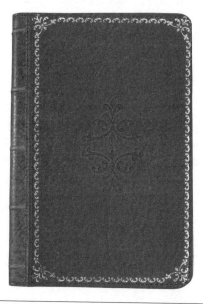

FIGURE 4-4   The Lightwedge Prologue cover for the Kindle Fire

messenger-style bag ($179.00) with a custom-sized, padded pocket for your tablet, plus other compartments for your cell phone, eyeglasses, and other belongings.

- **Zoogue** (www.zoogue.com)   The Kindle Fire Leather Case Genius ($39.99) offers more than you might expect from a typical case. The case will keep your tablet safe when it's being transported. In addition, the black or pink case can securely hold your tablet at six different angles when placed on a tabletop.

Using a Protective Film for Your Kindle Fire's Screen

You've probably discovered by now that your tablet's touch screen is very sensitive and reflective. As you use it, it's easy to get it dirty with fingerprints and smudges caused by the oils in your fingers. Plus, the touch screen can get scratched or cracked if it's not properly protected while being transported or if it accidentally gets dropped.

Several companies offer an ultra-thin, clear protective film that gets placed over the tablet, which will protect it from scratches or cracks, plus make it easier to wipe clean as it gets dirty or covered in fingerprints. These protective films are custom-cut to the exact size of the Kindle Fire's screen, take just five to ten minutes to apply, and are meant to be kept on the screen at all times. However, the film can be removed from the screen in seconds, without leaving any sticky residue. Some protective films require that you wet them down prior to applying them. This takes a few minutes extra in terms of preparation, but offer a stronger and airtight, (but removable) seal between the tablet and protective screen.

Depending on what the protective film is made from, it might also offer antiglare protection, making the screen easier to see in bright light or in the sun, or it could offer a privacy filter, which makes it easy for you to see what's on your tablet's screen, but if someone is looking over your shoulder or from the side, all they'll see is a blank gray screen.

Regardless of whether you use a case and/or a cover for your tablet, investing in a protective film for the screen is a low-cost and nonintrusive way to protect your Kindle Fire at all times. These protective films are typically less than one millimeter thick, crystal clear, and made from extremely durable, military-grade material.

 Tip   In addition to a protective film for your tablet's screen, be sure to keep a microfiber cleaning cloth on hand, so you can wipe down and clean your screen at any time. Refer to Chapter 2 for more information.

You can find a protective film that's specifically designed for use with your Kindle Fire on Amazon.com or at retailers that sell Kindle tablets, such as Best Buy. On the Web, some of the companies they're available from include

- **Zagg** (www.zagg.com)   This company's InvisibleSHIELD protective film ($34.99) covers the entire tablet (front, sides, and back) with a military-grade, scratchproof film.
- **3M** (www.shop3m.com/98044051534.html)   Choose between an antiglare and a privacy protection protective film that can be cut to fit over your Kindle Fire's

Did You Know?

You Can Customize the Look of Your Tablet with Skins

In addition to using a clear protective film over the tablet's screen, you can purchase a highly durable and ultra-thin protective film that will cover the rest of your tablet as well. These skins are printed with artistic designs or artwork that allows you to dress up your Kindle Fire in a way that showcases your own personal taste and style. Several companies will even create custom-made Kindle Fire skins using your digital photos.

To learn more about custom skins for your tablet, visit www.decalgirl.com, www.skinit.com, www.zagg.com, or www.uniqueskins.com. The easily removable skins are designed to be kept on your tablet at all times. They're priced between $9.99 and $19.00.

screen. The 3M Natural View Screen Protector ($31.99), for example, reduces reflections and glares, plus it's smudge resistant.

- **BodyGuardz** (www.bodyguardz.com)   This company offers its HD Anti-Glare Screen Guardz and the UltraTough Clear ScreenGuardz ($15.95 each). Both are precut to fit the Kindle Fire's screen and offer scratch-resistant protection.

Tip If you search eBay or Amazon.com, you'll often find quality screen protectors for under $10.00 that can work nicely with your Kindle Fire.

Battery Charging and Power Options for Your Kindle Fire

The one accessory that your Kindle Fire comes with is an AC adapter that plugs into the Micro-B USB port on the bottom of the tablet. It's used to plug your Kindle Fire into an AC electrical outlet in order to recharge its battery. However, if you're often on the go, sitting around an electrical outlet to recharge your Kindle Fire's battery may not always be possible.

Some of the alternate options available to you that will keep your Kindle Fire powered up include a car charger and/or external battery pack. Kensington (www.kensington.com), for example, offers a handful of useful accessories for the Kindle Fire, including the Kindle Fire PowerBolt Duo USB Car Charger ($29.99). This device plugs directly into the cigarette lighter of your vehicle and offers 2.1 amps of power for quickly charging your tablet or using the tablet while its internal battery is being recharged. The charger comes with a detachable Micro-USB–to–USB cable that can also be used to sync your tablet with a computer.

Several companies offer external battery packs compatible with the Kindle Fire, including Brookstone (www.Brookstone.com) and RichardSolo (www.RichardSolo.com).

FIGURE 4-5 The Richard Solo 9000 is an external battery that will keep your Kindle Fire operational for two to four times longer than the tablet's internal battery.

These battery packs are ideal when you need to keep your tablet charged and operational for long periods and no electrical outlet is available.

The Richard Solo 9000 mAh Mobile Charger ($69.95) is a handheld, rechargeable battery that connects to the Kindle Fire via its Micro-USB port (shown in Figure 4-5). When fully charged, the Richard Solo 9000 can recharge your Kindle Fire's internal rechargeable battery multiple times, and keep the tablet running for an extra 20 to 30 hours (possibly longer).

External batteries that work with the Kindle Fire come in a variety of sizes. The Richard Solo 9000 measures 3.76" × 1.57" × 1.57" and weighs 10.2 ounces. Be sure to purchase a USB-to–Micro-B USB cable or adapter to work with any external battery pack that's compatible with the Kindle Fire. What's great about the Richard Solo 9000 is that it also works with a wide range of smartphones. The external battery can be recharged using any AC outlet or car charger with the proper adapter.

 Brookstone's PowerCup Power Inverter ($39.99, www.brookstone.com) is designed to fit into the cupholder of your vehicle and is plugged into the vehicle's cigarette lighter. It then offers two 120V AC outlets and a USB port that can be used for powering and/or charging multiple mobile devices at once. To keep your Kindle Fire running, you can plug in the AC power adapter that came with the device into this Coffee Cup Power Inverter, or plug a micro-B USB–to–USB cable (sold separately) between your tablet and this inverter.

Optional Accessories That Enhance the Tablet's Functionality

Aside from protecting your tablet and keeping it running, additional accessories can be used to enhance its functionality. For example, a variety of different laptop and tabletop stands are available that can position your tablet at the perfect angle for hands-free reading or watching video content.

Or, to dramatically improve the sound quality of the music and audio generated by your Kindle Fire as you're watching video content, listening to music, or playing games, you can either attach external speakers to the tablet that are capable of filling the room you're in with stereo sound, or you can attach stereo headphones to the tablet and use it as a personal, mobile entertainment device (without disturbing those around you).

While the Kindle Fire is not meant to serve as a full-featured word processor, using apps, you can use it to compose and send e-mails, view and annotate Microsoft Word documents, or even use a text editor to compose documents. Touch-typing using the Kindle Fire's virtual keyboard in portrait mode (shown in Figure 4-6) isn't too practical. Theoretically, however, by attaching an optional external keyboard, data entry becomes easier, but the mobility of your handheld tablet is hampered. While not available as of early 2012, an optional keyboard may be released for the Kindle Fire in the future. It would connect to the Micro-B USB port of the tablet.

Tabletop or Laptop Stands for Your Kindle Fire

A variety of different companies offer stands for the Kindle Fire that can be placed on any flat surface, such as your desk or the tray table of an airline seat, and used to position the device at the perfect angle to read or watch video content, without physically having to hold the device.

FIGURE 4-6   The Kindle Fire's virtual keyboard shown with the tablet held in portrait mode

Another type of stand takes the form of a pillow with a built-in shelf, which is ideal for using your tablet while sitting on a couch or lying in bed. This type of stand also holds your tablet at the right angle for reading or watching video content, for example, without your having to hold it in your hands.

 When lying in bed or sitting in your favorite chair to use your Kindle Fire, the Canvas Kiss Pillow ($39.00) from Levenger (www.levenger.com) is a pyramid-shaped pillow that will comfortably hold your tablet on your lap (or on a tabletop) as you're reading. This pillow also has three side pockets for your eyeglasses, note cards, pens, or other accessories. It measures 10.75" × 12.5" × 10.5" and weighs 0.5 pounds. It comes in a denim color.

Levenger also offers its extremely colorful and soft India Cloud Book Pillow ($49.00), which is handcrafted in India, and comfortably holds your tablet once the pillow is positioned on your lap or a tabletop. It measures 16" × 8" × 12", weighs 0.7 pounds, and has two side pockets.

eReader stands that work with the Kindle Fire are available from companies such as

- **Alibaba** (www.alibaba.com)
- **Beso** (www.beso.com/kindle-fire-stand/search)
- **BookBeanie** (http://stores.bookbeanie.com)
- **Boxwave** (www.boxwave.com)
- **iGearUSA** (www.igearusa.com)
- **Kradle for eReaders** (www.kradle.com)
- **Levenger** (www.levenger.com)
- **Moleskine** (www.Moleskine.com)
- **OmniMount** (www.omnimount.com)
- **Speck Products** (www.speckproducts.com)

Enhance the Sound Generated by Your Tablet

Many companies offer external speakers that can connect to your Kindle Fire. Plus, with the right optional cable, you can connect your tablet to your home or car stereo system. Or you can invest in a pair of good-quality headphones (or ear buds) and enjoy the audio generated by your Kindle Fire in private.

Any external speakers or headphones that can be plugged into a 3.5mm audio jack can be used with your tablet. When it comes to portability, however, there are a few external speakers, like the Jawbone Jambox ($199.00, www.jawbone.com), that are battery powered, extremely portable, and can fill a room with high-quality stereo sound. The Jawbone Jambox is shown in Figure 4-7.

By adding a good-quality external speaker to your tablet when watching a TV show episode or movie, for example, you can create a true home theater–like experience that's portable. Of course, these speakers are also ideal for listening to music or other audio content.

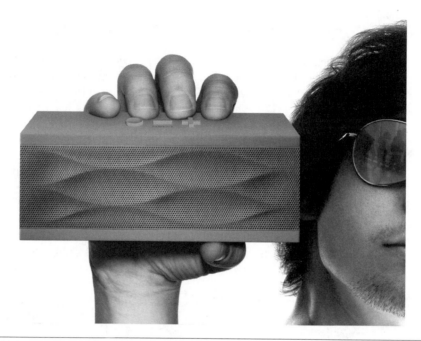

FIGURE 4-7   The Jawbone Jambox is a highly portable, but powerful external speaker that works with the Kindle Fire.

 Tip   While stereo headphones can be purchased for as little as $10.00, if you're an audiophile or simply want to enjoy the best sound quality possible using headphones or ear buds, consider investing in headphones or ear buds with noise-cancelling technology and that offer superior sound. Some of your options are described within this chapter.

Altec Lansing (www.alteclansing.com/ae/us/tablet-speakers/icat/tabletspeakers), Brookstone (www.Brookstone.com), iHome (www.ihomeaudio.com), and Bose (www .bose.com) are just a few of the companies that offer external speakers, some of which are battery powered, that can be connected to a Kindle Fire via its 3.5mm headphone jack.

As for optional headphones, companies like Bose (www.Bose.com), Shure www .shure.com), Beats by Dr. Dre (www.beatsbydre.com), Brookstone (www.Brookstone. com), JVC (www.jvc.com), Sennheiser (www.sennheiserusa.com), and Sony (http:// store.sony.com) offer a selection of noise-cancelling headphones and ear buds with 3.5mm jacks that can plug directly into the headphone jack of your Kindle Fire. They range in price from $99.00 to $399.00, depending on the design and quality. Of course, you can also find extremely inexpensive headphones or ear buds at any consumer electronics store, such as Radio Shack or Best Buy, for example.

Connect an Accessory to Your Kindle Fire

With the exception of cases or covers, the majority of available accessories will connect to your Kindle Fire in one of two ways: using the built-in Micro-B USB port or the headphone jack, both of which are located on the bottom of the device. The original model of the Kindle Fire does not offer wireless Bluetooth capabilities, so to connect an accessory to your tablet, a compatible cable needs to be used.

For between $5.00 and $25.00, you can purchase a Micro-B USB–to–USB cable from a computer or consumer electronics store if the appropriate cable does not come with the accessory you purchase.

For $14.95, Belkin (www.belkin.com) offers its 2-In-1 USB Kit, which includes a six-foot USB cable. On one end of the cable is a full-size USB connector. On the opposite site is a Mini-B USB connector. It comes with an adapter, however, to transform it into a Micro-B USB connector, so it can be used for connecting your Kindle Fire to a computer or other USB device with ease.

Keep in mind there's a difference between the various USB cable connectors and ports found on various devices. The port on the bottom of your Kindle Fire is a Micro-B USB port (not to be confused with a type A, type B, Micro-A, Mini-A, or Mini-B USB port). So, if you're connecting your Kindle Fire to an accessory with a typical (full-size) USB port (type A), you'll need a type A–to–Micro-B USB port in the appropriate length.

To connect any type of audio-related accessory to your Kindle Fire, such as external speakers, stereo headphones, ear buds, or stereo headphones with noise cancellation, you'll need to use headphones that come with a 3.5mm audio jack (not to be confused with 0.25" or 2.5mm audio jacks that are also commonly used by stereo headphone manufacturers). An inexpensive adapter may be needed to convert a .25" or 2.5mm stereo jack to a 3.5mm jack, so it will fit into your tablet's built-in headphone jack.

Make Touch-Typing Easier: Use an External Keyboard

As of January 2012, an optional, external keyboard that could connect to the Kindle Fire via its Micro-B USB connector had not yet been released, and external keyboards designed for other tablet devices are not compatible with the Kindle Fire, since it does not offer wireless Bluetooth functionality.

 Until an external keyboard accessory is released specifically for the Amazon Kindle Fire, you'll find it much easier to type quickly and more accurately with your thumbs if you place the tablet in landscape mode when entering text via the on-screen virtual keyboard (as shown in Figure 4-8).

FIGURE 4-8   When you hold the Kindle Fire in landscape mode, the on-screen virtual keyboard becomes slightly larger, making it easier to type.

Save Money When Shopping for Kindle Fire Accessories

Amazon.com typically offers low prices for its Kindle Fire accessories, including those manufactured by third-party companies that are being sold on Amazon.com. However, if you visit the websites for the manufacturing companies directly (many of which are listed within this chapter), you'll typically find a broader selection of available accessory products.

To save money on your Kindle Fire accessories, once you know exactly what you're looking for, try using a price comparison website, such as NexTag (www.nextag.com), to find multiple online merchants that sell the product you're looking for, and then compare prices. When choosing which merchant(s) to shop from, however, in addition to the price of the accessory or product itself, pay attention to how much the online vendor charges for shipping, as well as their overall customer ratings.

PART II

Your First Week Using a Kindle Fire

5

See What the Kindle Fire's Built-In Apps Are All About

HOW TO...

- Discover what your Kindle Fire can be used for, right out of the box
- Use the apps that come preinstalled on your tablet
- Listen to audiobooks, browse the Web in a new way, access documents, and more using your tablet

One of the features that set the Kindle Fire apart from the other Kindle eBook readers is that it can run apps. These apps, which are like programs used on a computer, dramatically increase the functionality of the tablet, beyond just allowing you to read eBooks. Right out of the box, your Kindle Fire has a handful of apps that come preinstalled and ready to use.

 As you'll discover in Chapter 14, an ever-growing library of third-party apps can be downloaded and installed on your Kindle Fire.

Some of the apps that come preinstalled on your Kindle Fire include:

- **Audible**   Gain access to the world's largest online audiobook store to shop for the audiobook editions of thousands of bestsellers and literary works from well-known authors. You can purchase, download, and then listen to audiobooks in all genres, using your Kindle Fire's built-in speakers, or by plugging external speakers or headphones into the tablet via its headphones jack. You can set up an Audible membership and purchase audiobooks at a discount, or purchase one title at a time. Audiobooks are offered in abridged or unabridged editions, and range in price from under $10.00 to upwards of $50.00, depending on the publisher and content.

- **Contacts**   This is a contact management app that allows you to create and maintain a personal database of people you know and companies you do business with. You can also import contacts from your existing contacts database into this Contacts app, or export Contacts entries you create on your Kindle Fire to your primary computer.
- **Email**   Use this app to manage one or more e-mail accounts. You can read incoming e-mail or compose and send outgoing e-mail messages directly from your Kindle Fire, as long as a Wi-Fi Internet connection is available.

 The entire focus of Chapter 7 is on sending and receiving e-mails and managing multiple e-mail accounts using your Kindle Fire.

- **Gallery**   Once you load digital images or photos into your tablet, this app allows you to view them on the tablet's screen.
- **Quickoffice**   This is one of the apps available that allow you to view and manage Microsoft Office documents and files directly on your Kindle Fire.
- **Amazon Shop**   With the Amazon Shop app, you can shop online for any products sold on Amazon.com: music, TV shows, movies, apps and other content for your tablet—just about anything. Using this app, you can often save money on purchases versus shopping at traditional retail stores.
- **Pulse**   Use this app to gather and present information from a variety of online sources on one, easy-to-navigate screen.

 When you purchased your Kindle Fire and set up an Amazon.com account, it included a free, 30-day trial of the Amazon.com Prime service, which among other things, entitles you to free two-day shipping for all products you purchase from Amazon.com.

In addition to the apps that come preinstalled on your tablet, your Kindle Fire comes with core apps, called Newsstand, Books, Music, Video, Docs, and Web, that allow you to handle the primary functions of your tablet. These apps are accessible from the Home screen's Navigation bar. You read descriptions of what these apps are used for in Chapter 2. Each of these core apps has at least one chapter dedicated to its use later in this book.

 A "core app" is one that is accessible from the Navigation bar, comes preinstalled on your Kindle Fire, and handles one of the main functions your tablet was designed to be used for, such as reading an eBook, listening to music, watching a video, launching a third-party app, or surfing the Internet.

This chapter, however, offers an overview of the apps that come preinstalled on your tablet, which are accessible once you tap the Apps command option from the Home screen's Navigation bar.

Enjoy Listening to Audiobooks on Your Kindle

One of Amazon.com's subsidiaries is Audible.com. It's an online-based store that sells audiobooks, as well as other specialized audio content, including audio versions of magazines and newspapers, radio shows, podcasts, stand-up comedy, and recordings of famous speeches. The Audible library comprises more than 100,000 titles, including abridged and unabridged editions of printed bestselling books and novels from well-known authors.

Your Amazon Kindle Fire comes with the Audible app preinstalled. It's used to browse and shop for audio content from Audible.com, which you can then listen to anytime and anywhere on your tablet, also using the Audible app.

To access the Audible app on your Kindle Fire, tap the Apps command option displayed on the Navigation bar of the Home screen. The Home screen will be replaced by the Apps screen (shown in Figure 5-1), which is a virtual bookshelf that displays app icons representing the apps currently stored on your tablet or that you own and have access to via your Amazon Cloud Drive account.

Tap the Cloud or Device command tab, displayed near the top-center area of the Apps screen, to display apps you own that are either stored online (but not on your tablet) or that are actually stored on your tablet and ready to use.

Because it's a preinstalled app, starting the very first time you access the App screen, you'll discover the Audible app icon displayed. Tap its icon to launch the Audible app. You will be given the option to sign into your existing Audible.com account, create a new account, or sample the Audible app for free without creating an account.

You Can Save Money with an Audible.com Membership

Instead of purchasing individual audiobooks and audio programs, Audible .com (which is owned by Amazon.com) offers memberships that entitle you to discounts on audiobook purchases. The regular monthly AudibleListener Gold membership fee of $14.95 includes one audiobook of your choice per month, plus a 30 percent discount on all additional audiobooks or audio programs purchased during the month. Members also receive free access to the audio edition of *The New York Times* and *The Wall Street Journal* newspapers.

Audible.com offers new members an introductory rate of $7.49 per month for the first three months. The membership can be cancelled at anytime. The alternative to becoming an AudibleListener Gold member is to purchase individual audiobooks and programs from Audible.com at their regular prices.

Audiobooks and content purchased from Audible.com can be enjoyed on your Kindle Fire, your computer, any digital audio player (including Apple iPods), and most smartphones.

FIGURE 5-1 View apps installed on your tablet, and launch them from the Apps Library screen.

If you opt to sample the Audible app, a handful of sample audiobook excerpts will instantly become available to you, which you can download for free and listen to using your tablet. When the listing of sample audiobook excerpts appears, tap the downward-pointing arrow icon to the right of any listing to download and listen to that audiobook or program excerpt.

To use the Audible app to browse or shop for audiobook titles, your Kindle Fire must have access to the Internet. Once an audiobook or audio program has been purchased and downloaded, you can listen to it without requiring an Internet connection.

Displayed near the top-left corner of the Audible app's main My Library screen is a shopping cart icon. It's used to access the online Audible.com store in order to browse and shop for audiobooks and audio programs. Near the upper-right corner of the Audible app's main screen is a Create Account icon. It's used to either establish an Audible.com membership or make it so you can purchase one audiobook or program at a time with a few taps on the screen. You can use your existing Amazon.com account information as your Audible.com account information, but it must be registered separately with Audible.com.

Once you set up an account with Audible.com, the Create Account icon is replaced by a Refresh icon that is used to display an up-to-date listing of your personal audiobook collection on your tablet's screen (shown in Figure 5-2).

Just below the Refresh icon is an icon composed of three horizontal lines. Tap it to reveal a menu screen that allows you to sort your personal audiobook collection based on all audiobooks you own, titles stored on your tablet, and free titles you've acquired from Audible.com.

FIGURE 5-2 The main My Library screen of the Audible app

 If you were listening to an audiobook but temporarily exited out of it to access the My Library screen of the Audible app, along the top of the screen will be a gray bar. To the extreme right of this bar will be a right-pointing arrow (>). Tap it to return to the Now Playing screen and resume playing the audiobook or audio program you were previously listening to. You'll pick up exactly where you left off.

As you look toward the bottom of the main My Library screen of the Audible app, you'll see four command tabs, labeled Recent, Title, Author, and Length. The Recent command tab displays the most recent audiobooks you've listened to. The Title command tab rearranges and displays your audiobook collection alphabetically, based on book titles. The Author command tab rearranges and displays your audiobook collection alphabetically, based on author names. Finally, the Length command tab will display your audiobook library based on the length of each recording.

Located near the bottom-left corner of the screen is the familiar Home screen icon. Tap it at any time to return to your tablet's Home screen. Displayed near the bottom-center area of the Audible app are three additional command icons. The first is a left-pointing arrow. It's used to return to the Audible app screen you were previously on.

The Menu command icon reveals six additional command icons, labeled Shop, News, Stats, Search, Settings, and Quit (shown in Figure 5-3). These menu options change depending on where in the app you access the menu from. The Search icon is used to search your audiobook library based on a title, author name, or keyword.

After tapping the Menu icon, if you select the Shop option that appears, you will immediately be transferred to the Audible.com store via the Audible app, where you can browse or shop for audiobooks. The News command icon allows you to view special offers and information about newly released audiobooks and audio programs available from Audible.com. The Stats icon is used to display your Audible.com membership information and track how many hours you've spent enjoying audio content from this service. The Search command works just like the Search icon, and allows you to search your audiobook library based on a title, author name, or keyword.

When you tap the Settings command icon, this reveals a separate submenu screen that allows you to customize the app. For example, if you tap the General Settings option, a submenu allows you to disable the Auto Lock feature related to your tablet's screen, use the tablet's web browser to access the Audible.com store, or control the status bar notifications you receive from the app.

The Playback settings allow you to customize how the on-screen controls work as you're listening to audiobooks. For example, if you tap the Back button, you can set how many seconds the recording will rewind (between 1 and 300).

 From Audible's Settings menu, access the Playback Settings option, and then turn on the Seamless Multipart Play option if you are listening to a multipart audio title and want your Kindle Fire to automatically begin playback of all separate segments in order as the previous part comes to an end.

From the Download setting, you can select your preferred download format. The options here include Standard Quality or High Quality. While the sound quality of a high-quality recording will be better than a standard-quality recording, the file size of the high-quality recording will be significantly larger and require more storage space on your tablet. For spoken-word audio programs, the difference in quality probably won't be noticeable. If you're an audiophile listening to music or sound effects in

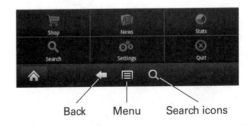

FIGURE 5-3   The menu icon reveals six additional command icons when accessed from Audible's My Library screen.

addition to the spoken word, chances are you will notice a difference between the standard and high quality settings.

 Unabridged editions of full-length books or novels also utilize large file sizes, since these audiobooks often run between 15 and 20 hours (or more) in duration.

 From Audible's Settings menu, if you select the Headset Settings option, you can set up and personalize the remote controls on your wired headset so you can control the audio being generated by your Kindle Fire using the headset's controls.

Once you download one or more audiobooks or audio programs from Audible.com using the Audible app, each audiobook or program will be displayed on the main My Library screen. To begin playing a specific audiobook or program, tap its listing.

Playing an Audible.com Audiobook or Program

As soon as you tap an audiobook or audio program listing from the My Library screen of the Audible app, that audio content will load and begin playing. What you see on the Audible app's screen will change accordingly. Displayed along the top of the screen when audio content from Audible.com is playing are four command icons (shown in Figure 5-4), labeled Now Playing, Details, Chapters, and Bookmarks. Now Playing reveals the on-screen controls used to play an audiobook.

By tapping the Details icon, you'll see a detailed description of the audiobook or program that's currently loaded and playing on your tablet. If you scroll down to the bottom of this Details screen, you'll see a Remove From Device icon. Tap it to delete the audiobook or program from your tablet when you're done listening to it. (The audiobook or program will still be accessible to you via your Amazon Cloud Drive account.)

The Chapters command tab reveals an interactive table of contents for the audiobook or audio program you're listening to. You can instantly fast-forward to a specific chapter by tapping its listing. Meanwhile, the Bookmarks icon reveals a listing of virtual bookmarks you've created as you were previously listening to the audiobook. By tapping a bookmark listing, you can instantly return to any manually bookmarked location within the recording.

As you listen to any audiobook or audio program using the Audible app, the Now Playing screen reveals the on-screen controls necessary to customize your listening experience. Displayed near the top of the screen, just under the Now Playing, Details, Chapters, and Bookmarks command icons is a Time slider. On the left side of this slider is a timer that displays how much of the audio program or audiobook chapter you've already listened to (displayed in hours, minutes, and seconds). On the right side of this slider is how much of the audio program or audiobook chapter remains. Between these two timers is a white line with a moving gray dot, which graphically depicts how far along you are in the content.

FIGURE 5-4 The Audible app's screen changes when you begin playing an audiobook or audio program.

 Using your finger, drag the dot on the slider to the left to rewind, or to the right to fast-forward through the recording.

Near the bottom-center area of the Now Playing screen are three command icons: Rewind, Play, and Bookmark. Tap the Rewind icon to rewind the recording between 1 and 300 seconds (depending how this setting is customized). Tap the Play icon to begin playing the audiobook or program. While the audio content is playing, the Play icon transforms into a Pause icon. Tap it to pause the playback.

At any time, you can create a bookmark to mark a specific location within an audiobook or audio program that you want to refer back to later. To do this, tap the Bookmark icon. Once you do this, you can use the virtual keyboard to add a note to yourself in regard to that bookmark (shown in Figure 5-5).

Below the Rewind, Play, and Bookmark icons are four additional control icons (shown in Figure 5-6). The Chapter Back icon on the extreme left (which is composed of two left-pointing arrows and a vertical line) is used to rewind the audiobook or recording to the beginning of a chapter. The Manual Rewind icon (composed of just two left-pointing arrows) is used to slowly rewind within the audiobook or recording. Additional control icons become visible if you place your finger on the grip strip displayed above the Play icon and drag it upward.

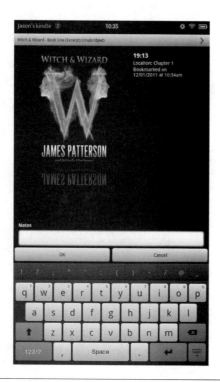

FIGURE 5-5   Just like when reading an eBook, you can create virtual bookmarks when listening to audiobooks as well.

The Manual Fast Forward icon (composed of two right-pointing arrows) is used to fast-forward within the recording, while the Chapter Forward icon (composed of two right-pointing arrows and a vertical line) is used to advance quickly within the audiobook to the next chapter.

 Hold down the rewind or fast-forward icons to move backward or forward more rapidly within the audiobook or audio program you're listening to.

Displayed along the bottom of the Audible app, regardless of which app screen you're looking at, you'll see the familiar Home, Previous Screen, Menu, and Search icons displayed. However, depending on which Audible app screen you're viewing, the menu options will change. For example, while viewing the Now Playing screen and listening to an audiobook, if you tap the Menu icon (found near the bottom-center area of the screen and shown in Figure 5-7), the command icons available to you include Share, Sleep, Button-Free, My Library, Narrator Speed, and Quit.

Tap the Share icon to post a message about the audiobook or audio program you're currently listening to on Facebook (assuming you have a Facebook account already set up and you're active on this online social networking site).

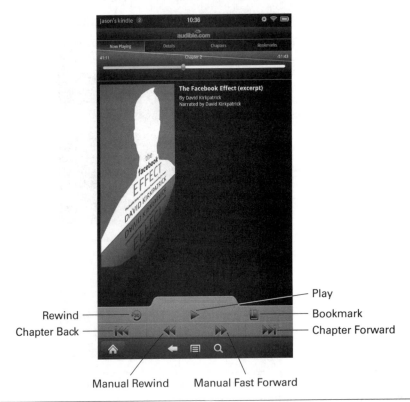

Play —
Rewind —
Bookmark —
Chapter Back —
Chapter Forward —
Manual Rewind — Manual Fast Forward

FIGURE 5-6   Control your audiobook listening experience using these on-screen control icons.

The Sleep command icon allows you to set an auto-shut-off, so the app will stop running and the tablet will go into Sleep mode at a predetermined time. Your Sleep mode setting options include Off (the audiobook will keep playing, nonstop, until the end), 15 minutes, 30 minutes, 60 minutes, End Of Chapter, or End Of Book Part.

Instead of using the on-screen command icons to play, rewind, fast-forward, add a bookmark, or perform other tasks within the app, tap the Button-Free command icon to begin using a series of on-screen finger swipes to control the app. A tutorial will show you how to use finger swipes to activate app commands.

Tap the My Library command to return to the My Library screen and view your personal audiobook library. Use the Narrator Speed icon to change the playback speed of the audiobook you're listening to. Your options include 0.5x, Full Speed, 1.25x, 1.5x, 2x, or 3x the normal playing speed. Tap the Quit icon to exit out of the app, which serves the same function as tapping the Home icon.

Note   Using these on-screen controls, you can listen to audiobooks and audio content stored within your Kindle Fire that was acquired from Audible.com.

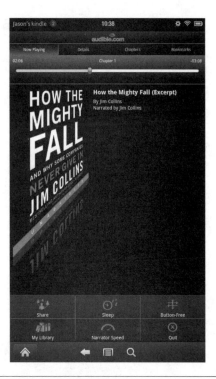

FIGURE 5-7 A different selection of options is displayed when you tap the Menu icon from the Now Playing screen.

Shopping for Audiobooks and Audio Content from Audible.com

Before you can begin listening to an audiobook or audio program using the Audible app, you must download content from Audible.com. You can begin by downloading free preview content or purchase and download an entire audiobook or audio program. Audible.com offers an ever-growing library composed of more than 100,000 full-length and abridged audiobook titles.

From the main My Library screen within the Audible app, tap the shopping cart icon (displayed near the upper-left corner of the screen) to access the Audible.com online store. To do this, your Kindle Fire needs access to the Internet via a Wi-Fi connection.

When the main Audible.com store screen is displayed (shown in Figure 5-8), you'll discover a Search field located near the top-center area of the screen. Tap this search field to quickly find any audiobook or audio program by entering its title, author, or a keyword.

Below the Search field are command options that allow you to browse the online store more leisurely. For example, you can tap Best Sellers, New Releases, Categories, or Special Features. By tapping the Best Sellers menu option, the Audible app will load a listing for the Top 50 audiobooks available from Audible.com. Each listing includes

FIGURE 5-8   Access Audible.com to shop for audiobooks and other audio programs.

the book's title, cover artwork, author, who narrates the audiobook, and its average star-based rating (between one and five stars, with five stars being the highest rating).

If you tap any audiobook listing, you can stream and listen to a brief sample of the audiobook or audio program. Or, you can tap the book cover graphic to reveal a more detailed description screen relating to that particular audiobook or program. From the detailed listing, you can purchase and download the audiobook with a single tap on the screen or read a description of the audiobook provided by the publisher.

Within each audiobook listing (below the book cover artwork) will be a section called Product Details. Here, the length of the audiobook, its release date, publisher, and average star-based rating are displayed.

 When viewing any audiobook listing, tap the left-pointing arrow that's displayed near the bottom-center area of the Kindle Fire's screen to return to the previous menu screen. Or, tap the Home icon to return to the Home screen and exit the Audible app.

Also as you're browsing the Audible.com store, near the bottom of the screen, you'll see menu options to manage your Audible.com account, view your Wish List, access online help, relaunch the Audible app, or manually sign out of the Audible.com store.

Between 9:00 A.M. and 10:00 P.M. (EST), Monday through Friday, or between 10:00 A.M. and 7:00 P.M. on Saturdays, you can call Audible.com directly at (888) 283-5051 if you have questions about shopping for audiobooks online or using the Audible app on your Kindle Fire.

 Some audiobooks include background music and sound effects. To fully experience the stereo audio effects included within the Audible audio content you're listening to, use stereo headphones or ear buds, or connect your tablet to external stereo speakers. Remember, with the right cable, you can also connect your Kindle Fire to your car's stereo system or home theater system/home stereo.

Manage Your Contacts with the Contact App

You might find the Contacts app to be somewhat minimal when compared to other contact management applications or software packages you may be accustomed to using; however, the app that comes preinstalled on your Kindle Fire does help you keep track of personal and professional contacts and access contact information via your tablet. In addition, you can import contact data from other software or applications and purchase and download additional apps that will enhance your tablet's ability to handle contact management-related tasks.

From your Kindle Fire's Home screen, tap the Apps command that's displayed as part of the Navigation bar. When the App screen appears, tap the Contacts app icon to launch the Contacts app. Unless you've already set up the Email app and entered contact information, initially, what you will see is an on-screen message that says, "You don't have any contacts to display." To begin populating your Contacts database with entries, or to import your preexisting contact database from another source (such as your primary computer), tap the Menu icon that's displayed near the bottom-center area of the screen.

 Once you begin to populate the Contacts app with entries, any time you launch the Contacts app, those entries will be displayed, in alphabetical order, on the main Contacts screen.

When you tap the Menu icon within the Contacts app, three app-specific command icons will appear near the bottom of the screen (shown in Figure 5-9). They're labeled New Contact, Settings, and Import/Export. Tap the New Contact icon to manually enter new contact entries, one at a time, into your personal Contacts database. By tapping the Settings icon, two additional Display Options are made available, allowing you to sort your Contacts list by first name or last name, and view contact names with first name first or last name first.

If you tap the Import/Export command, you'll have the ability to import contact entries from the Kindle Fire's internal storage or export contacts to the tablet's internal storage. This feature will be explained shortly.

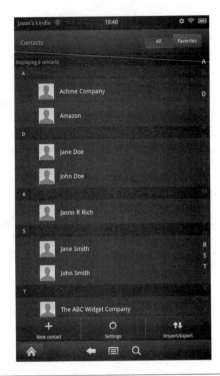

FIGURE 5-9 Tap the Menu icon within the Contacts app to reveal several options, including a command for creating new contact entries.

Creating New Contacts Entries

While you can import a preexisting contact database into your Kindle Fire from your PC, Mac, Microsoft Exchange account, or even your smartphone, to manually create a new entry within the Contacts app, tap the Menu icon within the app, and then tap the New Contact command icon. The New Contact screen will be displayed containing a handful of blank fields (shown in Figure 5-10). Tap one field at a time to enter the requested information using the Kindle Fire's virtual keyboard. The default fields included within the Contacts app include Name Prefix, First Name, Middle Name, Last Name, Name Suffix, Phone, Email, Postal Address, and Organization.

In the upper-right corner of the New Contact screen is a photo field. By tapping this field, you can attach a digital photo of the contact that's already stored within your tablet. When you look at the Phone and Email fields, you'll notice that each has a user-selectable label on the left, in addition to a plus and negative sign icon on the right.

Tap the Phone or Email label field to associate the phone or e-mail address with a specific label, such as Home, Mobile, Work, Other, etc. Then, enter the appropriate information within the blank field. Since most people or businesses have multiple phone numbers or e-mail addresses, tap the plus sign icon for that field to associate

FIGURE 5-10   One field at a time, enter relevant information to create a new entry within the Contacts app.

multiple phone numbers or e-mail addresses with that contact entry. Tap the negative sign icon to delete one of the Phone or Email fields.

 As you begin entering information into each field using the Kindle Fire's virtual keyboard, displayed just above the keyboard will be word suggestions. If the word you've started entering appears, tap it to quickly enter that word without having to finish typing it. Doing this will speed up your data entry.

When you tap the Postal Address field, it will expand into six separate blank fields, labeled Street, P.O. Box, City, State, Zip Code, and Country. Fill in the appropriate information for your contact using the tablet's virtual keyboard. Likewise, when you tap the Organization field, it will expand to display two blank fields, labeled Company and Title. Once again, use the virtual keyboard to enter the appropriate information into each blank field.

 As you populate your Contacts database, include as much or as little information about each contact as you desire. You are not obligated to fill in each field for every contact entry you create.

As soon as you're done entering the information related to the contact entry you're creating, it's essential that you then tap the orange Save Changes icon that's displayed near the bottom of the screen in order to save that entry within your Contacts database. Once you do this, it will be displayed on your Contacts screen, and any data stored within that contact entry will become searchable when you use the Search command built into the Contact app.

Note If you're a business person who maintains detailed information about all of your associates, clients, customers, coworkers, employees, friends, and relatives, for example, you will probably discover some drawbacks to the Contacts app in terms of flexibility when creating entries and the lack of available data fields. Other third-party apps for contact management will probably be better suited to your needs. The Contacts app is more basic in its functionality, database structure, and the information it can efficiently store.

Viewing Contacts Entries

From the main Contacts screen, you'll see an alphabetical listing of the contact entries currently stored within your personal Contacts database. This will include entries you've manually entered into your Kindle Fire and/or entries you've imported from other sources (shown in Figure 5-11). The contacts will be displayed in alphabetical order.

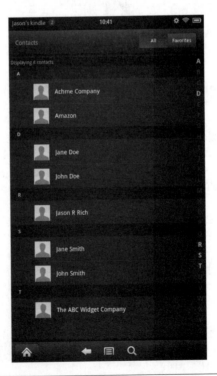

FIGURE 5-11 View listings for your contact entries in alphabetical order.

To view the details pertaining to a specific contact entry, tap its listing (shown in Figure 5-12). As you're viewing entries within the Contacts app, several of the fields within each entry are interactive. For example, if you tap an e-mail address that's associated with a contact, this will launch the Email app and allow you to quickly compose an e-mail to that person. (The e-mail will be preaddressed with the recipient's e-mail address in the To field.) Or, if you have an optional Maps app installed on your tablet, you can tap an address to view that location on a detailed map.

 The Contact app allows you to select specific contact entries to be your Favorites. To make a specific contact entry a Favorite as you're viewing it, tap the star-shaped icon that's displayed near the upper-right corner of the screen. When it turns orange, this indicates that the contact entry has been added to your Favorites list. Then, when you're viewing your contacts, you can sort them all alphabetically, or view just your Favorite entries (also in alphabetical order) by tapping the All tab or the Favorites tab in the upper-right corner of the Contacts screen.

When you're done viewing a specific contact entry, tap the left-pointing arrow icon that's displayed near the bottom-center area of the screen to return to the main Contacts screen (which lists all of your contact entries), or tap the Home icon to exit the Contacts app and return to the tablet's Home screen.

FIGURE 5-12   View the complete entry for any contact entry.

Edit, Share, and Delete Contact Entries

As you're viewing a contact, when you tap the Menu icon (displayed near the bottom-center area of the screen), three command options are displayed, including Edit Contact, Share, and Delete Contact.

Tap the Edit Contact icon to access the Edit Contact screen in order to add to or modify the contact entry you're looking at. When you're done editing, be sure to tap the orange Save Changes icon to save your modifications.

By tapping the Share icon, you can send the contact entry to someone else via e-mail, for example, assuming you have at least one e-mail account set up to work with your Kindle Fire and an Internet connection is present.

To delete the contact entry (erase it from your Kindle Fire and your personal Contacts database), tap the Delete Contact icon. Then, when the confirmation pop-up window appears, tap the OK icon.

From the main Contacts screen (which lists your contacts), use your finger to scroll up or down through the list to find the contact entry you're looking for. Or tap the Search icon that's displayed near the bottom of the screen. Using the virtual keyboard, enter a contact's first and/or last name, company name, or any information that's related to the contact you're looking for. As soon as you begin entering data into the Search field, related search results will be displayed on the screen. Tap any result to view that contact entry in its entirety.

Another way to quickly search through your Contacts database is to tap the letters displayed along the right margin of the screen (or as divider bars that go across the screen). When you tap a letter, such as "M," all contact entries beginning with an "M" will be displayed. As you look at the letters on the right side of the screen, only letters that have entries associated with them will be lit up and accessible.

Importing Contact Entries from Other Sources

Instead of manually entering your contact entries directly into your Kindle Fire via the Contacts app, you can save time by importing contact entries from other sources. Nearly every popular contact management software application or smartphone app allows you to export its contacts database in vCard format. This is an industry-standard data format for contacts that the Contacts app within your Kindle Fire understands.

Whether you use Microsoft Outlook on a Mac or PC, Address Book on a Mac, Contacts on an iPhone or iPad, Act! on a PC, or any other popular contact management software or app, begin by exporting your existing contacts database into a vCard-compatible format. Most contact management software packages offer an Export or Save As command that allows you to export your entire contacts database quickly.

Once your preexisting contacts database is stored in vCard format on your primary computer, for example, use your personal Send-To-Kindle e-mail address to e-mail that file to your Kindle Fire. Or connect your tablet to your primary computer via a Micro-B USB-to-USB cable, and then drag-and-drop the vCard file from your computer to your tablet. Directions for how to do this are provided in Chapter 12.

After the vCard file has been transferred to your tablet, from within the Contacts app, tap the Menu icon, followed by the Import/Export command. When the Import/Export Contacts pop-up menu appears, tap the Import From Internal Storage option. The contact entries you exported from your primary computer and then transferred to your Kindle Fire will be imported into the Contacts app. Now, when you look at the main Contacts screen of the Contacts app, all of your contact entries will be displayed and accessible to you.

View Digital Photos Using the Gallery App

The Gallery app that comes preinstalled on your Kindle Fire allows you to import and view digital photos and images.

 If you browse the Kindle Fire App Store, you'll discover additional photography-related apps that give you more functionality when it comes to viewing, sharing, editing, or enhancing the digital photos stored on your tablet. Chapters 14 through 18 focus on adding third-party apps to your tablet and showcase a handful of the best apps available.

When you first launch this app, the main Gallery screen will simply display the message, "There are no items in your collection." To populate your Gallery app with your own digital photos, use a Micro-B USB-to-USB cable to connect your tablet to your primary computer, and then drag-and-drop the digital images or image folders/albums to your tablet using the directions provided in Chapter 12.

Depending on how many photos you're transferring to your Kindle Fire, the resolution of the photos, and their file sizes, the process of importing them into the Gallery app could take several minutes.

 Once photos have been transferred to your tablet, thumbnails representing those albums and images will automatically be displayed when you launch the Gallery app and view the main Gallery screen.

The Gallery app divides up the digital images stored on your tablet into separate albums (shown in Figure 5-13). This allows you to import groups of photos simultaneously, and then easily organize them within your tablet. The main Gallery screen displays a thumbnail representing each album (along with the album's title and the number of images stored within that album below it).

 Although the Gallery app can be used while holding the tablet in portrait or landscape mode, you'll find it easier to view images and navigate your way around the app if you use it in landscape mode.

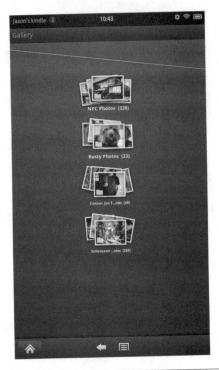

FIGURE 5-13 The Gallery app allows you to sort your digital images into separate albums.

Tap any album thumbnail to reveal thumbnail images for all of the photos stored within that particular album (shown in Figure 5-14). Use your finger to swipe left or right (or up and down) to see all of the thumbnail images. You can also use your finger to drag the slider that's displayed near the bottom of the screen left or right, just above the Menu icon. By tapping the View icon that's displayed near the upper-right corner of the screen, you can change the view of your album and quickly reorganize the images based on the date each was shot.

As you're viewing image thumbnails for a particular album, tapping the Menu icon (displayed near the bottom-center area of the screen) will reveal five command icons. Along the top of the screen, you'll see the Select All and Deselect All icons. Near the bottom of the screen, you'll see Share, Delete, and More icons.

At this point, you can tap any individual thumbnail images to select them. When you do this, a green and white check mark will appear in the upper-right corner of the image thumbnail. You can manually select as many images from an album as you desire (shown in Figure 5-15). Or tap the Select All icon to select all of the images at once.

FIGURE 5-14   View thumbnails representing all of the images stored within an album.

To unselect one image, tap it again. Or to deselect all of the selected images, tap the Deselect All icon. After selecting one or more image thumbnails, you have the option to share or delete those selected images by tapping the appropriate icons. If you tap the More icon, you can view details for the selected images or rotate them.

 When just one image is selected, if you tap the More icon, you'll also be given the option to crop that image.

FIGURE 5-15   You can manually select one or more images from an album. The Select All command is used to select all of the images.

How to... **View Individual Images Within the Gallery App**

Any time you're viewing image thumbnails within the Gallery app, tap an individual thumbnail to view a particular image in full-screen mode (shown in Figure 5-16). Then tap that image to reveal Play, Zoom In, and Zoom Out icons.

You can also use a reverse pinch or pinch finger motion to zoom in or out as you're looking at a photo in full-screen mode, or double-tap one area of the image to zoom in or out. Swipe your finger left to right (or right to left) to view the previous or next image within the album.

As you're viewing a single image, tap the Menu icon to reveal the Share, Delete, and More options. The More menu option once again reveals options to view image details, crop the image, or rotate the image.

Tap the Play icon when viewing a single image to begin watching an animated slide show composed of the images within the album you're viewing.

When you're done selecting images to share, delete, crop, or rotate, tap the left-pointing arrow icon that's displayed near the bottom of the screen, to the immediate left of the Menu icon, to return to the Gallery screen and view the thumbnails for the selected album once again.

FIGURE 5-16 View individual images in full-screen mode.

Quickoffice: One Option for Accessing Your Microsoft Office Documents and Files

The Quickoffice app that comes preinstalled on your Kindle Fire is used to view and manage Microsoft Office documents and files. Realistically, don't expect to use your tablet to compose complex Word documents or manage detailed spreadsheets. Between the small size of the tablet's screen and the limitations of its virtual keyboard, trying to create or heavily edit Microsoft Office–compatible documents or files is not at all practical. Instead, use this Quickoffice app to simply view documents and files. If you want more advanced features, upgrade to Quickoffice Pro.

 The first time you launch the Quickoffice app, you'll be required to read the License screen and accept the terms of use. Tap the I Agree icon to continue. You'll then be asked to register your software by entering your e-mail address.

 The Quickoffice app that comes preinstalled on your tablet is the basic edition of this app suite used for viewing Microsoft Office documents and files. From the Amazon App Store, you can upgrade to the premium Quickoffice Pro suite ($9.99), which offers enhanced functionality when it comes to creating and editing Microsoft Office files, as well as viewing them. You'll learn more about business and productivity apps in Chapter 15.

The main Quickoffice screen displays icons to launch three separate Quickoffice apps: Quickword, Quicksheet, and Quickpoint (shown in Figure 5-17). As you've probably surmised, Quickword is used to view Microsoft Word–compatible documents. Quicksheet is used to view Microsoft Excel spreadsheet files, and Quickpoint is used to view Microsoft PowerPoint digital slide presentations.

Displayed near the bottom of the main Quickoffice screen are seven additional command icons. Here's a brief explanation of what each is used for:

- **Browse**   Tap this command to access the Quickoffice File Manager screen and import documents or files from your Kindle Fire's internal storage into the app. Chapter 12 explains how to import or transfer documents and files into the tablet's internal storage. By tapping the disk drive–shaped icon at the bottom of the screen, you can also access files stored online within a Google Docs, Dropbox, Box, Huddle, SugarSync, or MobileMe (Apple iCloud) account.
- **Search**   Perform a search to quickly find a document or file you want to access and view using Quickoffice.
- **Accounts**   Manage any of your cloud-based file sharing accounts (such as Google Docs or Dropbox) that you plan to use with Quickoffice to quickly share and transfer documents, either between your primary computer and your tablet, or between yourself and other people. In addition to connecting your tablet to your primary computer via a USB cable, documents and files can be transferred

FIGURE 5-17 The Quickoffice app is really a suite of apps that allow you to view Microsoft Word, Excel, and PowerPoint documents and files.

wirelessly using your Send-To-Kindle e-mail address or a third-party cloud-based file sharing service that this particular app is compatible with.

- **Update** Upgrade to the Quickoffice Pro app suite by tapping this command icon to access the Amazon App Store.
- **Support** Access online technical support and a user guide for the Quickoffice app suite.
- **Explore** Learn more about Quickoffice by following the app's developer on Twitter, Facebook, or YouTube, or by reading the company's blog.
- **Up Arrow** Access the Home icon, Previous icon, Menu icon, and Search icon that isn't otherwise visible from the main Quickoffice screen.

Loading and Viewing a Document or File into Quickoffice

Once you've transferred your Microsoft Office document(s) or file(s) from your primary computer, for example, to your tablet by following the directions offered in Chapter 12, from the main Quickoffice screen, tap the appropriate app icon, based on the type of file or document you want to view.

If you want to view PDF files on your tablet, use the Adobe Reader app that's available for free from the Amazon App Store. You'll also discover other apps for viewing PDF and/or Microsoft Office files using your tablet, such as ezPDF Reader ($2.99), Smart Office ($4.95), and AlwaysOnPC Virtual PC with Office Suite ($24.99).

To view a Word document, for example, tap the Quickword icon. Then, tap Internal Storage to import the Word document that's currently stored within your Kindle Fire's internal storage into the Quickword app. When you tap the Internal Storage icon, a listing of folders is displayed. Choose the folder that contains your Word file. Which folder your Word document can be found in will depend on where you transferred it to earlier. Once the folder is open, tap the filename for the file you want to view. It will open within the Quickword app.

You can now view the document and see it similar to how it appears on your computer's screen (shown in Figure 5-18). Use your finger to scroll upward or downward within the document.

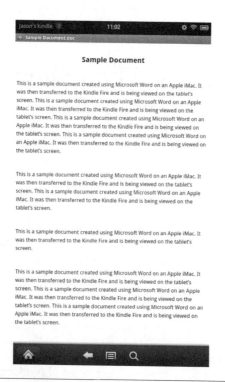

FIGURE 5-18   This sample Microsoft Word document was created on an iMac and transferred to the Kindle Fire.

Tap the Menu icon (displayed near the bottom-center area of the screen) to access several additional command icons used to manage the document you're viewing. These icons include

- **View**   View the document in full-screen mode.
- **Search**   Search for a keyword or phrase within the document.
- **Jump To**   Quickly jump to a specific page number within the document.
- **View With/Without Page Breaks**   Show page breaks within the document as you view it on the tablet's screen.
- **Narrator**   Have a computerized voice read the document to you.
- **Document Info**   Access details about the document, including its properties.

 Similar command icons are accessible if you access a Quicksheet or Quickpoint file.

 As you're viewing a document on the screen, you can use a reverse pinch or pinch finger motion to zoom in or out. This will increase or decrease the size of the text for viewing purposes on the Kindle Fire's screen, but it will not alter or reformat the actual document.

Find Great Deals When Shopping Online with the Amazon Shop App

In addition to being a pioneer in eBook readers and eBook publishing, Amazon.com has changed the way many people shop online. Amazon.com allows you to shop for virtually any product online and purchase it at a discount. Plus, if you maintain your Amazon.com Prime membership, you receive free two-day shipping on all of your online purchases.

 The Amazon Shop app is used for purchasing products from Amazon.com, not for acquiring content for your tablet, like music, TV show episodes, movies, or apps. To acquire content for your Kindle Fire, you'll use other apps to access the Amazon MP3 store or Amazon App Store, for example.

Whether you're shopping for yourself or for gifts, chances are you'll find any product available from Amazon.com that you'd find at your local mass-market superstore (for example, Wal-Mart, Target, or K-Mart) or consumer electronics superstore (like Best Buy). You'll also find books, audio CDs, DVDs, clothing, jewelry, cameras, consumer electronics, and many other types of products for sale from Amazon.com.

Using the Amazon Shop app that comes preinstalled on your tablet, you can use your Amazon.com account and Kindle Fire to shop for anything (and save money). When you launch this app, displayed near the top-center area of the screen is a Search

For Products field. To quickly find what you're looking for, enter a product name (including its manufacturer and model number, if applicable) or a product category to begin your online search.

You can also browse product listings directly on your tablet's screen using the Amazon Shop app. For example, you can begin your online shopping experience by tapping the Shop All Departments option displayed on the main Amazon Shop screen to display a list of product category options (shown in Figure 5-19). There are more than 35 categories to choose from, including appliances, automotive, beauty, clothing, electronics, home and garden, jewelry, movies and TV, office products, shoes, video games, and watches.

As you explore Amazon.com using the Amazon Shop app, you can view individual product descriptions and full-color product images. You can also read customer reviews of the product and perform all of the same tasks you can while shopping online from your primary computer.

When you're ready to make a purchase, because your Kindle Fire is already set up to make 1-Click purchases using your Amazon.com account, you can tap the appropriate Buy icon to have your selected and purchased item(s) shipped to your door within a few business days.

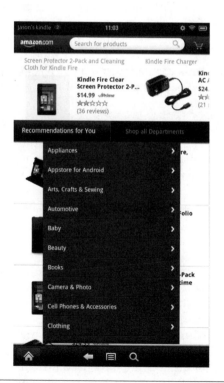

FIGURE 5-19   Using the Amazon Shop app, you can shop online for almost any product and often save money versus buying the item from a retail store.

Did You Know?

You Can Save Money by Shopping on Amazon.com

You already know you can save money when shopping for new products on Amazon.com; however, you also can sometimes purchase a used or refurbished product from an independent seller, often at a huge discount.

As you're looking at a product's description using the Amazon Shop app, look for the discounted New price, but also tap the New & Used From icon to see if that product is being sold by independent sellers even cheaper.

If you become a savvy shopper using Amazon.com and the Amazon Shop app, your Kindle Fire and ongoing Amazon.com Prime membership could pay for themselves quickly based on the money you'll save.

Access the Web Using the Pulse App

The Pulse app offers a new and more streamlined way to monitor dozens of different news sources, digital publications, webpages, online social networking sites, and blogs simultaneously using a simple interface that groups together headlines and web content and makes it easily accessible from a centralized screen.

Note Technically, Pulse can be called a "news reading application"; however, it offers more advanced features than a typical news reader app or software package.

In addition to browsing the Web using the Amazon Silk web browser or another specific app that's designed to help you easily utilize a particular website, the Pulse app that comes preinstalled on your Kindle Fire offers a way to access news and articles from the Web that are of direct interest to you on one customizable screen.

Note To use the Pulse app, your Kindle Fire must have access to the Internet.

When you initially launch the Pulse app, news headlines from *The Wall Street Journal, ESPN, Fast Company* magazine, *Popular Science,* and *Techcrunch* are displayed in a concise format. Simply tap a headline or photo that's of interest to load the full article or related multimedia content.

What's great about the Pulse app is that it's highly customizable. You can choose the websites, online sources, and digital publications the app will monitor, so when you view the main Pulse screen, only headlines that are of interest will be displayed.

To customize the Pulse app's Home screen, tap the gear-shaped icon that's displayed near the upper-left corner of the screen. Then, tap the X icon associated with each website or publication you want to delete from the online sources list that the app will monitor on your behalf. Next, tap the plus sign icon below the list of sources to add publications and websites.

At the top of the Add Sources screen, tap the Featured, Browse, or Search icon to find specific publications and websites that you want the Pulse app to monitor, and then select them one at a time. Tap the plus sign icon associated with each website or publication to add it to your monitored list. The Pulse app can monitor up to 12 sources simultaneously per page (shown in Figure 5-20). However, you can group sources together by subject (referred to as packs) and view them on separate pages, with access to a dozen topic-specific sources on each page.

If you opt to group together interests into packs, each will be displayed as a separate screen that's accessible from the main Pulse screen. Topic-specific tabs will be displayed near the top of the Pulse app's screen.

You can also manage your Pulse app sources by tapping the Menu icon that's displayed near the bottom-center area of the screen and then selecting the Manage Sources option. Also, by tapping the Menu icon, you can access a Refresh All icon (which will update the headlines being displayed on the screen) or adjust the app's settings.

FIGURE 5-20   Use the Pulse app to monitor multiple websites, digital publications, blogs, and social networking sites from one screen.

By registering your own .ME account from within the Pulse app, you can access Pulse content from any or all of your mobile devices, as well as your personal computer(s), and have the content synchronized. You can also save bookmarks for specific articles or content that you want to refer to later. Tap the .ME icon that's displayed in the upper-right corner of the Pulse app's main screen to set up and use your account. To learn more about using Pulse with other computers or devices, visit www.pulse.me.

In addition to using Pulse to monitor and display news stories and articles from popular publications and websites, you can have the app monitor your Facebook page and Twitter feed. To do this, once the app is launched, tap the Menu icon, and then select the Settings option. Toward the bottom of the Pulse app's Settings screen, tap the Logged In To Facebook or Logged In To Twitter option. You will be prompted to enter your Facebook user name and password or your Twitter user name and password. Once you do this, the content from those accounts will become part of your main Pulse news screen.

Once you've approved the link between Pulse and your Facebook or Twitter account, return to the main Pulse screen and tap the gear-shaped icon to reveal the source list. Tap the plus sign icon at the bottom of the list, and then tap the Browse tab that's displayed near the top of the screen. Scroll down to the Social option and tap it. Next, select the Facebook option, and then decide if you want to display Facebook links, Facebook Wall, or Facebook status updates.

Pulse can also monitor your YouTube, Flickr, Digg, Vimeo, and Reddit account and display all updates to these accounts on one centralized screen.

As you're viewing the main Pulse content pages, next to each source name will be a Refresh icon. Tap it to manually reload content with updated headlines as they become available. You can also tap the Menu icon, followed by the Refresh All icon, to manually refresh all of the web content being fed into the Pulse app.

Learn More About Additional Preinstalled Kindle Fire Apps

From the Home screen, when you first tap the Apps command icon from the Navigation bar and then tap the Device tab to view only apps already installed on your tablet, you'll also see app icons for IMDb and Facebook. IMDb (which stands for Internet Movie Database) is an app that serves as an interface for the IMDb.com website. From here, you can access information about almost any movie ever made (or that's in preproduction), or access details about almost any motion picture actor, actress, producer, director, or other crewmember. You can also see U.S. box office results, view movie trailers, and discover what's new on DVD or Blu-ray.

IMDb also offers a comprehensive database of television shows and TV actors, plus offers ongoing news stories and information related to the entertainment industry. All of this information is readily available from IMDb.com. However, the IMDb app makes accessing information and browsing the website on the Kindle Fire's screen much more efficient.

The Facebook app icon you see displayed on your Apps screen is simply a webpage shortcut for the mobile version of the Facebook website, which allows you to access your Facebook account via the Amazon Silk web browser. You'll learn about specific apps for accessing Facebook, Twitter, Google +, LinkedIn, and other online social networking services in Chapter 17.

Displayed at the top of the Apps screen on your Kindle Fire are the Cloud and Device tabs. This chapter has offered details about the apps that come preinstalled on your tablet and are ready to use. By tapping the Cloud tab, you'll see app icons for additional apps that are available to you via your Amazon Cloud Drive account. These are apps that come with your tablet, but are not preinstalled. To install any of these free apps, which include Comics, ESPN Scoreboard, Pandora, The Weather Channel, and Words with Friends, tap the relevant app icon to download and install it. You'll learn more about these and other apps in Chapters 14 through 18.

6

Use Amazon Silk to Surf the Web with Your Kindle Fire

HOW TO...

- Access and use the preinstalled Amazon Silk web browser to surf the Internet
- Adjust the settings for the Silk web browser
- Use tabbed web browsing to quickly switch between browser windows
- Create and access bookmarks

When you're within a Wi-Fi hotspot or within the signal radius of a wireless network, your Kindle Fire can be used to surf the Web thanks to the Amazon Silk web browser that comes preinstalled. Unlike Microsoft Explorer, Safari, Firefox, Chrome, and other popular web browsers available for PCs, Macs, and other devices, Amazon Silk is a proprietary web browser designed specifically for the Kindle Fire. It allows you to access virtually any website and then navigate your way around it using a series of finger gestures on the Kindle Fire's touch screen.

 To enhance your web surfing experience, it's possible to zoom in or out as you're viewing almost any webpage. Double-tap a specific area of a webpage to zoom in and then zoom out again. Or use a reverse-pinch finger motion to zoom in, and a pinch motion to zoom back out.

 One advantage the Kindle Fire has when it comes to surfing the Web is that it's Adobe Flash–compatible. This allows you to view animated graphics and Flash-based websites on the Kindle Fire's screen.

To help compensate for the screen size of the Kindle Fire, the Silk web browser utilizes tabbed browsing. This feature allows you to open multiple webpages simultaneously and then quickly switch between them with a tap of the finger. How to do this will be explained shortly. Plus, the Silk web browser allows you to create

FIGURE 6-1   If you attempt to surf the Web using Silk without the Kindle Fire being connected to the Internet, you will receive an error message.

custom bookmarks and then easily return to bookmarked webpages. To make your web surfing experience even more convenient, you can also create webpage shortcuts that appear on the Kindle Fire's Home screen. How to do this will also be explained later in the chapter.

How to Launch the Amazon Silk Web Browser

To begin surfing the Web, make sure your tablet is connected to the Internet via a Wi-Fi connection. Otherwise, when you attempt to launch the Amazon Silk app, you'll receive an error message (shown in Figure 6-1). To confirm that your tablet is connected to the Internet, access the Home screen and then look in the upper-right corner of the screen. Next to the battery life indicator, if you see a Wi-Fi signal icon displayed and at least one signal strength bar is visible, you're connected to the Internet.

Once your Kindle Fire is connected to the Internet, to begin surfing the Web, from the Home screen, launch the Amazon Silk web browser. To do this, tap the Web option, which is displayed to the extreme right of the Navigation bar shown in Figure 6-2. The app icon for Amazon Silk may also appear within the Home screen's Carousel or Favorites bar. If so, you can also tap this icon to launch Amazon Silk.

How to...   **Choose the Strongest Wi-Fi Signal**

Depending on where you are, multiple Wi-Fi hotspots or wireless networks may be available to you. If so, choose the hotspot or network with the strongest signal strength. From the Home screen, tap the Quick Settings icon (which looks like a gear). It's located in the upper-right corner of the screen. Next, tap the Wi-Fi option. Make sure the Wireless Networking option is turned on. Under the Connect To A Network heading, tap the Wi-Fi hotspot or wireless network listing that displays the best signal strength and that's unlocked (unless you have the password to access a locked network).

FIGURE 6-2   Amazon Silk is the web browser that comes preinstalled on your Kindle Fire. Tap the web option to launch it.

 The Amazon Silk app is used to surf the Web. To access and manage e-mail accounts, use the Email app that comes preinstalled on your Kindle Fire. How to use this app is covered in Chapter 7.

Surfing the Web Using Amazon Silk

If you already know how to surf the Web on your desktop or laptop computer (or even on your smartphone), the user interface for the Amazon Silk web browser will seem familiar, although somewhat less robust in terms of features. For example, you cannot print webpages or web content as you're surfing the Internet from your Kindle Fire.

When you launch the Amazon Silk web browser, you'll discover that the app's screen is divided into three sections. Near the top of the screen are tabs used for opening and then quickly switching between multiple web browser windows or webpages. To the extreme right of the tab bar is a plus-sign icon that's used for opening a new web browser window and to create a new tab. Just below the tabs is the web browser's Website Address and Search field. Tap the empty address field to make the tablet's virtual keyboard appear, and then manually enter the webpage address (URL) that you want to visit. Within this field, use any of these URL formats: http://www .WebsiteName.com, www.WebsiteName.com, or WebsiteName.com.

You can also use this field to search for the websites or content you're looking for simply by entering one or more keywords or search phrases into the field and then tapping the Go icon that appears to the right of the field, or as part of the virtual keyboard (shown in Figure 6-3).

 Tap the globe-shaped icon that's located to the immediate left of the address field in order to access your web surfing history.

FIGURE 6-3   Tap the Website Address and Search field to either initiate a web search or manually enter the URL for the website you want to access.

FIGURE 6-4 The Amazon Silk Bookmarks screen shows a listing of your favorite or more frequented webpages stored as bookmarks.

Below the Website Address and Search field is the main area of the Silk web browser, where website content is displayed. Or if you're looking at the Bookmarks screen, thumbnails representing bookmarked webpages will be displayed (shown in Figure 6-4).

Displayed along the bottom of the Amazon Silk screen are five command icons used for navigating the Internet. As shown in Figure 6-5, these command icons include the following:

- **Home** Tap this icon, which is displayed near the lower-left corner of the screen, to return to the Kindle Fire's Home screen and exit out of the Silk web browser.
- **Back** Tap this left-pointing arrow icon to jump back to the webpage you were previously viewing within that browser window.

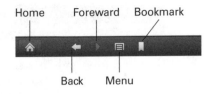

FIGURE 6-5 The Amazon Silk web browser's command icons

- **Forward**   Tap this right-pointing arrow icon to jump forward to a webpage you were previously viewing, if applicable. When there is no website to jump forward to, this icon will not be active.
- **Menu**   Access the Amazon Silk menu, which includes the following options:
  - **Add Bookmark**   Add a bookmark to your Bookmarks listing for the webpage you're currently viewing.
  - **Share Page**   Any time you discover a webpage that you want to share with other people, tap this command icon to post a message about it on Facebook or e-mail the website's link.
  - **Find In Page**   Search the webpage you're currently viewing for a specific word or phrase, which you enter into the search field that appears near the top of the screen.
  - **History**   Access a detailed listing of webpages you've previously visited that day and in the past seven days. To return to any of the previously visited webpages, tap its listing on the History screen, shown in Figure 6-6.

FIGURE 6-6   The History screen of the Silk web browser maintains a list of websites you've visited in the past seven days.

- **Downloads** Access files, documents, or content that you've downloaded from the Internet and saved within your tablet's internal storage.
- **Settings** Customize your web surfing experience by adjusting the various options offered from the Settings menu. These options are explained shortly.

 When you tap the various menu command icons offered within the Silk web browser, the main command icons displayed at the bottom of the web browser's screen will sometimes change. For example, a Search icon (which is shaped like a magnifying glass) may become available.

- **Bookmarks** Use this icon to reveal the Bookmarks screen, which is composed of thumbnails for the webpages you've already bookmarked. Tap a thumbnail to access the particular website each corresponds to.

Using the Amazon Silk Tabbed Web Browsing Feature

To make it easy to load multiple webpages and then quickly switch between them without having to manually close and then reopen them, the Silk web browser uses a tab-based interface. Each webpage you open when surfing the Web can be within a separate tab, which is displayed near the top of the screen. You can then switch between tabs (and webpages) by tapping the various tab icons. One webpage at a time can be visible and active on the screen, although using tabs, up to ten webpages can be open simultaneously.

 To open a new tab (browser window), tap the plus-sign icon that's displayed to the right of the Website Address and Search field near the top of the screen. A new tab, containing an empty browser window, will appear. You can then enter a website URL or access a bookmarked webpage within that browser window. To return to a previously opened tabbed browser window, simply tap its tab.

 At any given time, up to ten browser tabs can be open at once. However, when the tablet is held in portrait mode, only four tabs at a time appear at the top of the screen. Swipe your finger from left to right (or right to left) to quickly scroll through the tabs.

Within a single tabbed browser window, you can move forward or backward within a website to reaccess specific pages you've already viewed while that browser window was open. To do this, tap the left- or right-pointing arrow icons that are displayed near the bottom-center area of the screen.

Once a tab is open, the title of the webpage that appears within the browser window is displayed within the tab itself (shown in Figure 6-7). To the right of the title will be an "X" icon. Tap this "X" to close that browser window and remove its tab.

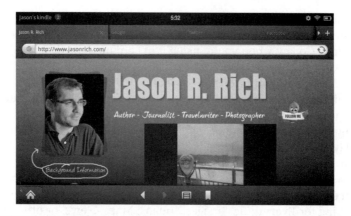

FIGURE 6-7   By opening multiple tabs, you can open multiple web browser windows simultaneously and then switch between them with a tap on the screen.

To return to a previously visited webpage, you can always access Silk's History screen, which maintains a detailed and chronological listing of websites you've visited. You can also manually re-enter the website's URL in the Website Address and Search field, or access a website from the Bookmarks menu, if you've saved the website as a bookmark.

The benefit to using tabs is that you can be viewing one webpage and decide to visit another webpage altogether without having to close the previous page. Then, when viewing the second, third, or fourth webpage, you can quickly switch back between open browser windows by tapping their respective tabs.

Search the Web for What You're Looking For

Unless you know the website URL (address) for the specific webpage, website, or content you want to access, the easiest way to find what you're looking for on the Internet is to use a search engine, such as Google, Yahoo!, or Bing. When surfing the Web with Amazon Silk, to quickly perform a web search, enter the appropriate keyword, keywords, or search phrase into the Website Address and Search field instead of typing a website URL, and then tap the Go icon.

As you are manually entering a website URL or search phrase into the Website Address and Search field, an "X" icon will appear on the right side of the field. Tap this icon to delete whatever text currently appears within the field, and then begin re-entering a keyword, search phrase, or website URL from scratch. Also, as you're typing a keyword, search phrase, or website URL into this field, possible website or content matches will be displayed below the field. Tap any of these matches to instantly jump to that website URL or content. Or when you're done entering a keyword, search phrase, or website URL into the field, tap the Go icon to initiate the desired web search.

The Go icon appears to the immediate right of the Website Address and Search field. However, the virtual keyboard that's displayed at the bottom of the screen also contains an orange Go key when you're using it in conjunction with the Silk web browser. Next to the Go key on the virtual keyboard is a .COM key (shown in Figure 6-8). Use this key to quickly add a .com extension to whatever website URL you are manually entering, assuming the website ends with a .com extension and not another extension, such as .net, .gov, .info, or .tv.

By default, your Kindle Fire will use Google to perform a web search and then display your search results in the main area of the Silk screen. Tap any search result listing to access that relevant website or online content.

Depending on which search engine you use to perform your web searches, when using Amazon Silk, you may have the option to narrow your search results by searching for Everything, Images, Videos, Maps, News, or other specific content that's relevant to your search parameters.

FIGURE 6-8 When using Amazon Silk, there's a Go icon located next to the Website Address and Search field, as within the virtual keyboard.

Did You Know?

You Can Select Your Default Search Engine

From within the Settings menu for the Amazon Silk web browser, you can select the default search engine that's used when you enter a keyword or search phrase into the Website Address and Search field. Your options include Google, Yahoo!, or Bing. Or you can manually access your favorite Internet search engine by entering its URL. For example, within the Website Address and Search field, you could enter www.Google.com, www.Yahoo.com, or www.Bing.com to access Google, Yahoo!, or Bing, respectively, and then perform a web search.

To make your web searching experience easier on the smaller screen of your Kindle Fire, by default, the "mobile" version of most Internet search engines will automatically load. These are optimized to offer the same features of the main search engines, but they format and display relevant content for a smaller-sized screen.

Tip Once a webpage is loaded and is being displayed within a tabbed browser window, it may periodically be necessary to refresh or reload that content. To do this, tap the circular Refresh icon that appears to the right of the Website Address and Search field.

As you begin using the Website Address and Search field repeatedly, all of the keywords and search phrases you've entered in the past are saved and will be displayed, as appropriate, when you begin entering new content into this field.

Access Websites You've Previously Visited from the History Screen

Like most web browsers, Amazon Silk keeps track of all webpages you visit, and can display them in reverse chronological order on the History page. To access the History page, tap the Menu icon while surfing the Web using Amazon Silk, and then tap the History icon.

Displayed at the top of the screen will be the Today heading. Below it will be listings for websites you've visited today. Underneath that listing, you'll see a heading labeled Last 7 Days. It displays a detailed listing of webpages you've visited during the past week. Tap the downward-pointing arrow icon to the left of the heading to view all of the applicable websites that you've visited during that time period. To revisit one of the listed websites, simply tap its listing. You will not have to manually retype its URL.

To the right of each listing is a bookmark icon. If you tap the plus sign within the bookmark icon, you'll be able to create a bookmark for a website that you previously visited. If the bookmark icon is already solid white, this means the URL has already been saved as a bookmark. Tap any of the bookmark listings to reopen and access that webpage.

 To manually clear your History screen and all of the URLs listed on it, tap the Clear All icon that's displayed near the upper-right corner of the History page. This can help you maintain your privacy if someone else uses your tablet. To manually delete an item from the Carousel, hold your finger on the item's thumbnail for a second or two and then tap on the Delete From Carousel option that appears.

 When you exit out of the Silk browser, a thumbnail graphic representing the last website you visited is automatically displayed on the Home screen's Carousel for anyone who picks up your tablet to see. In a future version of the Kindle Fire, you may be able to edit what appears on the Carousel, but when the tablet was first released, this was not possible. So, to keep your web surfing habits and history private, be sure to use the Clear All command that's displayed on the History page of the browser.

Use Options Found Within the Settings Menu to Customize Your Web Surfing Experience

The Silk web browser has its own Settings menu. By adjusting the options within this menu, you can personalize your web surfing experience. To access the Settings menu, first launch Amazon Silk. Then, at the bottom of the screen, tap the Menu command icon. The Settings command icon will be one of the additional command icons that appear. Tap the Settings icon to reveal the Settings menu, shown in Figure 6-9.

The Settings menu is composed of the following 24 menu options, shown in Figure 6-10. They are divided into categories and displayed under the General, Saved Data, Behavior, and Advanced headings that appear on the Settings screen.

The Settings Menu Options

As you'll discover, some of the menu options can either be turned on or off, while others allow you to access submenus or multiple options.

FIGURE 6-9 You can customize the Amazon Silk settings.

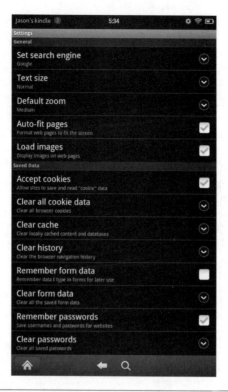

FIGURE 6-10   The Settings menu for Amazon Silk

Menu Options Under the General Heading

The following is a brief summary of each of the Settings options available below the General heading within the Silk web browser:

- **Set Search Engine**   Tap this menu option to choose between Google, Bing, and Yahoo! as your default search engine. The option you select will have an orange dot associated with it, shown in Figure 6-11.

FIGURE 6-11   The search engine you choose to be your default will have an orange dot displayed to the right of it.

- **Text Size** Set the default size of the text that's displayed within webpages on your Kindle Fire's screen. Your options include Tiny, Small, Normal, Large, and Huge. The default option is Normal. If you switch it to Tiny or Small, for example, additional information will fit on the tablet's screen, but it will be harder to read without zooming in on areas of certain webpages. Figure 6-12 shows a website with the Normal Text Size option selected. Figure 6-13 shows the same website with the Huge Text Size selected.

- **Default Zoom** This option determines the level of zoom that's applied when you double-tap on the screen when viewing a webpage. The three choices include Far, Medium, and Close. The default option is Medium.

- **Auto-Fit Pages** When turned on, this option will auto-format webpages so they fit on the Kindle Fire's screen. Often, to clearly view what's included within the webpage you're viewing, it will be necessary to zoom in on content when this feature is turned on. The benefit to turning on this feature is that you can see the full layout of a webpage, as if you were viewing it on a full-size computer screen or monitor.

- **Load Images** When turned on, this option will automatically load all graphics and photos that are part of a webpage. If you turn off this option, webpages will load significantly faster, but placeholder graphics will be used instead of the actual

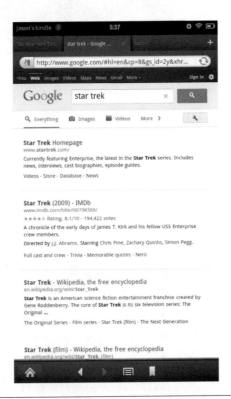

FIGURE 6-12 A website with the Normal Text Size selected.

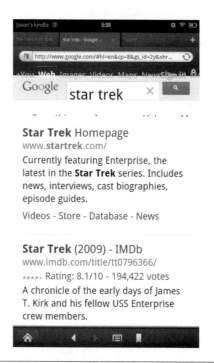

FIGURE 6-13   The same website, but with the Huge Text Size option shown

graphics or photos. You'll then need to tap the placeholder graphics to manually load and display the actual images, graphics, or photos.

Menu Options Listed Under the Saved Data Heading

The following is a brief summary of each of the Settings options displayed below the Saved Data heading within the Silk web browser:

- **Accept Cookies**   As you surf the Web, the websites you visit save tidbits of information within your tablet's internal storage that is associated with your personal preferences related to that website. When the Accept Cookies option is turned on, this data is stored. Thus, when you return to certain websites, those sites will remember you. If you turn off this option, each time you visit a website, it will be as if it's your first time visiting it, and none of your personalized preferences or settings will be remembered.
- **Clear All Cookie Data**   By surfing to hundreds or thousands of different websites, which is pretty common over time, the amount of cookie-related data stored on your tablet will accumulate. If you want to delete this data and free up internal storage space, tap this option, and then tap the OK icon to confirm your decision.
- **Clear Cache**   Also as you visit websites, content from those sites will be stored automatically within your tablet's internal storage. This will allow those webpages

to reload significantly faster when you revisit them. If you want to delete the cache and remove this data from your tablet, tap this Settings menu option, and then confirm your decision by tapping the OK icon.

- **Clear History** Tapping this menu option deletes the listing of webpages you've visited that's automatically stored within your Kindle Fire. Tapping this option will help to maintain your privacy in terms of what websites you've visited if other people access your tablet.
- **Remember Form Data** Like most web browsers, Silk is designed to remember data you manually enter into online-based forms. When this option is turned on, it can automatically insert the appropriate content into form fields that recur often, such as your fields for your name, address, and phone number.
- **Clear Form Data** Tap this option to delete the stored data that's associated with online forms.
- **Remember Passwords** When turned on, this feature will automatically remember passwords for websites you visit, so you don't constantly have to remember and re-enter the specific passwords. The benefit of this feature is that it saves time. The drawback is that if other people use your tablet, they'll be able to automatically log into password-protected websites using your personal passwords.

 If someone accesses your Kindle Fire without permission and you have your passwords automatically stored, they could potentially buy stuff from Amazon.com and have it shipped to them. This is particularly troubling if you leave your tablet unattended in a public place and someone picks it up. Even if they don't steal the tablet itself, in a matter of seconds, they can make a handful of costly purchases that get billed to your credit card.

   Likewise, if your kids start using your Kindle Fire while unsupervised, they could purchase and view TV shows, movies, digital publications, or eBooks or access websites that are not suitable for them.

- **Clear Passwords** Tap this menu option to delete the database of website passwords that Amazon Silk can automatically store. Before using this feature, be sure to write down all of your website-specific passwords so you don't forget them.

Menu Options Listed Under the Behavior Heading

The following is a brief summary of each of the Settings options displayed below the Behavior heading within the Silk web browser:

- **Show Security Warnings** If the web browser detects a problem with a website's security, you will be notified with a warning message. To help protect your privacy and ensure you don't accidently visit a fraudulent website that's posing as another website, keep this feature turned on.
- **Enable Plug-ins** Tap this menu option to select one of three options, labeled Always On, On Demand, and Off. This determines whether or not web browser plug-ins will automatically download, install, and be used as they're needed to

display the content of webpages you visit. The default option for this feature is Always On.

- **Enable JavaScript** JavaScript is one of many popular programming languages used to create and publish websites. This feature must be kept on if you want to be able to access and view websites created using JavaScript.

- **Open Pages In Overview** Turn on this feature to display an overview of newly opened webpages. This feature automatically shrinks down the content of a webpage as much as necessary so it fits nicely on the tablet's screen. This feature allows you to view the layout of a webpage as it's intended, but you'll often have to manually zoom in on content to view it clearly.

- **Open In Background** As you're surfing the Web, if you tap a link that requires the site to open a separate web browser window and a new webpage, when this feature is turned on, that new webpage will be opened using a separate tab. Thus, it will be faster and easier to switch between the original webpage you were viewing and the newly opened webpage.

- **Block Pop-up Windows** Some websites are designed to display annoying pop-up windows that automatically appear on the screen, but need to be manually closed. When turned on, this feature blocks pop-up windows from being displayed as you surf the Web.

 At the time the Kindle Fire was released, Amazon received some negative publicity over concerns that the Silk web browser not only tracks what people do when surfing the Web, but also reports this information to Amazon.com, so it can use it for various purposes, including marketing. In late December, Amazon released an updated version of the Kindle Fire operating system that addressed some of these privacy concerns. The company can still remotely track how you use the device, but now, this information is theoretically only used to improve performance of the tablet.

Menu Options Listed Under the Advanced Heading

The following is a brief summary of each of the Settings options under the Advanced heading within the Silk web browser:

- **Accelerate Page Loading** When turned on, this feature is supposed to speed up the webpage loading process. You might want to experiment by turning this feature on and then off when you're surfing the Web to see if you notice any significant changes. This feature's impact on web surfing speed may become more apparent in future versions of Amazon Silk.

- **Desktop Or Mobile View** Some websites, including the popular search engines, have both desktop and mobile editions. When you activate the Mobile View option, if Amazon Silk is given a choice, it will launch the mobile version of a website that's been designed to make navigating and web surfing on a device with a smaller screen easier. If you select the Desktop View, your tablet will always launch the version of a website that's designed to be seen on a full-size monitor or computer screen. While it will still be viewable on the tablet's seven-inch display, you will need to actually navigate your way around to see an entire webpage. In general, due to the Kindle Fire's screen size, you'll find it advantageous to access the mobile view of most websites. However, you can always switch to the desktop view of a specific webpage if you deem it necessary to improve your web surfing experience.

- **Text Encoding**   Based on your native language, you'll want to choose a text encoding option that's appropriate. For example, if you speak English, select the Latin-1 (default) option. If you want to view characters in Chinese or Japanese, select the appropriate option.
- **Website Settings**   If applicable, this menu option will allow you to adjust settings for specific webpages. Most of the time, however, this feature will be inactive.
- **Reset To Default**   Tap this option to restore all of the settings that are adjustable from this menu back to their factory defaults.

Creating and Accessing Bookmarks

As you surf the Web, if you want to revisit a website, you have multiple options. For example, you can tap the webpage icon that appears within the Carousel on the Home screen. Or while still using Silk, tap the Menu icon, followed by the History icon, to view a listing of websites you've visited within the last seven days.

However, to create, manage, and access your most frequently visited or favorite webpages, the easiest thing to do is create a bookmark for each of them. Amazon Silk allows you to create and maintain a personalized listing of website addresses, called bookmarks. When you view your Bookmarks menu, with a single tap on the screen, you can return to any webpage that has a bookmark associated with it.

Amazon Silk comes preinstalled on your Kindle Fire with a handful of popular websites already stored as bookmarks. You can manually delete any of these bookmarks and/or add your own. To view your personalized Bookmark list, tap on the Bookmark icon that's displayed near the bottom of the screen, to the right of the Menu icon. The Bookmark icon looks like a solid-white ribbon.

How to...   Create a Bookmark While Surfing the Web

As you're surfing the Web, if you come across a website you want to be able to revisit later easily, create a bookmark for it. To do this, tap the Menu icon that's displayed at the bottom of the Silk screen. Then, tap the Add Bookmark icon.

When the Add Bookmark window appears, you can manually enter a title or name for the bookmark, or leave the default title, as well as edit the website location (URL). To save the bookmark, tap the OK icon that's displayed near the bottom of the Add Bookmark window. That bookmark will now appear within your Bookmarks listing.

As soon as you tap the Bookmarks icon, the Bookmarks screen will replace whatever you were previously looking at on the tablet's screen. The Bookmarks screen is composed of graphic thumbnails (refer back to Figure 6-4), each of which represents one website. Tap any of the bookmarks to launch the webpage it's associated with within the Silk web browser. You will not have to manually retype the website's URL.

As you're looking at the Bookmarks screen, you can also hold your finger on any of the thumbnail icons that represent individual bookmarks to reveal a submenu that's associated with that bookmark. This submenu includes the following seven options (shown in Figure 6-14):

- **Open** Tap this option to open the bookmarked webpage within the currently open web browser window (or, if necessary, open a web browser window).
- **Open In New Tab** If one or more web browser windows are already open, tap this option to open the bookmarked webpage within a new tabbed web browser window. This allows the other webpages you have open to remain open. The newly opened bookmarked webpage will automatically become the active and viewable browser window.
- **Open In Background Tab** If you have one or more web browser windows already open, tap this menu option to open a new browser window and launch the webpage associated with the bookmark. However, whatever webpage you were previously looking at will remain the active browser window.
- **Share Link** Use e-mail or Facebook to share the link for the bookmarked website with other people.
- **Copy Link URL** Tap this command to copy the URL that's associated with the bookmarked website into your tablet's virtual clipboard. You can then paste that website address data into an empty field within Amazon Silk or another app.
- **Edit Bookmark** Manually edit the title or URL for a bookmarked website.
- **Delete** Delete the selected website from your Bookmark list.

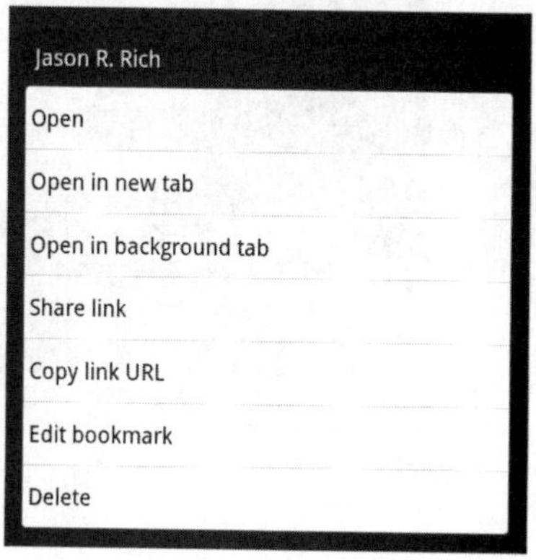

| Jason R. Rich |
| Open |
| Open in new tab |
| Open in background tab |
| Share link |
| Copy link URL |
| Edit bookmark |
| Delete |

FIGURE 6-14 Hold your finger on a bookmark thumbnail to reveal this submenu.

Did You Know?

You Can Change the Bookmark Screen's View

Instead of looking at thumbnails for each bookmarked website on the Bookmarks screen, tap the icon that's displayed near the upper-right corner of the Bookmarks screen that looks like three horizontal lines. This will transform the graphic thumbnails into a text-based listing of bookmarked webpages that displays the title and website URL for each bookmark (shown in the next illustration). You can then tap any listing to open that webpage within the Silk browser.

To return to the thumbnail view of the bookmarks, tap the other icon that's displayed near the top-right corner of the Bookmarks screen. This one contains four white squares.

A text-based listing of your Bookmarks menu

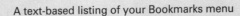

As you're viewing the Bookmarks screen, tap the Search icon (the magnifying glass icon that's displayed near the bottom of the screen) to search all of your bookmarks based on a keyword or search phrase that you enter using the tablet's virtual keyboard. Also as you're viewing the Bookmarks screen, you can create a bookmark for the last webpage you were viewing by tapping the thumbnail that's displayed near the upper-left corner of the screen, which contains a plus sign within it.

 To return to the main Amazon Silk screen from the Bookmarks screen without accessing any bookmarked webpages, tap the left-pointing arrow that's displayed near the bottom of the screen.

Navigate Your Way Around a Website That's Displayed on Your Kindle Fire

Once a webpage loads within the Amazon Silk browser, you swipe your finger from the bottom of the screen toward the top in order to scroll downward on the page. Or hold your finger somewhere near the top of the screen and drag it in a downward direction to manually scroll upward on a webpage. If applicable, you can also swipe or drag your finger from right to left, or from left to right, to scroll sideways on a webpage.

Any time you encounter an active link within a webpage, you can tap it to activate the link. This serves the same purpose as clicking a link with a mouse if you're surfing the Web on your computer.

As you're viewing a webpage, to enter data into blank fields or an online form, tap any empty field within the webpage. The Kindle Fire's virtual keyboard will appear, allowing you to manually input the requested data.

At any time, if you're having trouble viewing a portion of a webpage on your tablet's seven-inch screen, double-tap that area of the page to zoom in. Or use a reverse-pinch finger motion to zoom in on an area of a webpage to get a more detailed or closer view.

 After zooming in, to return a webpage to its normal size, either double-tap again on the screen or use a pinch finger motion.

When viewing most webpages, you can manually save any photo or graphic that's displayed by holding your finger on that graphic or photo for two to three seconds. A pop-up window will appear that displays two options: Save Image or View Image. Tap the Save Image option to store the image within your tablet's internal memory and view it using the Gallery app, for example. Or tap the View Image option to view just the image alone within an otherwise empty web browser screen. The image will not be saved, however. When you're viewing an image alone, you can hold your finger on it and then save it using the Save Image command.

When you're done surfing the Web, to return to your tablet's Home screen, tap the Home icon that's continuously displayed near the bottom-left corner of the screen. All of the browser tabs that you have open will remain open until the next time you launch the Silk browser. Your most recently visited websites, however, will also be displayed on the Home screen's Carousel. You can quickly relaunch Silk and open a particular webpage by tapping the icon that appears within the Carousel.

Once a webpage shortcut appears (temporarily) within the Carousel on the Kindle Fire's Home screen, you can add a permanent shortcut to the Favorites bar, which is displayed near the bottom of the Home screen. To do this, hold your finger on the webpage shortcut icon that appears on the Carousel for two to three seconds. When the Add To Favorites tab appears on the screen (shown in Figure 6-15), tap it. The webpage icon will immediately be added to the Favorites bar on the Home screen and remain there until you delete it.

FIGURE 6-15 Tap the Add To Favorites tab to create a shortcut for that webpage on the Home screen.

7

Send and Receive E-mail on Your Kindle Fire

HOW TO...

- Set up the preinstalled Email app to work with your preexisting e-mail account(s)
- Read incoming e-mails
- Compose and send e-mails
- Manage multiple e-mail accounts

You've already discovered that, thanks to the proprietary Amazon Silk web browser app, your Kindle Fire easily can be used to surf the Web and visit your favorite websites, as long as the tablet is connected to a Wi-Fi hotspot or wireless network.

Using the separate Email app, which also comes preinstalled, you can set up your Kindle Fire to access your preexisting e-mail account(s) so you can read incoming e-mails, as well as compose and send outgoing e-mails.

 The Email app that comes preinstalled on your Kindle Fire is compatible with many personal e-mail accounts, including Google Gmail, Yahoo! Mail, Microsoft Hotmail, AOL Mail, and most IMAP and POP e-mail accounts. However, if Microsoft Exchange is used to host your work-related e-mail account, for example, you'll need to use a separate third-party app, called Exchange By TouchDown Key. You'll learn more about this app in Chapter 15.

Before you begin sending and receiving e-mails using your Kindle Fire, the Email app needs to be initially set up with information pertaining to your preexisting e-mail account(s). This setup process is done just once for each account. Then, from one inbox screen, you'll be able to receive and access e-mails from multiple accounts simultaneously. Keep in mind that while you can view incoming e-mails from several accounts on one screen, your Kindle Fire actually keeps e-mails from your various accounts separate.

For example, if you have your Kindle Fire configured to manage your personal and work-related e-mail accounts, as you view your incoming e-mails, when you opt to reply to a work-related e-mail, that reply will automatically be sent from your work-related e-mail account, unless you manually change the From field of the outgoing e-mail. The ability to view all incoming e-mails on a single screen makes it more efficient to access and manage your e-mails, without having to constantly switch between e-mail accounts.

Once you've configured the Email app to work with your e-mail account(s), if you receive an incoming e-mail with an attachment, you will be able to open and access that attachment as long as your Kindle Fire has an appropriate app installed that is compatible with that attachment. For example, if someone sends you a Microsoft Word document via e-mail (shown in Figure 7-1), to open and view it, you'll need to use a third-party app, such as Quickoffice. Or, if someone sends you a PDF file, it's necessary to have the Adobe Reader app (or a similar app) installed on your tablet to open and view PDF files.

Tip   Digital photos sent as attachments via e-mail can be retrieved using the Email app and then viewed and managed on your tablet using the Gallery app. However, if the photo is embedded in the body of the e-mail, you can view it using the Email app.

How to...   # Set up a Free E-mail Account You Can Use with Your Kindle Fire

If you don't yet have your own e-mail account, or if you want to create a separate e-mail account to utilize exclusively on your Kindle Fire, Google, Yahoo!, and Microsoft are among the companies that allow you to set up and use free e-mail accounts. To create a free Google Gmail e-mail account, visit https://accounts.google.com/NewAccount. To create a free Yahoo! Mail e-mail account, visit https://edit.yahoo.com/registration. To create a free Microsoft Hotmail account, visit https://signup.live.com/signup.aspx.

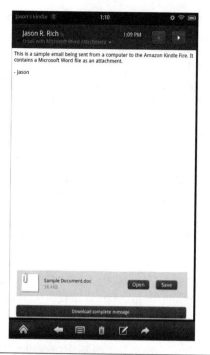

FIGURE 7-1   Your Kindle Fire can receive e-mails that contain attachments. You can open those attachments with specific apps, based on the type of file being sent.

Launch and Set up the Email App

When you're ready to set up your Kindle Fire to use the Email app so that you can send and receive e-mails from one or more preexisting e-mail accounts, from the tablet's Home screen, tap the Apps option that's displayed along the Navigation bar. As you know, the Apps screen displays app icons for all of the apps that are currently installed on your Kindle Fire (shown in Figure 7-2). To launch the Email app, locate

Email ——

FIGURE 7-2   Launch the Email app by tapping on the Email icon that's displayed on the Apps screen.

its app icon and tap it. Depending on how many apps you have installed on your tablet, the location of the Email app on the App screen will vary. By default, the app icons are displayed alphabetically.

When you launch the Email app for the first time, you'll see a white envelope graphic displayed in the center of the screen, with a "Welcome to e-mail setup" message (shown in Figure 7-3). Tap the orange Start icon that's displayed near the bottom-center area of the screen. Next, select your e-mail provider from the menu that's displayed on the screen. Your options include Gmail, Yahoo!, Hotmail, AOL, and Other.

Add an E-mail Account from the Displayed List

Assuming your preexisting e-mail account is a Gmail, Yahoo! Mail, Hotmail, or AOL Mail account, tap the appropriate icon from the Select Email Provider menu (shown in Figure 7-4). The Setup screen for that particular type of e-mail account will be displayed next. If you have a Yahoo! Mail account, for example, tap the Yahoo! icon.

 As with many apps, your Kindle Fire needs Internet access when you set up an e-mail account and/or attempt to access your e-mail accounts from your tablet.

FIGURE 7-3 The first time you launch the Email app, you'll need to configure your preexisting e-mail account(s) to work with it.

FIGURE 7-4   Select the type of e-mail account you're setting up.

If you select to set up a Gmail, Yahoo!, Hotmail, or AOL Mail account, you'll be prompted to enter your account user name and password for the preexisting account. Using the Kindle Fire's virtual keyboard, enter this information. Tap the orange Next icon to continue the e-mail account setup process, shown in Figure 7-5.

FIGURE 7-5   When prompted, enter the e-mail account–specific information that's requested, such as your user name and password.

After the Email app communicates briefly with your e-mail account's server to confirm your account information, two additional blank fields will be displayed. They're labeled Display Name and Account Name (shown in Figure 7-6). Within the Display Name field, enter your full name, exactly as you'd like it to appear within the From field of all outgoing e-mails you compose and send.

Within the Account Name field, create a nickname for the e-mail account so you can easily identify it. Only you will see this account nickname, which is optional. For example, you could enter, "Work E-mail," "Personal E-mail," or "Yahoo! E-mail."

Once you've filled in these two fields, tap the orange View Your Inbox icon that's displayed near the bottom-center area of the screen, just above the virtual keyboard. This will conclude the e-mail setup process for this account. The inbox for the account will be displayed on the screen, your incoming e-mails will be downloaded from the server, and you can begin managing your e-mail account.

Add an IMAP or POP E-mail Account

If you have an Internet Message Access Protocol (IMAP) or Post Office Protocol 3 (POP3) e-mail account that's not listed within the Select Email Provider menu, tap the Other option. In addition to providing your user name and password for the account,

FIGURE 7-6 Enter your full name and a nickname for the e-mail account when prompted.

be prepared to enter details such as the IMAP Server, Security Type, Authentication Type, Port, and IMAP path prefix (shown in Figure 7-7). You should obtain this information from your Internet service provider (ISP) or e-mail service provider. This information allows the Email app to find and then access your preexisting e-mail account's e-mail server. For example, the IMAP or POP3 server that you may be prompted to provide is equivalent to a website address for your particular e-mail server. In this field, you'd enter "mail.[yourservername].com," for example.

You will then be prompted to type your name within a blank field. This is what will appear in the From field of your outgoing e-mails. You'll also be prompted to provide a nickname for the e-mail account you're setting up. This name is for your own reference.

Once your Kindle Fire confirms your e-mail address information with the appropriate e-mail server, the inbox for that e-mail account will be displayed. It will contain your incoming e-mail messages. At this point, the e-mail account is set up and ready to use in conjunction with your Kindle Fire.

FIGURE 7-7 When configuring some IMAP or POP3 e-mail accounts, you'll need to provide more detailed information about the account than just your user name and password.

Set up Additional E-mail Accounts

After setting up one e-mail account, if you have additional e-mail accounts you want to be able to access from your Kindle Fire, from the Inbox screen, tap the Menu icon that's displayed near the bottom, and then tap the Accounts icon. When the Accounts screen appears, tap the Menu icon once again. This time, tap the Add Account icon.

Once again, the Select Email Provider menu will appear. Repeat the steps you just followed in order to set up your second e-mail account. You can then repeat the process again for each additional e-mail account that you want to access using the Email app on your Kindle Fire.

After entering your full name and a nickname for the e-mail account, you'll see an empty check box displayed next to the heading Send Mail From This Account By Default. By tapping this check box to add a check mark, you will make this the default "from" e-mail account when you opt to create an outgoing e-mail message from scratch, if you're managing multiple accounts from your tablet.

Read Your Incoming E-mails

The Email app's Inbox screen (shown in Figure 7-8) is pretty straightforward. At the top of the screen you'll see a pull-down menu that allows you to select just one of your e-mail accounts to view at a time. By default, the Unified Inbox option is

FIGURE 7-8 The Inbox screen with one e-mail account set up to work with the Kindle Fire

selected, which means that the incoming e-mails from all of your e-mail accounts that have been set up to work on the Kindle Fire will be displayed in chronological order on a single screen.

 Tap any e-mail listing within your inbox to view the entire message on your tablet's touch screen.

Near the top-left corner of the screen, a second pull-down menu is displayed. It's labeled Newest. When you tap it, a pull-down menu appears that allows you to sort your inbox's e-mail messages from newest to oldest; oldest to newest; or by subject, sender, flagged, read, unread, or attachments. As soon as you tap your selection, the message listing within your inbox will be re-sorted and displayed. Each incoming e-mail has its own listing within the inbox. This listing displays the subject, date, and the first two lines of the message's body.

 On the right side of each incoming e-mail's listing within the inbox, just under the date, will be a flag icon. Tap this icon to flag the message, which is equivalent to marking it as urgent. When you tap the flag icon, it will turn orange. If you tap the flag icon again, you can remove the priority flag you previously added.

As you're viewing your inbox, displayed along the bottom of the Email app's screen are six command icons, starting with the Home icon near the lower-left corner (shown in Figure 7-9). Here's a quick summary of what these command icons are used for:

- **Home**   Exit out of the Email app and return to the Kindle Fire's Home screen.
- **Back**   This icon looks like a left-pointing arrow. Tap it to return to the previous screen you were looking at within the Email app.
- **Menu**   Depending on where you are within the Email app, when you tap the Menu icon, a different selection of command icons will be displayed. For example, if you're looking at the inbox, six additional command icons will be displayed. (See the next section of this chapter for details about these command icons and the options associated with them.)
- **Refresh**   Tap this icon that looks like chasing arrows to check for new incoming e-mails and refresh the inbox display.
- **Compose**   Tap this icon to compose a new (outgoing) e-mail message from scratch. See the section of this chapter, entitled, "Composing and Sending E-mails from the Email App."
- **Search**   When you tap this magnifying glass icon, you can search your inbox for a specific keyword, search phrase, contact name, date, etc., that appears within a message.

FIGURE 7-9   These icons let you work with your e-mails quickly and efficiently.

When reading an individual e-mail, the displayed command icons at the bottom of the screen will change.

The Inbox's Menu Commands

As you're viewing the Email app's inbox, tap the Menu command icon to reveal six additional command icons, shown in Figure 7-10. Here's a summary of what these command icons are used for:

- **Edit List**   Using the Edit List commands, you can quickly mark as read, move, or delete multiple incoming e-mails that are displayed within the inbox listing. To do this, tap the Edit List icon. Each e-mail listing will now have an empty check box displayed to the left of it. One at a time, select an e-mail listing by tapping the empty check box to select it. An orange check mark will appear within the check box. You can select just one e-mail listing or multiple e-mail listings.

  After at least one e-mail message from your inbox is selected, four command icons will appear near the bottom of the screen. They're labeled Mark As Read, Move, Delete, and Done. Tap the Mark As Read icon to indicate that the selected messages have been read. As you look at your inbox, these messages will no longer be highlighted as new messages.

  Tap the Move icon to move the incoming e-mail from your inbox to another folder. A listing of available folders set up for that e-mail account will be displayed.

  To delete the e-mail from your inbox altogether, tap the Delete icon. Or to exit out of the Edit List mode and not do anything else, tap the Done icon.

- **Help**   Access on-screen help for the Email app.
- **Contacts**   Launch and access the Contacts app from within the Email app. While looking at a contact's listing, tap their e-mail address to compose an e-mail to that person without having to manually enter their e-mail address into the To field of the outgoing e-mail.
- **Accounts**   Access the Email app's Accounts screen and view details about each of the e-mail accounts you have set up to work with the app. When you tap any account's listing, the inbox for just that account will be displayed. Or, if you tap the Menu icon as you're looking at the Accounts screen, a selection of submenu options, including Contacts, Add Account, and Settings, will be displayed.
- **Folders**   Each of your e-mail accounts has a series of folders set up for it that allow you to organize your e-mail messages. In addition to an inbox, your e-mail account may have a Sent, Trash, Junk, Draft, and/or Notes folder. Depending

FIGURE 7-10   The Menu command icon within the Email app reveals six additional command icons.

on your e-mail service provider, you may be allowed to create additional folders and label them however you wish. For example, you might opt to create folders labeled "Personal," "Urgent," or "Work-Related."

While looking at the Folders screen for a specific e-mail account, tap the Menu icon to reveal a different selection of submenu command icons, including Empty Trash, Accounts, and Settings.

- **Settings** From the inbox, if you tap the Menu icon and then select the Settings option, you'll be given access to the Email app's main Settings menu. From here, you can customize the app's functionality. The settings options available to you will be explained shortly.

 If you tap the Settings icon from somewhere within the Email app aside from the Inbox screen, the Settings submenu options will vary.

The Email App's Settings Menu

From the inbox of the Email app, if you tap the Menu icon and then select the Settings option, the Settings menu screen will be displayed (shown in Figure 7-11). This menu offers over a dozen options that allow you to customize the Email app. These options include

- **Account Name** Change the account name you gave to each specific e-mail account when it was set up.
- **Default Account** If you have multiple e-mail accounts set up to work with your Kindle Fire, by placing a check mark within this menu option's check box, you will be able to select a default account. This will be the account e-mail messages you compose are automatically sent from, unless you manually change the From field within the outgoing e-mail. However, when you reply to a message, it will be sent from the e-mail account the original message was sent to. You can, however, manually change this if you're managing multiple e-mail accounts from your tablet by tapping the Send As field that's displayed below the Text Message window when you're composing a reply e-mail.
- **Always Show Images** You can opt to display all images, including graphics and photos, embedded within all incoming e-mails, or only show images within e-mails from people within your Contacts database. You can also opt to have the Email app not show any images or graphics that are embedded within incoming e-mail messages. If you're connected to a particularly slow Internet connection, not displaying images will speed up the loading process. However, since the Kindle Fire only uses a Wi-Fi connection, as opposed to a slower 3G Internet connection, adjusting this feature is not typically necessary.
- **Fetch New Messages** This option allows you to decide if your Kindle Fire should automatically and continually check for new incoming e-mails, or if you want to perform this task manually by tapping the Refresh icon while looking at the app's inbox. Having your tablet continually check for e-mails will drain its battery a bit faster.

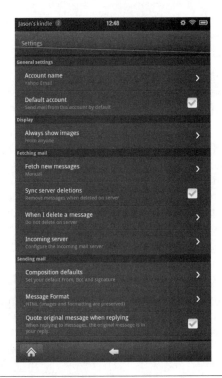

FIGURE 7-11   You can customize the Email app in a number of ways.

- **Sync Server Deletions**   When selected, this option will delete an e-mail from your tablet automatically if that message is deleted from the e-mail server as you're viewing it from another computer.

 As you're learning to use the Email app, refrain from turning on the Sync Server Deletion feature and be sure the Do Not Delete On Server option is selected. This way, if you accidently delete an important e-mail from your Kindle Fire, you'll still be able to retrieve it from your e-mail server.

- **When I Delete Message**   This menu option has three choices associated with it. When you delete an e-mail from your tablet, you can configure the Kindle Fire so the message either will or will not simultaneously be deleted from the e-mail server. If you choose not to delete messages from the server, you can opt to mark them as read. So, if you read an incoming e-mail on your Kindle Fire and then access that e-mail account from your primary computer, for example, messages you've already read on your tablet will no longer be marked as new messages.
- **Incoming Server**   This submenu option allows you to configure the incoming mail server that's associated with one of your e-mail accounts. If the e-mail account is working properly on your tablet, there should be no need to adjust any of these settings.

- **Composition Defaults**   Whenever you compose and send an e-mail from your Kindle Fire, the Email app will automatically insert your name and e-mail address in the From field, and can end each e-mail with a signature. You can customize or change these message composition options from the Composition Defaults submenu (shown in Figure 7-12). The Bcc All Messages To option allows you to forward a copy of all outgoing e-mails to a separate e-mail address without the recipients knowing this has been done.
- **Message Format**   You can choose to preserve HTML message formatting within e-mails you compose and send on your Kindle Fire, or choose to send them as plain text.
- **Quote Original Message When Replying**   When turned on, this feature will display the text from the incoming message you're responding to as part of the outgoing message. This makes it easier to follow e-mail–based conversations.
- **Outgoing Server**   Use this Settings menu option to edit or reconfigure the outgoing mail (SMTP) server information that's associated with your e-mail account.
- **Folders**   Displayed under the Folders heading of the Settings menu are five common e-mail folders that the Email app will utilize as you manage one or more

FIGURE 7-12   From the Settings menu, you can customize the signature that appears at the end of your outgoing e-mails.

You Can Create, Edit, or Remove E-mail Signatures

By default, e-mails composed on your Kindle Fire using the Email app will end with a signature that says, "Sent from my Kindle Fire." From within the submenu that's displayed when you select the Composition Defaults option from the Settings menu, you can modify this signature to say anything you'd like.

You can also remove the check mark from the Use Signature check box within Settings (refer back to Figure 7-12), which will disable this feature altogether, meaning that no signature will be displayed at the end of your outgoing messages. If you leave this feature turned on, however, as you're composing an individual message, you can tap the Signature field within the Compose Message screen and either edit or remove the signature just within that message.

e-mail accounts on your tablet. These folders are labeled Archive Folder, Drafts Folder, Sent Folder, Spam Folder, and Trash Folder. If you have custom folders set up for one or more of your e-mail accounts, you can customize the settings related to these folder options.

- **Notification Sound** When a new incoming e-mail arrives or the Email app needs to get your attention, it can alert you with an audible sound. From this menu option, select the sound you'll hear from a menu of sounds that are built into your tablet.

Composing and Sending E-mails from the Email App

One of the six command icons that are displayed at the bottom of the screen whenever the Email app is running is the Compose icon. It's located to the immediate left of the Search icon. When you tap the Compose icon, the Kindle Fire's screen will instantly be replaced with the Compose Email screen, shown in Figure 7-13. The To, Subject, and Message Text fields will be empty.

Tip To start quickly composing an e-mail that's addressed to a specific contact, from the Contacts app, tap the e-mail address included within a specific entry. The Email app will launch, and the Compose Email screen will be displayed. The To field of the message you're about to write will automatically be filled in with the recipient's name and e-mail address.

FIGURE 7-13   Use the Compose Email screen to create and send an outgoing e-mail.

 If you only have one e-mail account set up to work with your Kindle Fire, the From field will automatically be filled in with your name and e-mail address. However, if you are managing multiple e-mail accounts from your Kindle Fire, you will be able to choose which of your e-mail accounts the outgoing e-mail will be sent from. If you reply to an incoming e-mail, by default, it will be sent from the e-mail account the original message was sent to, unless you manually change the Send As field from the Compose Email screen.

At the top of the Compose Email screen is the To field. Tap it to use the virtual keyboard and enter the e-mail address for each recipient. If you're sending an e-mail to someone who has an entry within your Contacts database, tap the orange plus sign, and then select the appropriate contact from your Contacts database. It is mandatory to include at least one e-mail address for a recipient within the To field of an outgoing e-mail message.

 You can send an e-mail to multiple recipients by separating their e-mail addresses in the To field with a comma (i.e., Jason@jasonrich.com, jasonrich77@yahoo .com). Also, instead of filling in the To field with someone's e-mail address, if the recipient is included within your Contacts database, you can simply begin entering their name and then tap their e-mail address when it's matched up by the Email app and is displayed just below the To field.

Located to the right of the To field is the Cc/Bcc icon. Tap this to add a Cc and Bcc field to the Compose Email screen, and then tap one field at a time to fill in the appropriate e-mail addresses (shown in Figure 7-14). When an e-mail address is added to the Cc field, that person will receive a copy of the e-mail you're sending, and their e-mail address will be displayed at the top of the message for the main recipient(s) to see. When you enter e-mail addresses for recipients into the Bcc field, they will receive a copy of the e-mail, but the main recipients will not know the message was also sent to others.

Next, tap the Subject field of the outgoing e-mail message you're composing. Using the virtual keyboard, enter a subject for the message. You do, however, have the option to leave this field blank. Practicing good e-mail etiquette, however, dictates that you include a subject and make it intelligible and descriptive within your outgoing e-mails so the recipient can easily determine what the message is about.

Within the Message Text window, begin composing your outgoing e-mail message. This can be as long or as short as you desire. As you begin typing each word, above the top row of letters and numbers of the virtual keyboard, the auto-complete

FIGURE 7-14 You can send the same e-mail message to multiple recipients.

suggestions for what you're typing will be displayed. If you tap one of these words, you can include it within the e-mail's message without having to finish typing that word. Theoretically, this should increase your typing speed when using the Kindle Fire's virtual keyboard.

Note   The version of the Email app launched in conjunction with the Kindle Fire in October 2011 (Version 3.907) does not allow you to incorporate specialized formatting or to select fonts or typestyles within the body of the e-mail messages you compose. These are features that will most likely be added in later editions of the app.

Just below the Message Text window is the Signature field. By default, the signature your e-mail messages will end with will say, "Sent from my Kindle Fire." However, you can change this default message from within the Settings menu. Or, you can tap the Signature field, use the Delete button on the virtual keyboard to remove its contents, and then type a new signature message that will be used for just the outgoing e-mail you're composing.

Tip   As you're composing your e-mail, notice that the Kindle Fire's virtual keyboard looks very much like a traditional computer keyboard. However, above the top row of letters and numbers, you'll see a line of commonly used punctuation marks and symbols that you can tap to include within your message (shown in the illustration). While typing, the key tap sound will change based on which keys you're pressing. For example, letter and number keys will generate a different sound when pressed than the BACKSPACE, SPACEBAR, RETURN key, and CAPS LOCK/SHIFT key.

When you're done composing your message, tap one of the four command icons that are displayed between the Signature field and the virtual keyboard. They're labeled Attach, Send, Save Draft, and Cancel.

To add an attachment to your outgoing e-mail, tap the Attach icon. You can then choose between a photo or image stored within the Gallery app and a document stored within the Quickoffice app. However, if you have other apps installed on your tablet, such as Adobe Reader for PDF files, and those apps generate files or documents compatible with the Email app, these, too, will be displayed within the Choose Attachment From window that appears once you tap the Attach icon.

How to... **Save a Message as a Draft, Without Sending It**

As you're composing an e-mail, if you want to save it on your tablet but not send it out immediately, tap the Save Draft icon. The e-mail will be saved in your e-mail account's Drafts folder. You can access it at any time later to finish editing and/or composing it and then send it. After a message is saved to the Drafts folder, you will automatically be returned to the Email apps inbox.

To access the Drafts folder from the Inbox screen, tap the Menu icon and then select the Folders option. When the Folders menu appears, tap the Drafts option. A listing of messages saved as drafts will be displayed. Tap the listing for the e-mail message you want to view, edit, continue composing, and/or send.

After choosing the type of attachment you want to add, the Pick screen will appear, allowing you to select the specific photo, image, document, or file. As soon as you select the specific file to attach to the e-mail, a thumbnail representing that attachment, along with its filename and file size, will appear below the Signature field on the main Compose Email screen.

Whether or not you opt to include an attachment with your outgoing e-mail, when you're ready to send the e-mail, tap the orange Send icon. The e-mail message will be sent to its intended recipient(s), provided your tablet has access to the Internet. A copy of the message will be saved in your outbox or Sent folder.

 Note As you're composing an e-mail, if you tap the Cancel icon, you will be returned to the Inbox screen and the e-mail you were composing will be deleted and remain unsent.

Read and Reply to Incoming E-mails

From the Inbox screen of the Email app, tap any e-mail listing to open up that e-mail message and view the entire message on the tablet's screen. When you do this, you can use your finger to scroll up, down, left, or right, and use the Kindle Fire's zoom in and zoom out features. Likewise, if you tap a hyperlink within an incoming e-mail, the Amazon Silk web browser will automatically launch, and the webpage or web content associated with the hyperlink will be displayed.

As you're reading a single e-mail message (shown in Figure 7-15), notice the left- and right-pointing arrow icons that are displayed near the upper-right corner of the screen. Tap the left-pointing arrow to view the previous e-mail within your inbox. Or tap the right-pointing arrow to view the next message within your inbox in its entirety.

As you're reading an e-mail, along the bottom of the screen, six command icons are visible. The Home and Back icons you're already familiar with. The Menu icon

FIGURE 7-15 View individual e-mail messages, one at a time, on the Kindle Fire's screen.

will reveal three command icons, labeled Mark As Unread, Move, and Mark As Spam (shown in Figure 7-16). Tap the Mark As Unread icon to keep the message you're reading labeled as a new incoming message. Tap the Move icon to move the message you're reading from the inbox to another folder for safekeeping. If the e-mail message is unsolicited junk mail or spam, tap the Mark As Spam icon to move the message into the Email app's Spam folder.

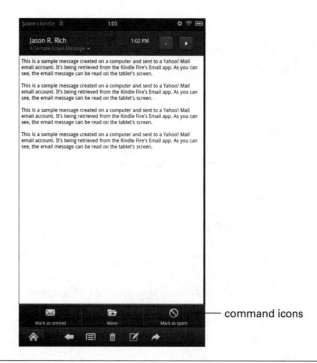

FIGURE 7-16 When reading an e-mail, here are the command icons you see when you tap the Menu icon.

Located to the right of the Menu icon as you're reading an e-mail is the Trash icon. Tap this icon to delete the e-mail message you're reading from your inbox and your Kindle Fire altogether. Displayed to the right of the Trash icon is the Compose Email icon. Use it to begin creating a new e-mail from scratch.

However, if you want to reply to the e-mail you're currently viewing or forward the e-mail to someone else, tap the right-pointing arrow that's displayed near the bottom-right corner of the screen as you're reading an e-mail message. When you do this, the Reply, Reply All, and Forward command icons appear.

Tap the Reply icon to respond to the e-mail message you're reading. The Compose Email screen will appear, and the To field will be filled in automatically with the recipient's e-mail address. If the original e-mail was addressed to multiple recipients (you being one of them), tap the Reply All icon to respond to the message and address your response to all of the original message's recipients. In this case, the To field, as well as the Cc and/or Bcc fields, will be filled in automatically. However, you also have the option to manually enter additional e-mail addresses to any of these three fields.

To forward the message you're reading to someone else, tap the Forward icon. In this case, the subject line and body of the e-mail will be filled in with the contents of the original message you're forwarding; however, you will need to manually provide the intended recipient's e-mail address. When you forward an e-mail, you also have the option to add to the body of the outgoing e-mail message you're forwarding.

How to...

Use the Select, Copy, Cut, and Paste Commands as You Compose an E-mail

While typing an e-mail message, hold your finger on any word that appears on the screen within the body of the message. The Edit Text dialog box will appear. This window includes the Select Word, Select All, and Paste commands. To select that one word, tap the Select Word option. Or to highlight and select all of the text within the Message Text window, tap the Select All option.

Once you tap the Select Word option, that word will be highlighted in orange and two upward-pointing arrows will appear on either side of the word. Using your finger, drag either arrow to the right, left, up, or down to highlight and select additional text. When the appropriate text is highlighted, tap it again. The Edit Text window will appear again, this time offering the Cut, Copy, and Paste commands. (The Paste command will only be displayed when content is being stored temporarily in the tablet's virtual clipboard.)

Tap Cut to delete the highlighted text. Tap Copy to copy that text to the Kindle Fire's virtual clipboard so you can paste it elsewhere in the e-mail, in another e-mail, or within another app altogether. Use the Paste command to paste the text stored within the virtual keyboard wherever the cursor is presently located on the screen.

Managing Multiple E-mail Accounts from Your Kindle Fire

Setting up multiple preexisting e-mail addresses to work with your Kindle Fire is just a matter of repeating the e-mail account setup process multiple times, once for each e-mail account. Once this setup process is completed for each account, you will be able to manage them from your Kindle Fire.

As you're looking at the Inbox screen, tap the Inbox pull-down menu icon displayed near the top-left corner of the screen to select just one e-mail account at a time from which to view incoming e-mails. You'll probably find it more convenient, however, to select the Unified Inbox option in order to view all of the incoming e-mails, from all of your accounts, within one Inbox screen.

To see how many messages you have within each account, tap the Menu option from the inbox and select the Accounts option. The Accounts screen will display each e-mail account your tablet is set up to work with and will display a number that indicates how many incoming messages are stored within the inbox within an oval displayed next to the account name. Tap the account listing from the Accounts screen to access the inbox for just that account.

When composing an e-mail, in addition to the To, Cc, Bcc, Subject, and Signature fields and the Message Text window, you will notice a Send As option displayed between the Signature field and the virtual keyboard if you're managing more than one e-mail account from your tablet. Tap this Save As pull-down menu to select which of your e-mail accounts you want the message you're composing to be sent from.

When responding to an e-mail, the e-mail account to which the original e-mail was sent will be the default e-mail account from which your response is sent, unless you manually change it. However, if you tap the Compose icon to create a new message from scratch, the e-mail account you have selected as your default account from the Settings menu will be used. Again, you can tap the Send As option to change the outgoing account.

Other E-mail Options

Aside from using the Email app that comes preinstalled on your Kindle Fire, if you visit the Amazon App Store, you'll discover a handful of third-party apps that can also be used for managing one or more e-mail accounts. You'll also discover apps specifically for using online social networking services, like Facebook. Use the Facebook app, for example, to manage the e-mails associated with your Facebook account.

Likewise, if your preexisting e-mail account allows you to access the account via the Web, you can use the Amazon Silk web browser to manage individual e-mail accounts, and perhaps have additional e-mail–related features and functions at your disposal. For example, to access Yahoo! Mail from the Amazon Silk web browser, you'd visit https://login.yahoo.com.

 Some of the more advanced e-mail–related apps available from the Amazon App Store include Enhanced Email ($9.99), Exchange by TouchDown Key ($12.99), MailDroid (free), Yahoo! Mail (free), and OneMail ($0.99). You'll learn more about several of these apps in Chapter 15.

8

Access, View, and Edit Microsoft Office Files on the Kindle Fire

HOW TO...

- Access and view Microsoft Office files
- Create, edit, and share Microsoft Office–compatible files

When it comes to accessing Microsoft Office files via your Amazon Kindle Fire, there's good news and bad news. Starting with the good news, if you utilize a third-party app, such as Quickoffice, it is possible to view Microsoft Word, Microsoft Excel, and Microsoft PowerPoint documents and files on your tablet's screen. The basic version of Quickoffice comes preinstalled on your tablet and can be used for this purpose.

If you want to create, edit, and/or share Microsoft Office documents and files, however, you'll want to upgrade to Quickoffice Pro ($9.99), OfficeSuite Pro 5 ($14.99), or another similar app via the Amazon App Store. When you upgrade to Quickoffice Pro, for example, you'll also be able to share documents and files easily between your Kindle Fire and several cloud-based file sharing services, such as Google Docs, Dropbox, and iCloud. Plus, the Pro version of the app allows you to view PDF files.

 Tip If you want to view and manage PDF files on your Kindle Fire, you'll want to install Adobe Reader (free), ezPDF ($2.99), Documents To Go Main App (free), RepliGo Reader ($1.99), qPDF View (free), Quickoffice Pro ($9.99), or one of more than a dozen other apps designed for this purpose.

As for the bad news associated with viewing, creating, editing, printing, and sharing Microsoft Office documents and files via your Kindle Fire, there are a few obstacles you'll need to overcome, as well as limitations you'll need to accept. For example, due to the size of the virtual keyboard, touch-typing (unless you use just your thumbs) is not that feasible on the handheld device, at least for large amounts of text. So, you won't want to do that much or any serious word processing. And if you're viewing a document or file on the tablet's seven-inch screen, you may find yourself zooming in on content and navigating your way around the document or file using finger swipes to be able to view it clearly and in its entirety.

 When the Kindle Fire was first released, there was no way to connect an external keyboard to the tablet. Any data entry needs to be done using the tablet's virtual keyboard. This may change in future versions of the Kindle Fire.

The Kindle Fire is ideal for certain tasks, like reading eBooks, watching TV shows or movies, or surfing the Web; however, it is not necessarily the best tool for word processing, spreadsheet management, creating and viewing digital slide presentations, or doing other work-related tasks that a desktop computer, laptop computer, or netbook could easily handle. But, if you utilize the right third-party apps, these tasks are certainly possible using your Kindle Fire.

In terms of practicality, you can use the version of Quickoffice that comes preinstalled on your Kindle Fire (or another third-party app) to view Microsoft Office files and documents on your tablet's screen. But if you want to do any serious editing or create Microsoft Office–compatible documents or files from scratch, you'll need to purchase an app that offers more robust features and functionality.

This chapter focuses on how to use the basic version of Quickoffice to view Microsoft Office documents and files on your Kindle Fire. It then offers additional details about Quickoffice Pro, as well as other third-party apps that offer added functionality beyond just viewing Microsoft Office files on your tablet's screen.

Using Quickoffice to View Microsoft Office Documents on Your Kindle Fire

The Quickoffice app, from Quickoffice, Inc., comes preinstalled on your tablet. To launch this app, from the Kindle Fire's Home screen, tap the Apps option from the Navigation bar. When the Apps screen appears, tap the Quickoffice app icon.

As you'll discover, the Quickoffice app has three separate modules: Quickword, Quicksheet, and Quickpoint. From the main Quickoffice screen, shown in Figure 8-1, tap the blue Quickword icon if you want to view a Microsoft Word document. Tap the green Quicksheet icon to view a Microsoft Excel spreadsheet file, or tap the orange Quickpoint icon to view a Microsoft PowerPoint presentation file. To access any Microsoft Office files using this app, they must first be transferred to the tablet and stored within the Kindle Fire's internal storage. How to do this is explained fully in Chapter 13. See Chapter 5 for additional information about the basic Quickoffice app, which comes preinstalled on the Kindle Fire.

 When using Quickoffice, at the very bottom of the screen is a "^" icon. Tap it to reveal the Home, Back, Menu, and Search command icons that are common to most Kindle Fire apps. These icons are not continuously visible on the app's main screen.

FIGURE 8-1   The main Quickoffice screen

When you tap the Quickword, Quicksheet, or Quickpoint icon, the screen will display options for accessing your tablet's internal storage, so you can select and open a compatible Microsoft Office file or document that you previously transferred to your tablet. There is no need to manually convert the Microsoft Office file or document into another format that's readable by your Kindle Fire. It is viewable as is using the Quickoffice app.

Tapping the Internal Storage option within the app reveals a directory of folders accessible from your tablet. This directory includes a Books, Documents, Music, Pictures, and Video folder. (You can, however, create your own folders and subfolders to organize the files or documents that you store on your tablet.)

When transferring Microsoft Office documents or files to your tablet, place them within the Documents folder (or within a subfolder within the Documents folder), so you can find and load them easily, and at the same time, keep your files organized. While you can place any files anywhere in your internal storage that you desire, it's easier to remember where they are if you place them in logically named folders or subfolders. Plus, some third-party apps that might need to access Word documents, for example, will automatically seek them out from the Documents folder unless you manually adjust the app to provide an alternate file location.

If you tap the Recent Documents option offered by the Quickoffice app, this will display a listing of Microsoft Office–compatible documents or files you've recently accessed. Tap any of the file listings to reload that file or document quickly.

Tapping the Browse icon that's displayed near the bottom of the main Quickoffice screen will direct you to the File Manager screen, from which you can tap the Internal Storage or Recent Documents option to load a file or document.

As you'll learn from Chapter 13, there are a variety of ways to transfer files, including Microsoft Office documents and files, to your tablet. These methods include

- Using a Micro-B USB–to–USB cable to connect your Kindle Fire to your primary computer (a PC or Mac) and then dragging-and-dropping files or documents between the tablet and the computer from the computer's desktop.
- Use your Send-To-Kind e-mail address to e-mail your Kindle Fire documents or files to be stored within the tablet's internal storage.
- Use Amazon Cloud Drive to transfer a document to your online-based account and then transfer it from the cloud to the tablet (or vice versa).
- Use a third-party cloud-based file sharing service, such as Google Docs, Dropbox, Box, Huddle, SugarSync, or iCloud, to transfer documents and files via the Internet.

Using any of these methods, you can transfer a Microsoft Office document or file from your primary computer (or any computer or mobile device, for that matter) to your Kindle Fire and then store it within the Documents folder of the tablet's internal storage. Once the Microsoft Office document or file is stored within your tablet, you can open it using a compatible app, such as Quickoffice, and view it on your tablet's screen. As you're then viewing the document or file, use your finger to swipe upward or downward to navigate your way around the document. You can also use a reverse-pinch finger motion to zoom in, or a pinch motion to zoom out.

Within Quickoffice, double-tapping the screen when viewing a document will not activate the zoom in or zoom out feature like it does within other apps.

To return to the internal storage screen and select a different file to view, tap the left-pointing arrow that's displayed near the bottom of the screen (shown in Figure 8-2). To exit out of Quickoffice altogether, tap the Home icon. To search the document or file you're viewing for a specific keyword or search phrase, tap the magnifying glass icon.

Tapping the Menu icon when viewing a document or Microsoft Office file within Quickoffice will reveal a submenu containing five additional command options, which were explained in Chapter 5.

If you use the basic version of the Quickoffice app to open and view a PowerPoint or Excel file, you will be able to view them on the tablet's screen but not edit them. For example, each slide of a PowerPoint presentation will be displayed, one after another, as part of a long document (shown in Figure 8-3).

You can also view a PowerPoint presentation one slide at a time once it's loaded into Quickoffice by tapping the Menu icon, followed by the Play icon, which looks

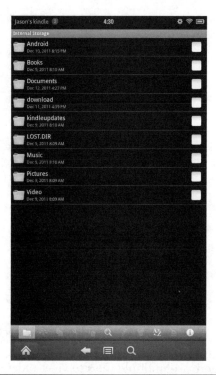

FIGURE 8-2   Access Microsoft Office files saved within the internal storage of your tablet, typically within the Documents folder (or a subfolder within Documents that you create).

like a right-pointing arrow. Any slide transitions or animations incorporated into the presentation when it was created on a PC or Mac, however, will not be viewable.

 Once a Microsoft Office file or document is loaded into your tablet and saved within its internal storage, you can share it with others using a cloud-based file sharing service or by attaching the file to an outgoing e-mail.

Upgrade to Quickoffice Pro

You can pay to upgrade to Quickoffice Pro either directly from the Amazon App Store or from within the basic version of the Quickoffice app. To do this, from the main Quickoffice screen, tap the Update icon that's displayed near the lower-left corner. When you do this, a pop-up window that says, "Update to Quickoffice Pro and get the most powerful mobile office suite available!" will be displayed, along with an OK and Cancel icon. Tap OK to begin the upgrade process. Follow the on-screen prompts that will direct you to the appropriate screen of the Amazon App Store, providing your Kindle Fire is connected to the Internet.

FIGURE 8-3 There are multiple ways to view slides on your tablet.

From the Quickoffice Pro app description screen within the App Store (shown in Figure 8-4), tap the orange price icon to purchase and download the app. When the price icon turns green and says, "Buy App," tap it again to confirm your purchase decision. A message that says, "Purchasing..." followed by "Downloading..." will be displayed.

After about 30 seconds, once the app has been downloaded to your tablet, tap the orange Open icon to launch it. The first time you launch Quickoffice Pro, a License screen will be displayed. Tap the I Agree icon to continue. You'll then be prompted to register the app by entering your e-mail address. Tap the Email Address field, enter your e-mail address using the tablet's virtual keyboard, and then tap the Register Now icon.

The Quickoffice Pro main screen looks somewhat similar to the basic Quickoffice app's main screen, except in addition to Quickword, Quicksheet, and Quickpoint icons, you'll discover a red QuickPDF icon. QuickPDF is used to view PDF files on your tablet (shown in Figure 8-5).

Note Because each module within the Quickoffice Pro suite is loaded with available features, depending on where you are within the app, tapping the Menu icon will reveal ten or more command icons, several of which will reveal submenus when you tap them. Once you learn the layout of the app's menu structure, you'll easily be able to find and access the Microsoft Office–related commands and features you want or need as you're working with documents or files.

FIGURE 8-4   You can upgrade to Quickoffice Pro from the Amazon App Store, and then be able to create and edit Microsoft Office documents and files, not just view them.

As you begin using Quickoffice Pro, you'll discover many additional menu options available to you that allow you to not just view Microsoft Office files and documents, but also create them from scratch or edit them.

 When you tap the Quickoffice Pro's Browse icon, or tap on one of the module icons to load a document or file, you'll be taken to the File Manager screen. In addition to the Internal Storage and Recent Documents options, an SD Card option is listed. Since the Kindle Fire does not have an SD Card slot, this will simply take you to the internal storage area of your tablet.

Now, if you open a document or file within Quickoffice Pro, in addition to simply viewing the document or file, if you tap anywhere within it, the virtual keyboard will appear, and you'll be able to edit the document. You'll also have access to the Select, Cut, Copy, and Paste commands, as well as a variety of formatting functions and other tools for word processing, managing a spreadsheet, or viewing a PowerPoint presentation.

After tapping the Quickword, Quicksheet, or Quickpoint icon, you also have the option to create a new document or file from scratch. After you do this, select a version number of Microsoft Office that you want the file to be compatible with.

FIGURE 8-5   The Quickoffice Pro app offers many additional features and functions not found in the basic edition, including the ability to view PDF files.

 Keep in mind that people using an older version of Word, for example, will not be able to open or access a document created using the Word 2010 format. However, the latest version of Word will open Word files created using older editions of this word processor. The same is true for Excel and PowerPoint files.

If you tap Quickword and then tap the Create New Document icon, for example, after choosing between a Word 2010, Word 2007, or Word 97–2003 document format, a blank document screen will be displayed, with the tablet's virtual keyboard shown at the bottom of the screen, as seen in Figure 8-6. You can now start typing your document.

To access the Quickword commands for formatting or saving the document, tap on the Hide Keyboard key that's located in the lower-right corner of the virtual keyboard, and then tap the Menu icon that's displayed near the bottom-center area of the screen. Ten command icons will become available to you, shown in Figure 8-7. Some of these command icons reveal submenus.

These command icons and submenus allow you to open an existing document, create a new document, save the document you're working on, use the Save As command to save the document you're working on, format your existing document

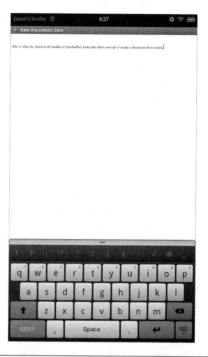

FIGURE 8-6   It may not look like Microsoft Word on your tablet's screen, but the Quickword module of Quickoffice Pro offers full word-processing capabilities, as well as many popular Microsoft Word features and functions.

(choose a font, typestyle, and font size), insert an image into the document, view the document in full-screen mode, or have a computer voice read the document you're working with aloud.

 Just above the keyboard, use your finger to drag open the formatting menu so you can quickly change fonts, font sizes, typestyles, or paragraph formatting.

Similar commands are available if you create or edit a Microsoft Excel spreadsheet file or PowerPoint presentation, although you'll also be given access to program-specific commands and features. It's assumed that if you're using Quickoffice, you're

FIGURE 8-7   Access a wide range of commands from command icons and submenus within the Quickoffice Pro app.

already familiar with Microsoft Word, Microsoft Excel, and/or Microsoft PowerPoint, as well as the features and functions of these PC or Mac software packages, which the Quickoffice app emulates and makes available on your Kindle Fire.

Tip When you save a document or file using Quickoffice, it is stored within your Kindle Fire's internal storage's Documents folder, by default. However, using this app, you can create custom folders by tapping the New Folder icon that's displayed when viewing your internal storage folders.

After you're done creating or editing a Microsoft Office–compatible document or file using Quickoffice Pro, return to the app's main menu screen, and tap the Accounts icon to access any of the nine cloud-based file sharing services the app is compatible with so you can easily transfer the document(s) or file(s) to your primary computer or share them with others. You can also load files or documents from other sources and view or edit them using Quickoffice, provided your Kindle Fire has Internet access.

Note To use a cloud-based file sharing service, you'll first need to set up an account with one of them. In some cases, this is free of charge. Some cloud-based file sharing services, however, have a fee associated with using them.

While Quickoffice Pro does not offer all of the features and functions of the Microsoft Office software applications available for your computer, this app does offer enough of the most important features and functions, so you can handle word processing, spreadsheet management, or digital slide show presentation creation and editing on your tablet. Assuming you're already familiar with how to use Microsoft Office, you'll find the Quickoffice app is loaded with familiar features that are easily accessible using a series of on-screen command icons, menus, and submenus.

If you want to perform work-related tasks on your Kindle Fire, Quickoffice Pro offers the tools you'll need to create from scratch or access Microsoft Office documents and files from virtually anywhere. And with so many different ways to import and export documents and files between your tablet and computer, you'll find the file transfer process to be straightforward and hassle-free.

Tip Once you return to your Kindle Fire's Home screen, the Carousel will display an app icon to quickly relaunch the Quickoffice or Quickoffice Pro app, as well as separate icons that are associated with the specific documents or files you were previously working with. Thus, you can tap any of these icons to relaunch the app and quickly regain access to your previous work.

Note If you upgrade to Quickoffice Pro, both the basic Quickoffice and Quickoffice Pro apps will be installed on your tablet. Because the basic Quickoffice app is considered a core (preinstalled) app, it cannot be manually deleted. In the future, be sure to launch the Quickoffice Pro app from the Home screen. The Quickoffice Pro icon has the word "Pro" displayed in the lower-left corner, as shown in the following illustration.

OfficeSuite Pro 5: Another Solution for Creating, Editing, Viewing, and Sharing Microsoft Office Files and Documents

Similar in functionality to Quickoffice Pro is the OfficeSuite Pro 5 app ($9.99) from Mobile Systems, Inc., which is also available from the Amazon App Store (shown in Figure 8-8). This app suite allows you to create, view, and edit Microsoft Word, Excel spreadsheet, and PowerPoint files, and view PDF files on your Kindle Fire's screen. (You cannot create PDF files using this app; you can only view PDF files created on other computers.)

Like Quickoffice Pro, OfficeSuite Pro 5 integrates nicely with a handful of cloud-based file sharing services, including Google Docs. This compatibility makes it easy to transfer documents and files between your computer and tablet, although you can also send files back and forth as e-mail attachments.

After purchasing, downloading, and installing the OfficeSuite Pro 5 app, launch it from the Apps screen of your tablet. Once launched, you'll discover a series of command icons along the left margin of the app's main screen, as well as along the top of the screen (shown in Figure 8-9).

The command icons available along the top of the main OfficeSuite Pro 5 app's screen allow you to create a new Microsoft Office–compatible document or

FIGURE 8-8   The OfficeSuite Pro 5 app adds a lot of functionality to your Kindle Fire, allowing it to serve more like a netbook and handle work-related tasks.

spreadsheet from scratch, find a file that's stored on your Kindle Fire, edit an existing document or file, sort or filter the Microsoft Office files stored on your tablet, adjust the settings related to the app, check for app updates, or obtain help related to using the app. The command icons running down the left margin of the app's screen allow you to locate and open recently used Microsoft Office files or documents, access the Documents folder within your tablet's internal storage area, or access files stored on cloud-based file sharing services that the OfficeSuite Pro 5 app is compatible with, such as Dropbox or Box.

 You can also transfer Microsoft Office files from your computer to your tablet using the methods described earlier in this chapter, and that are explored in greater detail in Chapter 13.

One nice feature of OfficeSuite Pro 5 is that from the main app screen, you can tap the My Documents command icon to open a file, and then from the Documents folder within the internal storage of your tablet, select any Word, Excel, PowerPoint, or PDF file you want to access. The file you select will open using the appropriate module of the app, and allow you to begin working with that file or document. You do not have to choose which module to launch. As you're looking at the My Documents screen, different file types are associated with different-colored icons for easy visual

FIGURE 8-9 The OfficeSuite Pro 5 app makes many Microsoft Office features and functions available from the main screen via command icons.

reference. For example, Word documents that are stored on your tablet will have a blue, diamond-shaped icon to the left of them. Excel files will have a green diamond-shaped icon to the left of them. PowerPoint documents will be accompanied by an orange diamond-shaped icon, and PDF files will have a red diamond-shaped icon. By default, the files displayed on the My Documents screen of OfficeSuite Pro 5 are listed in alphabetical order. However, by tapping the Sort command icon displayed near the top of the screen, you can rearrange the files by file type.

 By default, when you tap the My Documents icon to view your available Word, Excel, PowerPoint, and PDF files and documents, the app will search your tablet's Documents folder within its internal storage. However, you can tap the Settings icon, followed by the My Document Folder option, to change the path to what the app refers to as its My Documents folder. Thus, you can create a separate folder for all of your Microsoft Office files and use the Kindle Fire's default Documents folder to store other documents and files.

If you select the New command icon to create a document or file from scratch, you'll be prompted to choose between a Word document, Excel workbook, and PowerPoint presentation, allowing the app to load the appropriate module so you can begin working.

How to... Format Your Work on the Kindle Fire

When word processing, for example, OfficeSuite Pro 5 offers a robust set of features and commands, making it easy to create, edit, or view documents. As you can see in the illustration, just above the virtual keyboard is a selection of formatting icons, which look like those found within Microsoft Word. With the tap of an icon, you can switch between bold, italic, and/or underlined text; switch the paragraph justification between right-justified, center-justified, and left-justified; create numbered or bulleted lists; indent the margins of the paragraph; create highlighted text (using the color you select); or change the font color.

For a more extensive selection of formatting commands, tap the Remove Keyboard key that's located in the lower-right corner of the virtual keyboard as you're working with a document or file. Then, tap the Menu icon that's displayed near the bottom-center area of the screen. When the File, Edit, View, Format, Insert, and More menu icons are displayed, tap the Format icon. The Format menu will appear, which gives you access to several additional submenus, including the Font menu (shown in the illustration). The options available from the Font menu are used for selecting a font, font size, typestyle, and underline style, for example. Similar formatting commands suitable for working with spreadsheets are offered when creating, editing, or viewing a Microsoft Excel file.

To exit out of the submenus and return to your document or file, tap the Back icon (the left-pointing arrow) that's displayed near the bottom-center area of the screen. Then, to make the virtual keyboard reappear, tap anywhere within the document or file.

Just like in the real version of Microsoft Word, if you tap the Insert command within OfficeSuite Pro, you can incorporate a picture, table, hyperlink, bookmark, page break, comment, footnote, or endnote directly into a document. The photo or graphic, however, must already be stored within the internal storage of your tablet, within the Pictures folder, for example.

 Once a photo or table, for example, has been imported into the document, you can adjust its size and the formatting of text around it.

By tapping the Menu icon and then selecting the Edit command, you'll gain access to the Select, Cut, Copy, Paste, and Undo commands that make moving text or content around within a document or file (or between documents and files) a much faster process than having to retype that content.

While you're somewhat limited by the small size of the Kindle Fire's virtual keyboard, if you develop quick thumb-typing skills, you can achieve relatively fast and accurate data entry speeds using this powerful app. However, to slightly increase the size of the virtual keyboard, use the OfficeSuite Pro 5 app in landscape mode.

When you're done working with a document or file, it's important to save your work. (Although this is something you should get into the habit of doing more frequently.) Tap the Menu icon, and then tap the File command icon to reveal a File menu that offers a New, Open, Save, Save As, Protect, and Close command. These commands work just as they do when using Microsoft Office on your PC or Mac.

 The trick to being able to really utilize Quickoffice Pro or OfficeSuite Pro 5 is to get to know the layout of the app's menu structure so you can easily find and use the Microsoft Office commands and features you're already familiar with. Many of these commands and features are offered within these two apps, but they're organized differently and are accessible through command icons and submenus found within the apps.

Out of the handful of third-party apps available for the Kindle Fire that allow you to create, view, edit, and share Microsoft Office documents and files, OfficeSuite Pro 5 offers versatile and feature-packed functionality that most closely resembles what's possible using Microsoft Office on your computer. While it might take you a bit longer to adjust to the menu layout of this app, you'll discover it gives you the best selection of features when it comes to working with or creating Microsoft Office documents and files on your Kindle Fire. It's also easy to transfer and share files and documents using a variety of different methods.

Additional Options for Accessing Microsoft Office Files

If the idea of being able to create, view, edit, and share Microsoft Office files on your Kindle Fire is appealing, either the Quickoffice Pro or OfficeSuite Pro 5 app will probably meet your needs and most likely exceed your expectations in terms of what

You Have Other App Options for Accessing Microsoft Office Documents and Files

Another full-featured and robust app that's designed to give you Microsoft Office capabilities on your Kindle Fire is Documents To Go Full Version ($14.99). It, too, allows you to create, view, edit, and share Microsoft Office files, as does the Smart Office app ($9.99). To help you decide which app(s) to purchase, read their descriptions carefully, look at the sample screen shots offered within the Amazon App Store, pay attention to user ratings, and make sure the app you choose offers the functionality you need and a user interface you'll find intuitive, or at least useable in conjunction with the Kindle Fire's screen and virtual keyboard.

they're capable of. However, if you access the Amazon App Store and enter the search phrase "Microsoft Office" into the Search field that's displayed near the top-center area of the screen, you'll discover a handful of other apps that also give you the ability to work with Microsoft Office documents on your tablet.

Before purchasing and downloading any of these apps, keep in mind there's a difference between apps like Quickoffice Pro and OfficeSuite Pro 5 that allow you to create, edit, share, and view Microsoft Office files and documents, and apps that only allow you to view Microsoft Office documents but not edit or modify them in any way. Read the description of each app carefully in order to make sure it can handle the Microsoft Office–related tasks you're looking to accomplish on your Kindle Fire. Otherwise, you may wind up having to purchase and then switch between multiple apps in order to meet all of your word processing, spreadsheet management, and/or digital slide show presentation needs.

Printing from Your Kindle Fire

Unfortunately, there is no way to directly connect a printer to your Kindle Fire, either using a cable or Bluetooth wireless connection. However, several app developers and printer manufacturers have discovered ways to wirelessly print documents, photos, and files from your tablet via e-mail. This can be done through special online services or using printers that connect to the Internet or a wireless network.

To discover apps that offer you a variety of different printing options from your tablet, visit the Amazon App Store and enter the keyword "Printing" into the Search field. Keep in mind that some of the results will be apps designed to work with specific printer makes and/or models. Others will require you to sign up to use a special service, and fees may apply. Read each app's description carefully to find one that meets your needs and that's compatible with the printer and file types you'll be using it with.

EasyPrint is a free, ad-supported app that allows you to print documents from the Kindle Fire over the Google Cloud Print service, which can be configured to work with any HP, Kodak, or Epson printer that's connected to a PC or Mac. To work, the computer must have Internet access and have the Google Chrome web browser installed. The file, document, or image you want to print will need to be saved in the PDF format and sent to your free Google Cloud account via the Internet.

With EasyPrint, you can use your Kindle Fire anywhere, but whatever you opt to print will show up on your home or office printer. To learn more about the Google Cloud Print service, visit www.google.com/cloudprint/learn.

The Print Magic app ($1.99) will allow you to print documents and files wirelessly to any compatible printer that's utilizing the same Wi-Fi network as your Kindle Fire. The printer must also be connected to a PC or Mac.

For users of Kodak's All-In-One Printers, the free Kodak Pic Flick app allows you to print digital photos wirelessly from your Kindle Fire, as long as the tablet and printer are connected to the same Wi-Fi network.

In the future, Amazon may work with printer manufacturers to offer ways to directly connect the Kindle Fire, via a USB cable, to a printer by taking advantage of the tablet's Micro-B USB port. As of early 2012, this functionality was not yet possible.

9

Enjoy Video, Audiobooks, Entertainment, and Information on Your Kindle Fire

HOW TO...

- Download and watch TV shows and movies
- Stream video content from the Internet
- Download and listen to audiobooks and podcasts
- Stream audio content from the Internet

One of the tasks that your Kindle Fire is exceptionally good at is allowing you to experience audio and video entertainment from a variety of sources. In addition to the vast content library available from Amazon.com in the form of TV shows, movies, and music that can be purchased, downloaded, and enjoyed on your tablet at any time, whenever your Kindle Fire has access to the Internet, you can stream audio and video content directly from the Web. Streamed content can come from a wide range of sources, such as Amazon Prime, Netflix, Hulu Plus, YouTube, or Pandora Internet Radio, for example.

Whether you choose to purchase, download, and own your digital video or audio content, or stream it from the Web, literally hundreds of thousands of hours' worth of TV show episodes, as well as movies, documentaries, and music videos are available to you. Any time you purchase content from Amazon.com, in addition to that content being downloaded to your Kindle Fire, it is automatically stored for free within your Amazon Cloud Drive account. Thus, you can quickly access it for downloading or streaming without that content taking up any of your tablet's internal storage space when it's not being utilized.

When you purchase a DVD movie, it can be played using any DVD player you own. Likewise, once you purchase digital content from Amazon.com, you can watch or listen to it on your Kindle Fire, your computer, or another device at your leisure. You'll never have to repurchase that digital content again.

Did You Know?

The Difference Between Downloading and Streaming Content

After you purchase and download content from Amazon.com, such as a TV show episode or movie, you then own that content and can watch or listen to it as often as you like, whether or not your Kindle Fire is connected to the Internet. The content files can be stored within your Kindle Fire's internal storage or on your computer's hard drive.

When you stream content from the Internet, a specialized app is required to play that streaming audio or video. However, that content is not purchased, nor is it saved within your tablet's internal storage. As you're playing the content, it's possible to pause and restart it, but an Internet connection must be maintained. In addition to streaming content available directly from Amazon.com (if you obtain an Amazon Prime membership), you can stream content from a wide range of other sources, such as Netflix (using the Netflix app), Hulu Plus (using the Hulu Plus app), or Pandora (using the Pandora app).

Streaming Amazon Prime content to your Kindle Fire is done using the preinstalled Video app. However, accessing and viewing content from other services, like Netflix or Hulu Plus, requires you use a different app that was created specifically for that service. Streaming content does not require you to purchase specific content, but it does often require you to pay a membership or subscription fee to access content on an unlimited basis. For example, when you subscribe to Amazon Prime, Netflix, or Hulu Plus, you can watch as many TV show episodes or movies as you like during your membership period for a flat fee.

Downloading and Watching TV Shows and Movies

If you want to establish a digital content library that you own and that you can enjoy at any time, with or without an Internet connection (once the content is stored on your tablet), from the Kindle Fire's Home screen, tap the Video icon that's displayed along the Navigation bar.

The main Video screen is divided into several sections, shown in Figure 9-1. Along the top of the screen is a Search field that allows you to quickly search the Amazon Video Store for any TV show or movie, based on a title; genre; an actor, director, or producer's name; or any keyword or search phrase. Displayed to the right of the Search field is the Library icon. Tap this to reveal a listing of video content that you own and that's currently stored on your Kindle Fire (or available via your Amazon Cloud Drive account).

FIGURE 9-1   From the main screen of the Video app, you can access Amazon Prime Instant Videos, purchase or rent movies, or purchase TV show episodes.

Just below the Search field is a command tab for accessing Amazon Prime Instant Videos, which is a service offered as part of your paid Amazon Prime membership. This service is explained later in the chapter, and it's separate from content you can purchase and download from Amazon.com.

Below the Amazon Prime heading on the Video app's main screen, purchasable video content is displayed. This content is divided into two categories, labeled Movies and TV Shows. As you can see in Figure 9-2, just below the Movies heading, for example, are thumbnail graphics representing popular movies that you can purchase (or in some cases rent), download, and watch on your Kindle Fire.

FIGURE 9-2   Thumbnail graphics represent featured videos available for purchase and/or rent. The selection is constantly expanding.

Movies tab ———

FIGURE 9-3 You can browse Amazon.com's movie selection by category or find a specific movie using the Search field. Notice the Movies tab that's displayed near the top-left corner of the screen is orange.

Using your finger, swipe along this row of graphic thumbnails from right to left (or left to right) in order to view some of the featured movie releases. Or tap the View All command that's displayed to the right of the Movies heading to access and browse through all of Amazon.com movie offerings, which are categorized by Popular Movies, New Releases, Editor's Picks, All Genres, For The Kids, and Deals, shown in Figure 9-3. Just like when purchasing or renting DVDs, the price to acquire and download movies varies greatly, but starts at just $2.99 to rent a movie for 48 hours in standard-quality definition.

 When you purchase TV shows, or purchase or rent movies, you'll sometimes have two quality options. You can acquire the video content in standard or high definition (HD). Purchasing or renting HD quality video content typically costs a bit more, but the picture quality is significantly better. These HD files, however, are larger, take slightly longer to download, and will utilize more of your tablet's internal storage.

On the Video app's main screen, displayed just below the movie offerings, are the TV shows that you can purchase, download, and watch from Amazon.com. The

You Can Rent Movies to Watch on Your Kindle Fire

Depending on the movie title you access using the Videos app, you may be able to purchase it outright or rent it for 48 hours from Amazon.com. When you rent a movie, you can store it on your tablet or computer for up to 30 days before watching it. After 30 days, however, the file will automatically delete itself, whether or not it's been watched. Once you click Play to begin watching the movie, you can view it as often as you'd like for a 48-hour period. After the rental period, the movie will automatically delete itself from your tablet and/or computer.

When you rent a movie, it is downloaded to your Kindle Fire. Once it's stored within your tablet's internal storage, an Internet connection is no longer needed to watch it. So you can rent and download one or more movies before a long airplane flight, for example, and then enjoy watching them during the flight, when no Internet connection is available.

price to purchase a single half-hour or one-hour TV show episode starts at $1.99 for standard quality or $2.99 for HD quality. In addition to current TV show episodes from the major networks and cable TV channels, you'll discover that Amazon.com offers thousands of episodes from classic TV series, as well as episodes from past seasons of currently popular TV series.

Displayed just below the TV Shows heading, you'll see thumbnails for featured TV show offerings. However, to view Amazon.com's entire library of TV show episodes that are available for purchase and download, tap the View All command that's displayed to the right of the TV Shows heading, shown in Figure 9-4.

The selection of TV shows and movies that are available to purchase from Amazon .com is different from what's available for streaming with an Amazon Prime membership. Likewise, third-party services that offer video streaming, such as Netflix, offer their own collections of TV shows and movies, based on distribution deals they've worked out with the television networks and movie studios.

Selecting, Downloading, and Watching Movies from Amazon.com

While your Kindle Fire is connected to the Internet, if you tap one of the thumbnail graphics representing an available movie (displayed under the Movies heading of the Videos screen), you'll see a detailed description of that particular movie. To see a complete listing of movies available for purchase or rent, tap the View All command that's displayed to the right of the Movies heading.

TV tab

FIGURE 9-4 You can search through thousands of TV show episodes by browsing categories, like Latest TV Episodes, TV Channels, or Genres. Notice the TV tab that's displayed near the top-right corner of the screen is orange.

Near the top of the Movies screen, in addition to a Search field, you'll see an orange Movies heading. To the right are the Prime and All tabs, and to the right of that is a TV tab. If you have an Amazon Prime membership, tap the Prime tab to see movie offerings you can stream and watch on your Kindle Fire, on an unlimited basis, as part of your paid membership to this service. Or tap the All icon to see the movies you can purchase or rent from Amazon.com and download to your tablet.

To browse through the movies available for purchase or rent from Amazon.com, tap one of the category headings, which are also displayed near the top of the screen. These categories include Popular Movies, New Releases, Editor's Picks, All Genres, For The Kids, and Deals. Drag your finger from right to left to scroll through this listing, and then tap your selection.

When you tap a category tab, such as New Releases, displayed on the screen will be thumbnail graphics representing movies available for purchase and/or rent from Amazon.com that fit into that category. Scroll upward or downward on this screen using your finger to view all of the offerings.

Once you discover a movie you're interested in, tap its thumbnail icon to display its Description screen (shown in Figure 9-5). Near the top of the Description screen, you'll see the movie's title and thumbnail graphic, along with its average customer rating (between one and five stars), it's age-appropriateness rating (such as G, PG-13,

FIGURE 9-5   You can read a synopsis of a movie, view its cast list and ratings, and then purchase or rent a movie from its Description screen.

PG, R, etc.), and a series of orange icons that correspond to your purchase or rental options, including 48-Hour Rental, Purchase, and/or More Purchase Options.

If the Description screen has a 48-Hour Rental option associated with it, the price for that rental (in standard definition) is displayed within the corresponding orange icon. However, to view all of your purchase and/or rental options, tap the orange icon that says See All, which corresponds to the More Purchase Options icon, shown in Figure 9-6.

A pop-up More Purchase Options window will be displayed listing the prices to buy the movie outright or rent it in standard or HD quality. Tap your option to purchase or rent that movie. The cost will be billed directly to the credit or debit card you have on file in conjunction with your Amazon.com account.

 To purchase a movie from Amazon.com that will be downloaded onto your Kindle Fire, the average price will be between $14.99 and $19.99, but will vary. Many 48-hour rentals in standard definition are priced at $3.99, and most 48-hour rentals in HD quality are priced at $4.99.

As you're viewing a Movie Description screen, if you scroll downward, you'll be able to read a detailed synopsis of the movie, view its cast list and director, and see a listing for the movie's duration. Near the bottom of a Movie Description screen, you'll

FIGURE 9-6   Tap the More Purchase Options icon to see the price to purchase or rent a particular movie in standard or high definition.

see a row of additional graphic thumbnails under the heading Customers Who Bought This Item Also Bought. Tap any of these thumbnails to view the Description screens associated with these recommended movies.

   To exit out of the Description screen for a particular movie, tap the Back icon (the left-pointing arrow) that's displayed near the bottom of the screen. You can also tap the Home icon to exit out of the Videos app altogether and return to the Home screen. By tapping the Menu icon, a Settings and Help command icon will appear.

 If you're not sure what movie you're looking for, or if you just want to browse through your options, tap the All Genres category heading that's displayed near the top of the screen. This will display ten movie genre categories, such as Action & Adventure, Drama, Horror, Romance, or Sci-Fi & Fantasy. Scroll to the left or right to view all of the movie genre options. Then, tap your genre selection to see thumbnail graphics representing the Amazon.com movie offerings in that category.

Making Your Movie Rental or Purchase Decision

As you're viewing a movie's Description screen, tap either the 48-Hour Rental or More Purchase Options icon. If you tap 48-Hour Rental, the orange Price icon that's associated with this option will return green and say Rent. Tap it again to confirm your decision, and then download the movie or stream it from the Internet. Downloading the movie to your Kindle Fire's internal storage will take several minutes, depending on the file size associated with the movie and the speed of your Internet connection. HD quality movies and TV shows utilize larger file sizes than their standard definition counterparts. Thus, they take a bit longer to download.

 If you opt to root your Kindle Fire, which is a fancy name for hacking into it in order to broaden its accessibility to apps that are not associated with Amazon .com, chances are any content you purchase or rent from Amazon.com will not play properly. When you attempt to view, listen to, or stream content from Amazon, an error message will be displayed. To learn more about what rooting a Kindle Fire does and how to do it, visit www.tabletorials.com.

Selecting, Downloading, and Watching TV Shows from Amazon.com

From the Kindle Fire's Home screen, tap the Video option from the Navigation bar, and then scroll down toward the bottom of the Video app's screen to see the TV Shows heading. Using your finger, swipe right to left or left to right along the row of graphic thumbnails to view the list of featured TV shows, or tap the View All option that's displayed to the right of the TV Show heading to explore all of your viewing options. Amazon's selection of TV show episodes is constantly expanding.

Just like with the Movies option, when you tap the View All option associated with TV shows, you'll see a selection of thumbnail icons for popular TV shows. Along the top of the screen are additional category headings, including Latest TV Episodes, Editor's Picks, All Genres, For The Kids, Deals, and TV Channels. (Use your finger to scroll left or right along this headings bar.)

If you tap All Genres, for example, eight different genre categories will be displayed, shown in Figure 9-7. Choose one in order to view a selection of TV series episodes that fall within that genre. By tapping the TV Channels option, you'll see a listing of major network and cable TV channels to choose from. Tap a specific channel listing to see what TV shows from that network are available from Amazon.com.

FIGURE 9-7   Choose a genre for a television show you might want to watch. Action & Adventure, Comedy, Drama, Kids & Family, and Reality TV are among your options.

When you tap a specific thumbnail graphic that's associated with a TV series, at the top of the screen the name of that TV series, along with its graphic thumbnail, are displayed. Below the thumbnail graphic are tabs for each season of that TV series that's available from Amazon.com. The current or most recent season will be selected by default.

Below the Season tabs (shown in Figure 9-8) is a listing of individual episodes from the selected season of the TV show, along with any bonus or extra content related to the TV series that's available. Each specific episode listing includes the episode number, its title, its original air date, and a price option that's displayed in orange.

Unlike movies, TV show episodes available from Amazon.com can only be purchased. They are not available as 48-hour rentals. However, if you're an Amazon Prime member, you can stream thousands of TV show episodes on an unlimited basis. The selection of TV show episodes available to purchase from Amazon.com and to stream from Amazon Prime, however, are not identical.

Tap a specific TV show episode's price option to reveal a Description screen for that particular episode. Near the top of the screen will be a Buy icon along with a More Purchase Options icon. Depending on the TV series and episode, it may be available in standard quality ($1.99) and/or HD quality ($2.99). Tap the quality option you

FIGURE 9-8 If several seasons' worth of a TV series is available, tap the Season number to view a list of individual episodes from that season.

desire. The orange Price icon will transform into a green Buy icon. Tap this to confirm your purchase decision and begin downloading or steaming that TV show episode.

When you purchase a TV show episode, it can be downloaded to your Kindle Fire and stored on the device. In addition, it will be added automatically to your Amazon Cloud Drive account. From the cloud, you can use the Video app to stream the TV episodes you own without downloading them and saving them to your tablet. Streaming video content you own saves internal storage space on your tablet, but requires a constant Internet connection.

Watching TV Shows or Movies Acquired from Amazon.com

Once you've purchased a TV show episode or movie (or rented a movie) from Amazon.com, it will be displayed in your Video Library (shown in Figure 9-9), which is also accessible from within the Video app. From the Kindle Fire's Home screen, launch the Video app. Displayed near the top-right corner of the Video app's main screen, to the right of the Search field, is a Library command. Tap it.

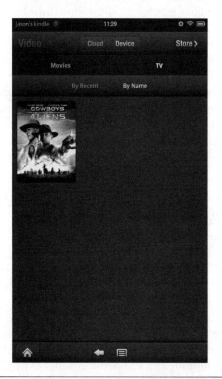

FIGURE 9-9   The Video Library screen displays thumbnails for TV show episodes or movies you own or have rented and that are either stored on your tablet or within your Amazon Cloud Drive account.

The Video Library screen will be displayed. At the top of this screen, tap the Cloud or Device tab to see a listing of content that's stored on your device versus content that's available for streaming or downloading from your Amazon Cloud Drive account.

Just below the Cloud and Drive tabs are separate Movies and TV show tabs, and below each of those are tabs labeled By Recent and By Name. Based on the selection of tabs you tap, thumbnail graphics representing the available and appropriate TV or movie content will be displayed on the tablet's screen.

Tap the thumbnail icon for the TV show or movie you want to watch. The Description screen for that content will be displayed. This time, however, near the top of the Description screen will be a Watch Now and Download icon. If you tap Watch Now and the content is already stored in your Kindle Fire's internal storage, it will begin playing. However, if the file is stored within the Amazon Cloud Drive account, you can either begin streaming it to your tablet by tapping the Watch Now icon, or tap the Download icon to download and store it within your tablet's internal storage before watching it.

Once the video starts playing, on the screen will be a selection of command icons for controlling the video's playback. For example, you'll see a Play icon, as well as a Back icon. When a video is playing, the Play icon transforms into a Pause icon. After a few seconds, the on-screen control icons will disappear, allowing you to view the video content in full-screen mode on your Kindle Fire.

To make the video playback on-screen control icons reappear, tap anywhere on the screen. Any time a TV show or movie is playing, tap Pause to pause the video. You can then exit out of the Video app. When you return to the Video app, you can continue the video from where you left off.

 Once you purchase a TV show or movie from Amazon, it is stored within your Amazon Cloud Drive account and can be viewed on your PC or Mac. There is currently no way to transfer a copyrighted TV show or movie directly from your tablet to your computer or TV, however.

Streaming Video Content from Amazon Prime

When you first purchased and registered your Kindle Fire, Amazon.com offered you a free, 30-day trial of its Amazon Prime service. One of the benefits to this fee-based service is that during your membership period, you have unlimited access to thousands of TV show episodes and movies, which you can stream (via the Internet) and watch on your Kindle Fire's screen, as long as an Internet connection is available.

The selection of TV shows and movies available from Amazon Prime (shown in Figure 9-10) differs from the video content that can be purchased or rented from Amazon.com. To access the selection of current and classic TV show episodes and movies available from Amazon Prime, launch the Video app from the Kindle Fire's Home screen by tapping the Video option that is displayed along the Navigation bar.

Just below the Search field of the Video app's main screen, you'll see a heading for Prime Instant Videos. While a few thumbnail graphics for featured TV shows and movies available from Amazon Prime are displayed just below the Prime Instant

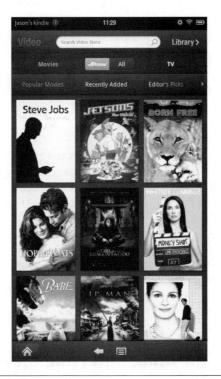

FIGURE 9-10   Amazon Prime allows you to stream an unlimited number of TV show episodes and/or movies to your Kindle Fire or computer screen.

Videos heading, tap the View All option to the right of this heading to browse the entire collection of video content that is available for streaming.

Keep in mind that video content from Amazon Prime is available on an unlimited basis as part of your Amazon Prime paid membership. The content, however, is streamed to your tablet, not downloaded and saved. So, to watch Amazon Prime video content, your Kindle Fire must have access to the Internet as you're watching your selected TV show or movie.

Upon tapping the View All option, near the top of the screen will be command tabs labeled Movies and TV. Tap one of these options to view available TV shows or movies. Next, tap the Prime icon to separate out content that can be accessed for free and streamed using your Amazon Prime membership.

Below the Movies, Prime, All, and TV tabs are category headings, which will vary slightly, based on whether you've tapped the Movies or TV tab. Select any category to browse for content to watch, or use the Search field at the top of the screen to find a TV show or movie based on its title or a keyboard. (Using the Search field, you can also enter an actor or director's name, for example, or any phrase that will help you find the TV show or movie you're looking for.) Tap a TV show or movie's graphic thumbnail to reveal its Description screen, and then tap the Watch Now icon to begin playing that content on your Kindle Fire.

How to... Search TV Shows or Movies by Genre

When viewing the Amazon Prime Movie option, you can browse the collection of movies either using the Search field or by tapping the Popular Movies, Recently Added, Editor's Picks, All Genres, For The Kids, or Holiday heading. If you tap All Genres, a submenu of movie genres, including Action & Adventure, Comedy, Documentary, Drama, Foreign Films, and Sci-Fi & Fantasy is displayed.

Likewise, when viewing the Amazon Prime TV episode option, you can browse the collection of TV show episodes either using the Search field or by tapping the Popular TV Shows, Recently Added, Editor's Picks, All Genres, For The Kids, Holiday, or TV Channels heading. If you tap All Genres, a submenu of TV episode genres, including Action & Adventure, Comedy, Documentary, Drama, and Sci-Fi & Fantasy, is displayed. Tap TV Channels to see a listing of major TV networks and cable channels, including ABC, CBS, NBC, Fox, and PBS, and then view available programming from those broadcasters.

Did You Know? What an Amazon Prime Membership Includes

After the initial 30-day trial of the Amazon Prime service expires, you can opt to pay for an annual membership, which includes unlimited streaming of Amazon Prime video content, as well as instant access to thousands of free Kindle-formatted eBooks and free two-day shipping on anything you purchase from Amazon.com.

The Amazon Prime video streaming service includes an ever-growing library of current and classic TV shows and movies, which you can view on an unlimited basis during your membership period. In other words, there are no per-view or 48-hour rental fees. The drawback to this service is that your tablet must be connected to the Internet to watch streaming video content. Remember, streamed content is sent to your Kindle Fire to be viewed or played, but is not downloaded or stored within the tablet's internal storage.

If you do not sign up and pay for an ongoing Amazon Prime membership, you can still purchase and download (and also stream) TV shows and movies from Amazon.com using the Video app, as well as rent certain movies for a 48-hour period. You also have the option to sign up for and use other video streaming services, such as Netflix or Hulu Plus.

Streaming Video Content from Netflix, Hulu Plus, and Other Services

From the Amazon App Store, you can acquire third-party apps from Netflix, Hulu Plus, and other video streaming services. While the apps associated with these services are free, to stream TV show and video content from them, a monthly membership fee will typically apply.

 A monthly membership to the Netflix video streaming service costs $7.99 per month, which includes unlimited access to Netflix's library of content that's available for streaming. For the same $7.99 per month, you can sign up for the Hulu Plus video streaming service, which works the same way as Netflix, but offers a slightly different library of TV show episodes and movies. Both services offer a free trial period, so you can try them both out and see which one you prefer to use with your Kindle Fire.

If you already have a Netflix or Hulu Plus membership that you utilize with your computer, video game system, Internet-compatible TV or DVR, that same membership can be used with your Kindle Fire at no additional cost. You will, however, need to download the free Netflix or Hulu Plus app. To download the Netflix or Hulu Plus app, from the Kindle Fire's Home screen, tap the Apps option that's displayed along the Navigation bar. When the Apps screen appears, tap the Store icon that's displayed near the upper-right corner of the screen. Your tablet will need access to the Internet to continue.

From the main Amazon App Store screen, tap the Search field that's displayed near the top-center area of the screen. When the virtual keyboard appears, type either **Netflix** or **Hulu Plus**, depending on which app you want to download and install.

Select the Netflix app from Netflix, Inc. (not from another third-party), and from the app's Description screen, tap the Free icon to download and install it (shown in Figure 9-11). When the orange Free icon turns green and says Get App, tap it again to confirm your decision. The free app will be downloaded and automatically installed on your tablet. This process is the same for the Hulu Plus app.

 When downloading the Hulu Plus app, make sure you select the Kindle Fire edition and not the Android or Android Tablet edition.

When the download process is complete, tap the orange Open icon to launch the app. The Netflix or Hulu logo screen will appear, followed by the sign-in screen. To use either the Netflix or Hulu Plus app, you'll need a pre-established account, which you can create and pay for by visiting www.Netflix.com or www.Hulu.com, respectively, from your computer, or using the Amazon Silk web browser.

When prompted, enter your e-mail address and password to log into the Netflix or Hulu Plus app. Once you've signed in, browse the available TV show and movie content, and then tap the graphic thumbnail that represents the content you want

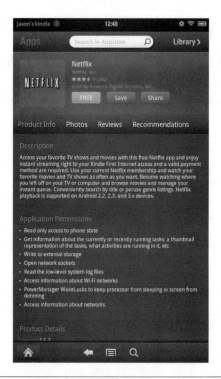

FIGURE 9-11 Download the Netflix or Hulu Plus app to stream TV shows and movies from a source other than Amazon Prime. A monthly membership fee applies.

to watch, shown in Figure 9-12. Within a few seconds, assuming your Kindle Fire is connected to the Internet, your selected content will begin playing in full-screen, landscape mode.

Tap anywhere on the screen to make a series of on-screen command icons appear that allow you to control the video content's playback (shown in Figure 9-13). For example, the Play/Pause icon is displayed near the lower-left corner of the Netflix app's screen. Tap the "^" icon that's constantly displayed at the very bottom of the Netflix screen when a video is playing to make the familiar Home, Back, Menu, and Search icons appear.

Tap the Back icon to return to the main Netflix app's screen in order to seek out additional content to watch, or tap the Home icon to exit out of the Netflix app and return to the tablet's Home screen. As you'll discover, Netflix, Hulu Plus, and Amazon Prime offer tens of thousands of TV show episodes and movies, each of which is rated by fellow members using a one-to-five-star rating system.

 When using the Netflix app, tap the Browse icon that's displayed in the upper-left corner of the app's main screen to see 14 genre and category headings to help you find a TV show or movie to watch. You can also use the Search field that's displayed in the upper-right corner of the Netflix app's main screen to find what you're looking for by entering a title or keyboard.

FIGURE 9-12 For a flat monthly fee, Netflix offers thousands of TV shows and movies you can stream on an unlimited basis using the Netflix app.

FIGURE 9-13 Use the on-screen controls to play, pause, fast-forward, or rewind as you're watching streamed Netflix content.

Also available from the Amazon App Store are separate apps from other content providers that allow you to stream TV shows and/or movie content, in some cases for free. Like Netflix and Hulu Plus, some have a monthly fee associated with them. For example, there's the free TV.com app, which works with the TV.com streaming service that is owned and operated by CBS. Using this app, you can stream free TV shows and video clips from CBS, The CW, Showtime, CNET, CBS News, CBS Sports, and other affiliated networks. A growing number of other TV networks, including E!, G4, and truTV, have also released their own apps for streaming content using the Kindle Fire.

 YouTube, which is accessible using the Amazon Silk web browser and by visiting www.youtube.com, also offers a vast collection of free video content, including entertaining and instructional videos produced and uploaded by everyday people, TV networks, and motion picture studios. Content from YouTube is streamed from the Internet to your Kindle Fire. To get the most out of the YouTube service, be sure to set up a free account.

Downloading or Streaming Audiobooks and Podcasts

You probably already know that your Kindle Fire can serve as a feature-packed digital music player. It can store thousands of songs within its internal storage and/or stream additional music content that you own from your Amazon Cloud Drive account. You'll discover how to use your Kindle Fire as a digital music player in Chapter 12.

In addition to playing music and video content, your tablet can be used to download and listen to audiobooks and podcasts. Audiobooks are typically audio versions of traditional printed books that feature a recording of one or more actors reading the book, word for word, like a storyteller. Many audiobooks include sound effects and background music.

Some audiobooks are unabridged, which means the entire book is read by the actor. A full-length audiobook can run between 8 and 20 hours, depending on the length of the book itself. Abridged versions of some traditional books are also available. These run much shorter and are edited to convey the main story or key points of the book.

Your Kindle Fire comes with the Audible app preinstalled. Audible is an online service that's owned by Amazon.com, which has become the largest audiobook store on the Web. Audible offers audiobooks based on current bestsellers, timeless classics, and other audio content.

 See Chapter 5 for more information on purchasing and listening to audiobooks using the Audible app on your Kindle Fire. Audiobooks from Audible are downloaded to your tablet. Podcasts, however, can be downloaded or streamed.

While audiobooks are considered premium audio content, since this content typically needs to be purchased, your Kindle Fire also has access to thousands of free podcasts. These are audio programs created by everyday people, radio stations, celebrities, TV networks, and other media outlets that are offered for free.

The easiest way to find and listen to podcasts is to download a free podcast app from the Amazon App Store. Use the Search field within the App Store, and enter the search phrase **podcast** to find one of the many free apps available for this purpose. Some of your options include Stitcher, TuneIn Radio, ACast, OnAir, BeyondPod Podcast Community, MyPOD Podcast, and Podcast Player. Any of these should work just fine for your needs. Some of the more popular podcasts have their own proprietary app available.

A podcast might sound like a professional-produced radio show, or it could be recorded and produced by some random guy sitting in his basement who wanted to rant about something and use the Internet as his soapbox. As you begin exploring what podcasts are available, you'll discover thousands upon thousands of hours' worth of free audio programming available at your fingertips.

Depending on the app you use, a podcast can be streamed from the Internet and played on your Kindle Fire (as long as an Internet connection is available), or it can be downloaded and stored on your tablet and listened to anytime, with or without an Internet connection, once it's been downloaded.

Instead of podcasts or audiobooks, with the right third-party app, you can stream music and/or radio stations from the Internet and listen to that audio content on your tablet. Many streaming music services have a monthly fee associated with them. However, they allow you to listen to any song on demand. Internet radio stations, on the other hand, offer free content that is streamed to your tablet, but you can't control what songs you hear or when your hear them.

The Pandora Internet Radio app, shown in Figure 9-14, comes preloaded within your Amazon Cloud Drive account, but is not installed on your Kindle Fire. To download and install this free app, from the Kindle Fire's Home screen, tap the Apps icon. Displayed near the top-center area of the Apps screen is the Cloud tab. Tap it. A listing of apps that you own and that are stored within your Amazon Cloud Drive account is displayed. This includes the Pandora app.

Tap the Pandora app's icon to access its Description screen. At the top of the Description screen is an orange Install icon (shown in Figure 9-15). Tap it to download and install the free Pandora Internet Radio app. Once it's downloaded, tap the Open icon to launch the app for the first time. You will be prompted to either enter your existing Pandora account information or to set up a new account.

Establishing a new account requires you to enter your e-mail address, create a password, and provide your birth year and ZIP code. Once the account is established, you can begin using this app to listen to radio programming, music, talk radio content, or news. While you can select the type of programming you want to hear, just as you can when listening to the radio, you cannot select specific songs to hear on demand.

Pandora app

FIGURE 9-14 The Pandora Internet Radio app allows you to create custom radio stations that broadcast only music or programming you'll enjoy listing to. It's not exactly on-demand programming, but it's free.

After establishing a Pandora account, use your computer's web browser (or Amazon Silk on your tablet) to visit www.Pandora.com in order to customize your listening experience and create personalized Internet radio stations based on your interests and favorite musical artist(s) or band(s).

 As you're listening to audio content using the Pandora app, as long as you do not manually quit the app, you can use other apps on your tablet while listening to Pandora audio content at the same time.

In the Amazon App Store, you'll discover a handful of other apps that allow you to stream other Internet-based radio stations to your Kindle Fire. Some of the apps you might want to check out include TuneIn Radio (free), Live365 (free), All Radio Stations ($1.50), FindFM (free), Nobex Radio ($1.99), iRadio Plus ($3.99), and the apps available from specific terrestrial radio stations.

FIGURE 9-15 You can download the free Pandora Internet Radio app from your Amazon Cloud Drive account or the Amazon App Store.

Tip To find news/talk radio stations that you can stream for free from the Internet and listen to on your Kindle Fire, within the Amazon App Store's Search field, enter the search phrase **News/Talk** or **Radio News**.

Did You Know?

You Can Transfer Your Own Videos to Your Tablet

If you have noncopyrighted home video files that you'd like to store and view on your Kindle Fire, as long as you first convert them to a compatible MP4 or VP8 video format using your computer, you can then transfer them to the Video folder within your Kindle Fire's internal storage using an optional Micro-B USB–to–USB cable and watch them on your tablet. The process for doing this is explained in greater detail in Chapter 13.

10

Use Your Kindle Fire as a Powerful eBook Reader

HOW TO...

- Find, purchase, and download eBooks from Amazon.com's Kindle Store
- Find and download free eBooks from Amazon.com and other sources
- Use the Kindle Fire's Books app to read eBooks

Amazon.com is a digital publishing pioneer when it comes to developing and selling its extremely popular Kindle eBook readers, as well as distributing eBooks through Amazon.com, which is now the world's leading eBook bookseller. As a result, not only can your Kindle Fire access several million eBook titles, it can also serve as a feature-packed and highly customizable eBook reader.

Using the Book app that comes preinstalled on your Kindle Fire, you can access Amazon.com's Kindle Store and discover free and low-cost eBooks, as well as normally priced bestsellers and other eBook titles from the world's leading authors and publishers. While your typical bookstore might offer a selection of thousands of traditionally printed book titles in stock, Amazon.com's Kindle Store offers an ever-growing library containing more than one million eBook selections—all available with a few taps on the tablet's screen.

When it comes to reading eBooks, your Kindle Fire offers a truly customizable reading experience, plus the ability to store your entire library of eBooks right on your tablet, so your favorite books can always be carried with you, and are accessible from virtually anywhere.

If you've grown up reading traditionally printed books, the concept of holding a tablet and reading an eBook may seem odd, at least initially. However, with just a little bit of practice, you'll soon feel comfortable and begin to enjoy reading eBooks on your Kindle Fire's screen.

Tip Because the Kindle Fire offers a full-color touch screen, a wide range of interactive children's books, picture books, photo books, and cookbooks, for example, are available from Amazon.com. These full-color eBooks (an example of which is shown in the next illustration) offer a wonderfully immersive reading experience for people of all ages.

Whether you enjoy reading the latest fiction from bestselling authors like John Grisham, David Baldacci, Lee Child, George R.R. Martin, Stephen King, Stephenie Meyer, or James Patterson; delving into a steamy romance novel; revisiting timeless classics; learning new skills from how-to books; or expanding your knowledge by reading nonfiction, Amazon.com's Kindle Store and your Kindle Fire are the perfect combination to make your reading experience a pleasure. So, when you're cuddled up in bed, sitting on your favorite couch, relaxing at a beach or poolside, riding a train or bus to or from work, or sitting on an airplane during a long flight, you can enjoy reading your favorite books.

Did You Know?

You Can Read eBooks Without an Internet Connection

If you want to use your Kindle Fire as an eBook reader in areas where an Internet connection is not available, be sure to purchase and download eBooks and load them into your tablet while an Internet connection is available. Internet access is required to visit Amazon.com's online eBookstore (the Kindle Store) and to purchase and download books. However, an Internet connection is not needed to actually read eBooks once the digital files are saved on your tablet.

The Cost of eBooks

Just like traditionally printed books, the price of eBooks varies greatly. However, the average price of a current *New York Times* bestseller, as well as most new releases from major publishers, is $9.99. At Amazon.com, you'll also discover tens of thousands of eBooks priced anywhere from $0.99 to $4.99, which have been published by well-known authors and publishers, as well as self-published authors.

Before purchasing almost any eBook from the Kindle Store, you can tap the Preview icon that's displayed on the eBook's Description page in order to download and read a free preview of that book. Or if you're a member of the Amazon Prime service, with some eBooks, Amazon gives you the option to borrow an eBook title for free, once per month. This gives you unlimited access to that eBook to read at your leisure during that one-month period.

Also available from the Kindle Store are thousands of popular classics, which are offered for free. You'll also discover more than 2.5 million free eBooks available from the Internet Archive, a nonprofit organization that offers access to historical collections and out-of-copyright eBooks. While browsing Archive.org using your personal computer, when you discover a free eBook you want to download and read on your Kindle Fire, click the Kindle (Beta) link to download it to your computer. Then, attach the tablet to your computer via a Micro-B USB–to–USB cable, and drag the eBook file to the Documents folder of your tablet's internal storage. You can then open the eBook file by opening the Doc app from the Navigation bar on your Kindle Fire, select the appropriate eBook file, and begin reading it. In this case, the Books app will automatically launch. However, you can't open an eBook acquired from a non-Amazon source directly from the Books app.

Did You Know?   Other Sources for Free eBooks

Three other sources for free eBooks include the Open Library (www.openlibrary .org), which offers more than one million titles; Project Gutenberg (www .gutenberg.org), which offers more than 30,000 titles; and ManyBooks.net (www.manybooks.net), which offers a collection of more than 26,000 titles. When visiting any of these sites, be sure to download the Kindle-formatted edition of the eBook(s) you want to read on your Kindle Fire.

Did You Know?

Choose a Compatible eBook Format

While there has been an effort throughout the publishing industry to create a standard eBook publishing format, called ePub, this has not yet been fully adopted by the various eBook publishers or eBook reader manufacturers. As a result, eBooks come in a variety of different formats.

When you purchase an eBook from Amazon, it's automatically provided in the appropriate Kindle file format. However, if you were to purchase an eBook from Apple's iBookstore, for example, those eBooks are formatted to be read using an Apple iOS device, such as an iPhone, iPad, or iPod touch. Thus, they're offered in a different file format that is not compatible with your Kindle Fire.

The Books app that comes preinstalled on your Kindle Fire is designed to access eBooks published using the Kindle eBook format. However, between the Books and Docs apps, your Kindle Fire can also access TXT, PDF, unprotected MOBI, DOC, and DOCX file formats. Using free third-party apps, such as EzReader, Unlimited Stores – Wattpad, or TradePub, you can acquire and then read eBooks from other sources that are offered in different file formats. As a general rule, if given a choice, download eBooks in the Kindle format to ensure full compatibility with your Kindle Fire without having to use third-party apps.

Note When acquiring eBooks from Amazon's Kindle Store, you'll discover the process for downloading or transferring eBooks to your tablet is much easier, and it can be done wirelessly, using Amazon's Whispernet service or the Amazon Cloud Drive file sharing system. You can also shop for and acquire eBooks directly from your tablet.

Shopping for Books from the Kindle Store Using Your Computer

Amazon.com has made it easy to shop its online store in order to purchase eBooks (or acquire free eBooks) for your Kindle Fire. You can visit www.Amazon.com from your computer, click the Kindle menu option that's displayed on the left side of the screen (under the Shop All Departments heading), and then choose Kindle Books from the submenu, shown in Figure 10-1.

FIGURE 10-1 Shop for eBooks for your Kindle Fire using your computer that's connected to the Internet (shown here), or shop for eBooks directly from your tablet.

You'll find yourself within the Kindle Store, which categorizes eBooks into sections, just like a traditional bookstore. In addition to searching for eBooks by browsing various sections or categories, you can use the on-screen Search field to quickly find what you're looking for when shopping for eBooks from the web browser of your PC or Mac to visit Amazon.com.

Once you purchase eBooks online via your computer, they are stored within your Amazon Cloud Drive account. From anywhere that your Kindle Fire can connect to the Internet, you can then launch the Books app, tap the Cloud tab that's displayed near the top-center area of the Library screen, and access your eBook purchases. Doing this will display eBook titles stored within your online-based Amazon Cloud Drive account. Tap the eBook title you want to download and read on your tablet in order to transfer it to your Kindle Fire and begin reading it.

How to... **Transfer eBooks Purchased on a Computer to Your Kindle Fire**

When you purchase an eBook from Amazon's Kindle Store via your computer, just below the Buy Now With 1-Click icon is a Deliver To pull-down menu (shown in the next illustration). Select your Kindle Fire from this menu to have the eBook automatically sent to your tablet wirelessly, via Amazon Whispernet (as long as it has access to the Internet). Within a minute or two, the downloaded eBook title will be displayed when you tap the Device tab that's displayed near the top-center area of the Book app's Library screen.

Shopping for eBooks from the Kindle Store Using Your Kindle Fire

eBooks can also be purchased directly from your tablet, which is often the quickest and easiest method when it comes to expanding your personal eBook library. To begin browsing Amazon Kindle Store's selection of more than one million eBooks that are available for purchase or for free, from the Kindle Fire's Home screen, tap the Books option that's displayed on the Navigation bar (shown in Figure 10-2). Doing this will launch the Books app.

Books option ——

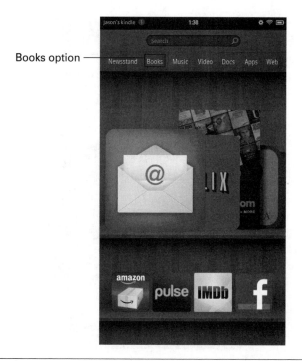

FIGURE 10-2 Launch the Books app by tapping the Books option. It is displayed along the Navigation bar.

When the Books app launches, you'll see a virtual bookshelf, referred to as the Library screen. It displays all of the eBook titles currently stored on your tablet or that are available to you from your Amazon Cloud Drive account, based on which option is selected at the top of the screen shown in Figure 10-3.

Displayed near the top-center area of the Library screen are two tabs, labeled Cloud and Device. The one that's displayed in orange is the selected option. Tapping the Cloud tab will display thumbnail book covers for all of the eBooks currently available from your Amazon Cloud Drive account; tapping the Device tab will display thumbnail book covers for all of the eBooks currently stored on your Kindle Fire.

 Your Kindle Fire's 8GB of internal storage space can be used to store upwards of 6,000 eBooks at any given time, assuming no other data or content (such as music, TV show episodes, and movies) is stored on the device. Thus, you truly can carry around an entire personal library and have it available to you virtually anywhere.

To access the Kindle Store and begin browsing Amazon's selection of eBooks, tap the Store option that's displayed in the upper-right corner of the Book app's Library screen. Remember, your Kindle Fire will need access to the Internet, since the Kindle Store is an online-based service.

When the Kindle Store launches on your tablet (shown in Figure 10-4), near the top of the screen will be a heading labeled Recommended For You. Below

FIGURE 10-3 The Book app's Library screen looks like a virtual bookshelf.

FIGURE 10-4 The main screen of the Kindle Store

this heading, you'll see book cover thumbnails for eBook titles that Amazon.com recommends for you based on your past purchases and searches. Use your finger to scroll from left to right, or right to left, in order to view these offerings. To view all of Amazon's recommendations, tap the See All option that's displayed to the right of the Recommended For You heading.

Below the Recommended For You heading, you can see additional headings by scrolling downward on the main Kindle Store screen. They're labeled Top 100 Paid, Children's Picture Books, Best Fiction Of 2011 (2012), New & Noteworthy, Kindle Singles, and Top 100 Free. Just below each heading will be a few book cover thumbnails, and to the right of the heading will be a See All option. Tap the See All option to view a more comprehensive selection of eBooks that fit into the category heading you select.

To the right of the headings, you'll see additional category options, such as Browse Books, Browse Kindle Singles, Visit The Kindle Newsstand, Editor's Picks, 100 Kindle Books For $3.99 Or Less, Kindle Owners' Lending Library, NY Times (*New York Times*) Best Sellers, Children's Picture Books, and Comic Books. Tap any of these options to view eBooks that fit into the selected category. Figure 10-5 shows the screen that's displayed when you tap NY Times Best Sellers, for example.

When you tap Browse Books, for example, a pop-up window displaying more than two dozen categories will be displayed, including Fiction, Nonfiction, Arts &

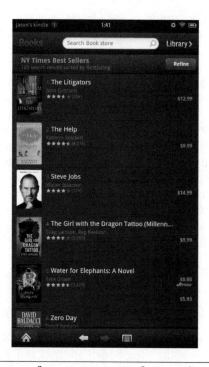

FIGURE 10-5 View a listing of current *New York Times* bestsellers that are available in Kindle eBook format.

How to... # Quickly Find the eBook(s) You're Looking For

If you already know what book you're looking for, you're looking for works by a particular author, or you want to find eBooks that cover a specific subject matter, the fastest way to find what you're looking for is to use the Search Book Store field that's displayed near the top-center area of the Kindle Store screen. Upon tapping this Search field, the virtual keyboard will be displayed. Enter the title of a book, author's name, or any keyword or search phrase that will help you find what you're looking for.

When you're done entering information into the Search field, tap the orange Go icon that's displayed in the bottom row of keys on the virtual keyboard. Suggestions for matching book titles will be displayed below the Search field. Tap on any of the search results to make a selection.

Entertainment, Computers & Internet, Humor, Mystery & Thrillers, Parenting & Families, Reference, Romance, and Travel. Tap any heading to see eBooks that fall into that category. These categories, and the eBook titles found within them, are similar to how printed books in a traditional bookstore are organized.

The process for acquiring free eBooks from the Kindle Store is virtually identical to purchasing eBooks; however, you will not be charged for your acquisitions.

Also as you're browsing the Kindle Store via your Kindle Fire, displayed at the bottom of the Book app's screens will be four familiar command icons: the Home, Back, Forward, and Menu icons. Tap the Home icon to exit out of the Books app (and the Kindle Store) and return to the Kindle Fire's Home screen. Tap the Back or Forward icon to return to a previous Kindle Store screen you were viewing.

Tap the Menu icon to reveal four additional command icons, labeled Storefront, Books, Kindle Singles, and Kindle Account. Regardless of where you are within the Kindle Store, tap the Storefront icon to return to the main Kindle Store screen. Tapping the Books icon reveals a vertical listing of bestselling eBooks, while the Kindle Singles command icon displays a selection of bestselling Kindle Single eBooks. A Kindle Single is a short eBook priced between $0.99 and $2.99.

The command icons that are displayed when you tap the Menu icon as you're browsing the Kindle Store are different from the command icons that are displayed when you tap the Menu icon while actually reading an eBook.

To manage your Amazon.com account, tap the Kindle Account icon. You'll be prompted to sign in using your e-mail address and Amazon.com password. You can then change the credit card information that's associated with your account, or perform a handful of other account-related tasks directly from your Kindle

Fire's screen. When you tap Kindle Account, the Silk web browser will launch and automatically direct you to the appropriate webpage of the Amazon.com website.

Regardless of which eBook browsing option or category you choose, what you'll see displayed on the screen is a collection of book cover thumbnails, listed by popularity, along with the eBook's title, author, average rating, and price. You can adjust how the eBook titles are sorted after choosing a category or genre by tapping the Refine icon that's displayed in the upper-right corner of the screen, shown in Figure 10-6.

 To view a detailed Description page for a specific eBook, tap its book cover thumbnail, title, or price.

Learn More About an eBook from Its Description Page

When you tap any eBook listing, the Kindle Store will display a detailed Description page for that title (shown in Figure 10-7). At the top of the Description page, you'll see the book's cover graphic. Tap the book cover thumbnail to see a larger version of it displayed on the tablet's screen.

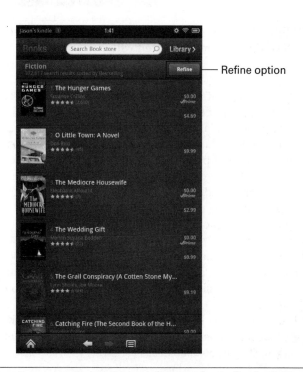

Refine option

FIGURE 10-6   After selecting a category or genre, listings for individual eBook titles will be displayed. Tap the Refine icon to reorganize the listing you're looking at.

FIGURE 10-7 Every eBook available from the Kindle Store has a detailed Description screen associated with it.

To the right of the book's cover graphic, the book's title, author, and average rating (between one and five stars) will be displayed. You'll also see the digital list price and Kindle price displayed, along with a You Save listing. The digital list price is the price the book's publisher (or self-published author) has set for the book. The Kindle price is the discounted price that Amazon.com's Kindle Store actually charges for the book. Next to the You Save listing, you'll see the price difference between the digital list price and the Kindle price, which is what you'll actually pay if you opt to purchase and download the eBook.

Displayed below the price of the eBook are two or three command buttons, labeled Buy For [Price], Try A Sample, and/or Borrow For Free. Tap the orange Buy For [Price] icon to purchase and download the book. Unless the eBook is free, the credit or debit card you have associated with your Amazon.com account will automatically be charged for the purchase, and the book will begin downloading.

 Due to security concerns, future versions of the Kindle Fire operating system or the Books app may require you to manually enter your Amazon.com password prior to making eBook purchases.

If you change your mind about purchasing a book while it's downloading, tap the Cancel Order option (displayed below the Downloading ... progress icon) to reverse the purchase and stop the download process. You will not be charged for the unwanted purchase. If the eBook has already downloaded to your tablet but the purchase was made by accident, contact Amazon's Technical Support Department to arrange for a refund.

Almost every eBook offered by the Kindle Store has a Try A Sample icon associated with it. Tap this icon to download a free sample of the eBook that you can read at your leisure before actually purchasing it. The publisher decides how long the sample you receive is, however, you'll typically be given access to the book's table of contents, along with at least one full chapter.

If you view the Description page for the book *How to Do Everything: Digital Photography* (McGraw-Hill, 2011), for example, when you tap the Try A Sample icon, in addition to the front matter for the book, the free sample includes the table of contents, introduction, and first chapter of the book. You can find this eBook listing using the Search field by typing in the book's title, the author's name (Jason R. Rich), or the subject matter, which is digital photography.

When an eBook's Description page displays a Borrow For Free icon (shown in Figure 10-8), you'll be able to tap it and "borrow" the eBook for one full month if

FIGURE 10-8 If you're an Amazon Prime member, you can borrow one eBook per month for free and read it at your leisure. Thousands of eBooks have a **Borrow** option associated with them.

you're a member of the Amazon Prime service and you don't have any other eBooks currently on loan. Your Amazon Prime membership includes one free eBook that you can borrow per month. At the end of the one-month lending period, the book will be deleted from your tablet automatically, unless you choose to purchase it.

Displayed below the Buy For [Price], Try A Sample, and Borrow For Free icons, you'll see a detailed, text-based description of the book, along with the length of the book's print edition and the eBook's publication date. As you're reading the book's description, you may need to tap the blue Read More option to view the complete description, depending on its length.

As you scroll downward on an eBook's Description screen, you'll see a heading that's labeled Customers Who Bought This Item Also Bought. Below this heading is a handful of book cover thumbnails for related books you might also be interested in.

Below the recommended books, the customer reviews for the eBook you're interested in will be displayed, shown in Figure 10-9. Here, you'll see the average rating (between one and five stars), as well as a breakdown of how many one-, two-, three-, four-, and five-star ratings a book has received. Below this ratings chart, text-based reviews from other Amazon.com customers are displayed.

FIGURE 10-9   Ratings and reviews for every eBook are displayed as part of its Description page within the Kindle Store.

Finally, near the bottom of the eBook's Description page are the eBook's product details. This includes the eBook's sales rank within the Kindle Store, language, print length, release date, publisher, sold by (distributor), file size, and ASIN number. The ASIN is a unique number given to every book that's published, similar to a product bar code, that makes it easier to identify.

After reading the contents of an eBook's Description screen, if you decide to purchase and download the eBook, tap the orange Price icon. Within 60 seconds or so (depending on the eBook's file size), the eBook will be downloaded to your Kindle Fire and appear within the Book app's Library screen. From the Library screen, tap the book's cover thumbnail to begin reading it.

 When you download a new eBook from the Kindle Store and then see it displayed on the Library screen for the first time, until you open that eBook and begin reading it, the book cover thumbnail will display a yellow banner that says "New." If you tapped the Try A Sample icon to download a sample of an eBook, on the Library screen, that eBook's cover thumbnail will display a silver banner that says "Sample." Books that are borrowed are displayed on the Library screen as normal eBooks, but will automatically disappear after one month.

The information provided within an eBook's Description page can be very helpful in determining if a book will be of interest to you, especially if the book was written by a self-published or unknown author, or if you're not sure the eBook covers the subject matter you're interested in. Keep in mind that an eBook's text-based description is supplied by the book's publisher or self-published author. It is usually written in a way that's designed to sell books.

However, the star-based ratings and full reviews for that book are provided by Kindle eBook readers, like yourself, who have purchased and read the book, and who have chosen to share their opinions on it. Often, reading these reviews, or at least taking into account the book's average rating (if that average rating is based on dozens, hundreds, or thousands of individual ratings), will help you determine if a particular book is worth downloading and reading.

 If given the opportunity, consider downloading the free sample of an eBook and reading that sample content for yourself before making the purchase decision. This is the best way to determine if a book's content will be of interest to you.

As you'll discover, eBook editions of popular books from bestselling authors and well-known publishers are typically released at the same time as their traditionally printed counterparts. So, if you see a book that you want to read in the New Releases section of your favorite bookstore, chances are it's already available as an eBook from the Amazon Kindle Store. Amazon.com has worked out eBook distribution arrangements with virtually all of the major book publishing houses around the world, as well as with thousands of smaller publishers and individual self-published authors.

The Kindle Store Also Sells eBooks Written by Self-Published Authors

The Kindle Store sells thousands of eBooks by self-published authors that may not be available in printed book form. Any up-and-coming or aspiring writer can publish an eBook relatively easily and inexpensively and have it distributed via the Kindle Store. Thus, as you browse the Kindle Store, you may discover some hidden literary gems from obscure or unknown authors, or you may discover eBooks written and published by aspiring writers still developing their writing skills. This is where reading an eBook's reviews and paying attention to their average star-based ratings can come in handy.

If you've written a book that you want to self-publish and make available for sale as an eBook from the Kindle Store, visit Amazon's Kindle Direct Publishing website (https://kdp.amazon.com/mn/signin) for details on how to do this. Bookbaby (www.bookbaby.com) is a reputable company that makes self-publishing an eBook a straightforward process once you've written the manuscript for the book using Microsoft Word, for example. eBooks that are self-published using this service are made available to customers via the Kindle Store and other online booksellers.

Reading eBooks Using the Books App

Once you've acquired one or more eBooks to read on your Kindle Fire, those eBook titles will be displayed on the Library screen within the Books app. To access and begin reading any of these eBooks, from the Kindle Fire's Home screen, tap the Books icon that's displayed along the Navigation bar. The Book's Library screen will be displayed, shown in Figure 10-10.

Next, tap the Device tab that's displayed near the top-center area of the Library screen to view the book cover thumbnail graphics for the eBooks that are currently stored on your tablet. You can also tap the By Author, By Recent, or By Title tabs—displayed below the Cloud and Device tabs—to reorganize the eBooks listed on the Library screen.

To begin reading an eBook that's stored on your tablet, tap its book cover thumbnail. As you're about to discover, the eBook reading experience on your Kindle Fire is highly customizable. Your experience will begin with the book's cover or title page being displayed on your tablet's screen. Tap anywhere on the screen to make a series of command icons appear along the bottom of the screen, shown in Figure 10-11. In addition to the familiar Home, Back, Menu, and Search icons, you'll see an "Aa" command icon displayed. This is the command icon used to customize your eBook reading experience.

Cloud option
By Author option
Device option
By Title option
By Recent option

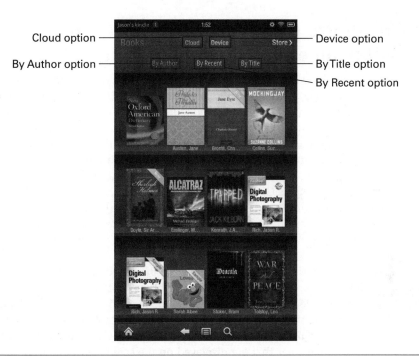

FIGURE 10-10   The eBooks on the Library screen are sorted by author, as opposed to by title or by recently purchased.

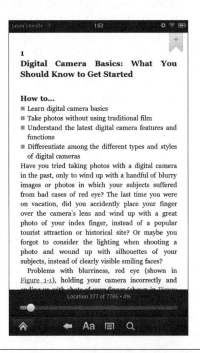

FIGURE 10-11   Format your eBooks so the text is visually appealing to you.

Customize the Appearance of the Text Within an eBook You're Reading

When an eBook opens on your tablet's display, the text is displayed using a default font, font size, typestyle, margin setting, and color mode that the publisher selected for you. However, by tapping the Aa command icon, you can customize any of these settings.

Under the Font Style option, choose the font size, line spacing, margins, and color mode that's used to display the text that comprises your eBook. Hundreds of personalized combinations are possible. To further customize the appearance of the eBook's text, tap the Typeface command tab, and choose from at least eight different fonts, such as Georgia, Caecilia, Trebuchet, Verdana, Arial, Times New Roman, Courier, and Lucida. These fonts are particularly easy on the eyes for reading purposes. As you customize the font style and typeface settings, the eBook you're reading will reformat itself almost instantly to reflect your changes.

 By tapping the gear-shaped icon that's displayed near the upper-right corner of the screen and then choosing the Brightness option, you can manually adjust the brightness level of the screen. When you're reading in a dark or dimly lit room, making the screen dimmer may be more comfortable for your eyes. However, you can also adjust the color mode from the Font Style menu to change the font and background color that are displayed on the screen as you're reading.

To exit out of the Font Style or Typeface command menu, tap the Back icon that's displayed near the bottom of the screen, and begin reading your eBook. The layout of the eBook will often be similar to the printed page of a traditional book (shown in Figure 10-12). Using your finger, swipe from right to left to advance to the next page of the book, or swipe your finger from left to right to go back one page at a time.

To demonstrate some of the ways you can customize the appearance of the text as you're reading an eBook, Figure 10-13 shows the same page of the eBook as Figure 10-12, but with different formatting options selected.

Whenever you want to take a break from reading, or simply mark a page for later reference, you can add a virtual bookmark to that page by tapping anywhere on the screen to make the command icons appear and then by tapping the bookmark icon that's displayed near the upper-right corner of the eBook's page, shown in Figure 10-14. The bookmark icon will transform from opaque to light blue, indicating that a bookmark has been saved.

Navigate Your Way Around Any eBook

In addition to swiping your finger to turn the page, one at a time, forward or backward, when the on-screen icons are displayed, place your finger on the dot that's associated with the slider at the bottom of the screen, and drag it left or right to quickly jump forward or backward within the book. Just above the slider, you'll see your location within the book displayed. The page number you're on, along with the total number of digital pages in the eBook, are displayed, as is a percentage that indicates how far along in the book you've read.

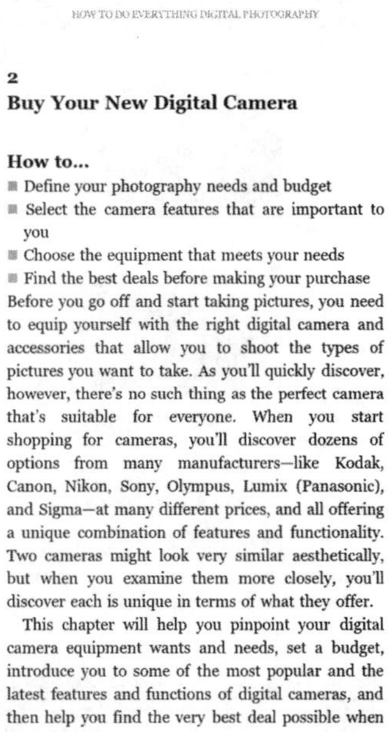

HOW TO DO EVERYTHING DIGITAL PHOTOGRAPHY

2
Buy Your New Digital Camera

How to...
■ Define your photography needs and budget
■ Select the camera features that are important to you
■ Choose the equipment that meets your needs
■ Find the best deals before making your purchase

Before you go off and start taking pictures, you need to equip yourself with the right digital camera and accessories that allow you to shoot the types of pictures you want to take. As you'll quickly discover, however, there's no such thing as the perfect camera that's suitable for everyone. When you start shopping for cameras, you'll discover dozens of options from many manufacturers—like Kodak, Canon, Nikon, Sony, Olympus, Lumix (Panasonic), and Sigma—at many different prices, and all offering a unique combination of features and functionality. Two cameras might look very similar aesthetically, but when you examine them more closely, you'll discover each is unique in terms of what they offer.

This chapter will help you pinpoint your digital camera equipment wants and needs, set a budget, introduce you to some of the most popular and the latest features and functions of digital cameras, and then help you find the very best deal possible when

FIGURE 10-12   The layout of an eBook is similar to its printed counterpart; however, you can choose the font, font size, and color that the text is displayed in.

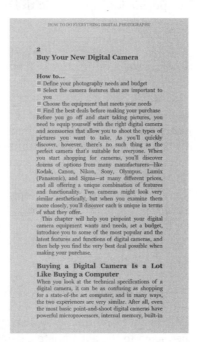

FIGURE 10-13   You can dramatically alter the appearance of text within an eBook so it's more visually appealing to you and easier on your eyes.

Bookmark icon

FIGURE 4-10 A moving subject shot using a camera's Continuous Shooting or Burst mode

FIGURE 10-14 Adding a virtual bookmark is like bending the corner of a printed book's page to mark a specific location within the text.

Another way to quickly move around within an eBook is to access the table of contents, which is almost always interactive. So, when you tap a chapter number or chapter title, for example, within the table of contents, you'll be sent directly to the appropriate page of the eBook.

To quickly access the eBook's cover or table of contents, to return to the beginning of the eBook, or to jump to a specific page number within the eBook you're reading, tap the Menu icon that's displayed near the bottom-center area of the screen and choose the appropriate menu option, shown in Figure 10-15.

When you tap the Menu icon, there's also a Sync To Furthest Page and My Notes & Marks option. The Kindle Fire automatically keeps track of the pages you've read in an eBook. At any time, to return to the last page you've read, tap the Sync To Furthest Page menu option. Or if you've manually placed virtual bookmarks on specific pages, tap the My Notes & Marks option to see a list of those bookmarks. Tap one of the bookmark listings to return to that page.

Tip

Another way to move around within an eBook is to use the Search icon. Tap it, and then use the virtual keyboard to enter any word or phrase that may appear within the book. If matches are found, they'll be displayed in a list of search results, and you can then jump to the appropriate page within the eBook by tapping the desired search result listing.

FIGURE 10-15   Some of the command options displayed when you tap the Menu icon as you're reading allow you to quickly navigate your way within the text.

As you're reading, if the text within an eBook appears as a hyperlink, when you tap that hyperlink (which is underlined and displayed in blue, if you have the default settings selected), the Amazon Silk web browser will launch and display the appropriate website. If an e-mail address is displayed, the Email app will launch and the Compose Message screen will be displayed with the appropriate e-mail address already filled in within the To field.

Discover the Definition of Words and More as You're Reading

In addition to customizing how the text within an eBook appears on your Kindle Fire's screen, as you're reading, if you place your finger on a single word and hold it there for a second or two, a pop-up window will appear that displays the definition of that word. Within the Word Definition window will be three additional command tabs, labeled Note, Highlight, and More.

Tap the Note command tab to annotate the book and create a custom note that will be stored in conjunction with that word or page (shown in Figure 10-16). This is equivalent to writing a note to yourself within the margin of a traditionally printed book. However, when you annotate an eBook, the note is digital and it can be edited or deleted at any time. Type your note and then tap the Save icon that's displayed next to the Note field.

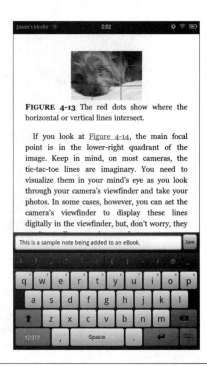

FIGURE 10-16   As you're reading, you can type notes to yourself and refer to them later.

To review your notes later, tap anywhere on the screen to make the command icons appear. Then, tap the Menu icon, and select the My Notes & Marks option. Or as you're re-reading that text, tap the highlighted word that has a blue note icon to the right of it. Your note will be displayed in a window, along with Edit, Delete, and Close command icons that relate to the note.

By tapping the Highlight command tab that appears within the Word Definition window, you can highlight that text in yellow so you can quickly find it again later. If you tap the More icon, you can search for recurrences of that work within the eBook you're reading, or perform a web search related to that word using Wikipedia or Google.

When photos or graphic images appear within an eBook, hold your finger on the image for a second or two. A Note, Highlight, and Zoom command tab will be displayed above the image. Tap the Zoom command tab to view that image or graphic in full-screen mode.

To exit out of the Books app at any time, tap the Home icon that appears near the bottom-left corner of the screen. To make this icon appear as you're reading an eBook, first tap anywhere on the screen. Once you've returned to the Kindle Fire's Home screen, within the Carousel, the book cover thumbnail image for the eBook you

FIGURE 10-17   Book cover thumbnails for the last eBooks you've read are displayed within the Carousel.

were reading will be displayed. In the upper-right corner of that thumbnail will be an orange banner that displays how far along in the book you are, shown as a percentage.

To relaunch the Books app and immediately pick up reading where you left off, simply tap the eBook's cover thumbnail that's displayed on the Home screen's Carousel (shown in Figure 10-17).

After you've experienced reading an eBook on your Kindle Fire, chances are you'll probably be pleasantly surprised how similar the experience is to reading a traditionally printed book. However, the added features when reading an eBook, such as the ability to use hyperlinks, look up the definition of a word, or annotate the text, will become welcome features once you get the hang of using them.

eBooks aren't the only type of published content you can experience reading on your Kindle Fire. Using the Newsstand app, you can acquire, download, and read newspapers and magazines as well. To do this, you'll use the Newsstands app as opposed to the Book app. How to acquire and read the digital editions of newspapers and magazines using the Newsstand app is the focus of Chapter 11.

 Once an eBook is saved in the internal storage area of your tablet, an Internet connection is no longer needed to actually read the eBook. However, some of the features available when reading an eBook, such as the ability to perform a Google or Wikipedia search, will be disabled if no Internet connection is available.

Did You Know?

eBooks Are Available from Additional Sources

Aside from the Amazon eBookstore, there are dozens of smaller and independent eBookstores on the Web, some of which offer Kindle-compatible eBooks (when you use a third-party app). For example, using the free Aldiko app, you can shop for eBooks from the BooksOnBoard.com eBookseller. To learn more about how to use the Aldiko app instead of the Books app that comes preinstalled on your Kindle Fire, watch the free online-based Aldiko video tutorial at www.youtube.com/watch?v=MD5X78Dxjg0.

Fictionwise (www.fictionwise.com) is another online bookseller that offers Kindle-compatible eBooks. To learn how to find and transfer Kindle-compatible eBooks to your Kindle Fire, visit www.fictionwise.com/help/kindleFaq.htm.

To find other sources for free and paid eBooks that can be acquired for or from your Kindle Fire, access any search engine (such as Google, Yahoo!, or Bing), and enter the search phrase **Kindle-compatible eBooks**.

Unless you're using a specific third-party eBook reader app, in most cases, you will need to transfer the eBook(s) you acquire from a non-Amazon source to your tablet's Documents folder, and then open it using the Docs app. When you do this, the eBook's cover graphic thumbnail may not appear on the Library screen or on the Carousel of the Home screen in conjunction with the eBook's title.

11

Read Your Favorite Newspapers and Magazines Using Newsstand

HOW TO...

- Use the Newsstand app to find, purchase, download, and read your favorite newspapers and magazines
- Use publication-specific apps to read certain magazines and newspapers
- Manage your digital subscriptions

Due to the increasingly busy lifestyles of most people and the fast-growing popularity of eBook readers with full-color screens, paid subscribers to traditionally printed newspapers and magazines are dwindling quickly. As a result, more and more of these publications are launching digital editions, making them available to be purchased, downloaded, and read on a tablet.

Most publications allow you to purchase one issue at a time, like you would at a traditional newsstand. However, to save money, and also to ensure that the latest issues of your favorite publications are downloaded to your tablet automatically as soon as they're published (via Amazon's Whispernet), a paid subscription is also available.

Every newspaper and magazine publisher has taken a different approach to adapting their publication to be read on a tablet. As a result, the digital editions of some publications look virtually identical to the layout and design of their printed counterparts and offer the same content. In some cases, however, the digital editions of publications are enhanced with multimedia content or interactive elements, which allow you, as the reader, to delve deeper into the articles and advertising featured in that publication.

For example, when you tap the individual photographs included within an article, an entire collection of images, or even related video clips and multimedia content, may become viewable on your tablet's screen. Or, in some cases, the content becomes truly interactive or highly personalized.

When you're reading a newspaper, the weather forecast, sports coverage, television listings, and/or movie listings can be customized to your exact location, and the horoscope, for example, will be based on your birthday.

The 8GB of internal storage built into your Kindle Fire is capable of storing thousands of newspaper and magazine issues, so if you subscribe to the digital editions of your favorite publications, they can be downloaded, stored, and read on your tablet at your leisure. The individual publishers, however, often limit the number of back issues you can store on your tablet simultaneously.

Also depending on the publication, you may be able to perform keyword searches in order to seek out only articles that are of interest, access past issues of the publication, save specific articles in your tablet's internal storage for later review, quickly access web-based content pertaining to articles by tapping hyperlinks that are embedded in what you're reading, or share articles with others via e-mail.

As you're about to discover, many newspaper and magazine publishers have gone to great lengths, not just to offer entertaining, informative, and well-written content, but also to showcase that content on your tablet in a visually appealing, easy-to-navigate, and immersive way. This allows you to experience some of your favorite newspapers and magazines in an entirely new way, and have them available to you whenever and wherever you want to read them.

Just as with eBooks, an Internet connection is required to find, purchase, and download digital editions of newspapers and magazines. However, once the content is stored on your tablet, in most cases, an Internet connection is no longer required, unless you want to access the interactive elements of a digital publication.

The per-issue and subscription rates for the digital editions of newspapers and magazines vary greatly, and new publications are launching digital editions that are compatible with the Kindle Fire every week. Plus, a growing number of digital-only publications are launching. A sampling of popular newspapers and magazines is listed in the next section of this chapter.

One challenge many newspaper and magazine publishers are facing is the ability to make their publication's content fully compatible with all of the popular tablets on the market, since the screen sizes and capabilities of each tablet vary greatly. As a result, some digital publications will look perfect on the seven-inch screen of your Kindle Fire, while others will require you to use your finger in order to navigate your way around more often on each page, and to zoom in on text or images more frequently in order to view content more clearly.

To find, purchase, download, and read, as well as subscribe to your favorite digital newspapers and magazines, you'll use the Newsstand app that comes preinstalled on your tablet. In some cases, the Newsstand app will instruct you to download and install a proprietary, publication-specific app that will allow you to read a newspaper or magazine's content on your Kindle Fire. Otherwise, the Newsstand app will be used to acquire and read issues of digital publications.

Discovering Some of the Digital Publications Currently Available

In addition to major daily newspapers and popular consumer-oriented magazines being offered digitally so that they can be read on a tablet, such as the Kindle Fire, many industry-oriented publications, as well as publications offered by special-interest groups and associations, are now being offered in a digital format.

Fifty Popular Magazines Available in Digital Form

The following is a sampling of the digital publications currently available via the Newsstand app to be purchased, downloaded, and read on your Kindle Fire. When applicable, the per-month subscription fee for the publication is listed. Individual issue rates are higher.

Free Trial Subscriptions Are Available for Many Publications

In some cases, the publisher of the digital edition of a newspaper or magazine offers a free trial subscription that allows you to sample one or more issues of the publication on your tablet before you pay for individual issues or a subscription.

Take advantage of these offers so you can experience what it's like reading a variety of different publications on your Kindle Fire. When you launch the Newsstand app (by tapping the Newsstand icon from the Navigation bar on the Home screen), displayed near the top of the main Newsstand screen, you'll see a heading that says Exclusive 90-Day Free Trial. Tap the See All option that's associated with this heading. At any given time, at least 20 magazines offer free trial subscriptions (shown to the right).

If your favorite publication does not offer a free trial, begin by purchasing just one issue to make sure that the digital format of the publication is to your liking before investing in an annual or recurring subscription.

When no price is listed, this means the publication has its own proprietary app for downloading and acquiring content. Paid subscribers to the print edition of the publication may be able to receive the digital edition (via the Kindle Fire) for free. Digital subscription and individual issue prices vary and are listed within the app itself. Content acquisitions (subscriptions and single-issue purchases) are done using in-app purchases. How you manage a subscription using a publication-specific app will also vary.

General and Special Interest Publications

- Billboard ($9.99 per month)
- Bon Appétit ($1.99 per month)
- Conde Nast Traveler*
- Consumer Reports ($2.00 per month)
- Entertainment Weekly*
- Family Circle ($1.50 per month)
- Food Network Magazine ($1.99 per month)
- MacLife ($0.99 per month)
- National Geographic ($1.99 per month)
- National Geographic Traveler ($1.33 per month)
- Newsweek ($2.99 per month)
- Parents Magazine*
- PC Magazine ($1.49 per month)
- People Magazine*
- Popular Photography ($1.99 per month)
- Popular Science ($1.99 per month)
- Prevention ($1.25 per month)
- Road & Track ($1.99 per month)
- Robb Reports ($4.25 per month)
- Rolling Stone ($2.99 per month)
- Star ($4.46 per month)
- The Atlantic ($1.99 per month)
- The Hollywood Reporter ($7.99 per month)
- Time Magazine*
- TV Guide ($0.99 per month)
- U.S. News Weekly ($1.99 per month)
- US Weekly ($5.99 per month)
- Wired Magazine*

Women's Magazines

- Better Homes and Gardens*
- Brides ($1.99 per month)
- Cosmopolitan ($1.99 per month)
- Glamour*
- Martha Stewart Living ($1.65 per month)
- O, The Oprah Magazine ($1.99 per month)
- Vanity Fair*
- Women's Health ($1.16 per month)

Sports Publications

- ESPN The Magazine ($2.99 per month)
- Golf Digest*
- Ski ($0.99 month)
- Sports Illustrated*

Men's Magazines

- Details ($1.99 per month)
- GQ*

- Maxim ($1.25 per month)
- Men's Health ($2.07 per month)

Financial Publications

- Barron's ($10.99 per month)
- Fast Company ($2.49 per month)
- Forbes ($2.49 per month)

- Fortune*
- Inc. ($2.49 per month)
- The Economist ($9.99 per month)

 When you subscribe to a publication, you will be billed either each month for the current issues or just once for the annual subscription price. However, at the end of the subscription period, it will automatically renew, and the new charges will be billed to the credit card that you have linked to your Amazon.com account, unless you manually cancel the subscription. You'll discover how to cancel a subscription shortly.

Major Daily Newspapers Available for Your Kindle Fire

The advantage to subscribing to a digital newspaper is that each daily or weekly edition will be downloaded automatically to your tablet as soon as it becomes available (via Amazon's Whispernet), so it will be waiting for you and ready to read when you take your first sip of morning coffee.

 In addition to these and other U.S.-based newspapers, a wide range of newspapers from other countries are available via the Newsstand app. A growing number of small-town newspapers, as well as regional newspapers and weeklies, are also available as digital publications that are accessible using your Kindle Fire.

The following is just a sampling of 20 major daily newspapers that you can subscribe to and read on your tablet:

- Chicago Tribune ($9.99 per month)
- Detroit Free Press ($6.99 per month)
- Financial Times ($14.99 per month)
- Los Angeles Times ($9.99 per month)
- New York Daily News ($0.99 per month)
- Newsstand ($9.00 per month)
- Orlando Sentinel ($5.99 per month)

- San Francisco Chronicle ($5.99 per month)
- The Arizona Republic ($9.99 per month)
- The Boston Globe ($14.99 per month)
- The Denver Post ($5.99 per month)
- The Jewish Advocate ($1.99 per month)

- The Miami Herald ($9.99 per month)
- The New York Times ($19.98 per month)
- The Philadelphia Inquirer ($9.99 per month)
- The Sacramento Bee ($6.99 per month)
- The Salt Lake Tribune ($5.99 per month)
- The Seattle Times ($9.99 per month)
- The Washington Post ($11.99 per month)
- USA Today ($11.99 per month)

Use the Newsstand App to Access Your Favorite Publications

Because the Newsstand app is considered one of the core preinstalled apps that comes with your Kindle Fire, you can launch it directly from the Home screen by tapping the Newsstand option that's displayed along the Navigation bar, shown in Figure 11-1. You'll see the Newsstand option listed first, near the upper-left corner of the Home screen.

Once you've read a digital publication, an icon for that publication will also appear on the Home screen's Carousel, shown in Figure 11-2. Tap the magazine or newspaper's cover thumbnail icon to relaunch it and continue reading where you left off.

Newsstand icon ——

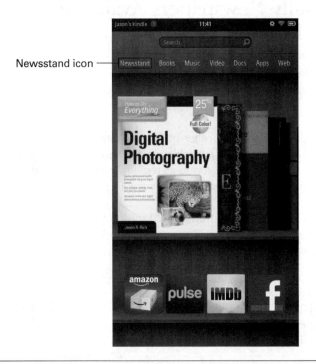

FIGURE 11-1 The Newsstand app provides quick access to a wide range of digital publications.

FIGURE 11-2 Cover graphic icons for recently read publications appear in the Carousel.

Like the Books app, the Newsstand app displays a main Library screen when it's launched. This virtual magazine/newspaper rack displays cover thumbnails for the various digital publications that are either stored in your tablet or that are paid for and accessible to you via your Amazon Cloud Drive account.

Displayed near the top-center area of the Newsstand's Library screen are two command tabs, labeled Cloud and Device (shown in Figure 11-3). Tap the Cloud option to access publications that are stored within your Amazon Cloud Drive account on the Internet but that have not been transferred to your tablet. Tap the Device icon to display publications currently stored on your tablet.

To download publications one at a time to your tablet, after selecting the Cloud command tab, tap a publication's cover thumbnail. It will display a small downward-pointing arrow in the lower-right corner of the thumbnail. Depending on the publication, the download process will take one to three minutes. During this process, the word "Downloading" will be displayed on the cover thumbnail. When the Downloading message disappears, tap the cover thumbnail graphic to open and begin reading that issue of the publication.

 Tip A newly downloaded publication that has not yet been read will display an orange New banner in the upper-right corner of its cover thumbnail (Figure 11-4).

Cloud icon

By Recent icon

Store icon

Device icon

By Title icon

FIGURE 11-3 The Newsstand's main Library screen

Located directly below the Cloud and Device command tabs are two additional command tabs, labeled By Recent and By Title. This determines how the publications are sorted and displayed on the screen.

As with most Kindle Fire apps, along the bottom of the screen, you'll see the now-familiar Home, Back, Menu, and Search icons. While viewing the Library screen of the Newsstand app, when you tap the Menu icon, only two additional command icons are displayed. They're labeled Grid View and List View. They also determine how the publications are displayed on the Library screen.

When you subscribe to newspapers or magazines, the latest issues will be made available automatically within your Amazon Cloud Drive account and will be downloaded to your tablet via Whispernet.

To find additional newspapers or magazines to purchase on a per-issue or subscription basis, tap the Store option that's displayed in the upper-right corner of the Newsstand's Library screen.

Whispernet is a free service offered by Amazon that transfers purchased content from Amazon.com to your Kindle Fire wirelessly, via the Internet. The process happens automatically.

FIGURE 11-4 The New banner helps you identify quickly publications you have not yet read.

How to...

Save, Delete, and Add Publications to Your Favorites Area

While viewing the Library screen of the Newsstand app, hold your finger down on any cover thumbnail for a publication for between one and three seconds. This will reveal a pop-up menu that offers three options, including Add To Favorites, Remove From Device, and Keep (shown in Figure 11-5).

Tap Add To Favorites to add an icon for the publication to the Home screen's Favorites area, displayed near the bottom of the Home screen. Tap the Remove From Device option to delete the publication from your tablet's memory. Tap the Keep option to save the issue on your Kindle Fire, even after new issues are downloaded. Unless you tap the Keep option, when new issues of that publication are made available, the older issues will be deleted automatically from your tablet to save internal storage space.

Add to Favorites icon
Remove from Device icon
Keep icon

FIGURE 11-5 Hold your finger on a cover thumbnail to access options for storing, deleting, and more.

Acquiring New Publications to Read

When you tap the Store option that's displayed in the upper-right corner of the Newsstand's Library screen, your tablet will access the Newsstand section of the online-based Kindle Store, allowing you to browse, purchase, and download additional publications to read on your Kindle Fire (shown in Figure 11-6). Remember, to browse or shop for publications, your tablet requires an Internet connection.

FIGURE 11-6 The online-based Newsstand section of the Kindle Store is where you can browse for, purchase, and download digital publications.

Displayed at the very top of the Newsstand's main screen when you access the Kindle Store is a Search Newsstand Store field. Tap it to manually enter the title or subject of a newspaper or magazine you're interested in so you can quickly find, purchase, and download it.

To the right of the Search field is the Library option. Tap this to immediately return to the Newsstand app's Library screen, from which you can begin reading any of the publications you've downloaded.

Just below the Search field is a section labeled Exclusive 90-Day Free Trial, along with a selection of cover thumbnails that represent popular magazines. At any given time, at least 20 publications offer free trial subscriptions via the Kindle Store. Tap the See All option (displayed to the right of the section heading) to view all of the free offers.

Along the left side of the Newsstand screen, you'll see additional category headings displayed in orange type, shown in Figure 11-7. They're labeled Featured Magazines; Featured Newspapers; Fashion & Entertainment; Men's Interest; Cooking; Home & Lifestyle; Sports & Fitness; General Interest; and News, Finance & Technology.

Below each heading are three cover thumbnails representing sample publications from that category. Tap the See All option (displayed to the right of each heading) to see the full selection of publications that fit into that category.

Category headings

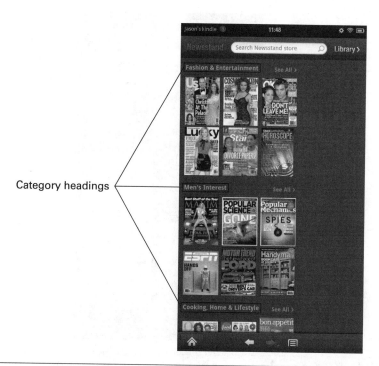

FIGURE 11-7   Search for publications based on their subject matter.

Tip In order to view all of the headings on this Newsstand screen, use your finger to scroll downward. Tap any publication's cover thumbnail to access details about a specific publication.

Displayed about halfway down and to the right as you're looking at the main Newsstand Kindle Store screen, you'll see four text-based headings in white type that are labeled Browse Magazines, Browse Newspapers, Visit The Kindle Bookstore, and Interactive Magazines. Tap the Browse Magazines option, shown in Figure 11-8, to view a pull-down menu containing nine magazine categories, including:

- Kindle Magazines
- Arts & Entertainment
- Business & Investing
- Internet & Technology
- Lifestyle & Culture
- News, Politics & Opinion
- Regional & Travel
- Science
- Sports

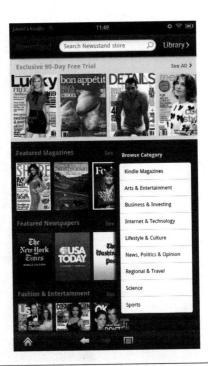

FIGURE 11-8 You can browse for publications by genre or by category.

Tap any of these category options to view a selection of digital magazines for your Kindle Fire that fall into that genre.

Tap the Browse Newspapers option to view a pull-down menu containing six newspaper categories, including Kindle Newspapers, Asia, Europe, North America, South America, and International.

If you tap the Kindle Bookstore option, the Books app will launch and you'll automatically be connected to the Kindle Store to browse Amazon's vast selection of eBooks. See Chapter 10 for more information about finding, purchasing, downloading, and reading eBooks on your Kindle Fire.

A typical digital edition of a magazine offers the same content as its printed counterpart. However, some publishers have created truly interactive digital magazines, which offer a broader range of multimedia content, not just printed articles, photographs, and illustrations. These publications typically require their own proprietary app.

To see a listing of the interactive magazines available for the Kindle Fire, tap the Interactive Magazine option. You'll see listings for more than 20 popular publications, like *People, Reader's Digest, Wired, Better Homes and Gardens, Time, GQ, Sports Illustrated,* and *Golf Digest.*

Interactive magazines typically require that you download a free app in order to acquire single issues or a subscription to that publication and then be able to read it on your tablet. While the publication-specific apps are free, you will need to pay for the content on either a per-issue or subscription basis.

As you're browsing the Newsstand area of the Kindle Store using the Newsstand app on your tablet, tap any publication's cover thumbnail to view a detailed Description screen related to that publication, or, if it's an interactive magazine, to learn more about the publication and then download and install the required app.

Explore a Publication's Description Page

Just like when viewing eBooks offered from the Kindle Store, when you tap a cover thumbnail graphic for a digital newspaper or magazine, a detailed Description page for that publication will be displayed, shown in Figure 11-9. Near the top of a publication's Description page, the current issue's cover graphic is displayed, along with the magazine's title and publisher.

Displayed just below the title and publisher, the publication's frequency is listed in conjunction with the Delivered heading. For example, it will say Daily, Weekly, Monthly, or Quarterly, based on how frequently new issues of that newspaper or magazine are published. The monthly price of the publication (if you subscribe), as well as the current issue price are also displayed near the top of a publication's

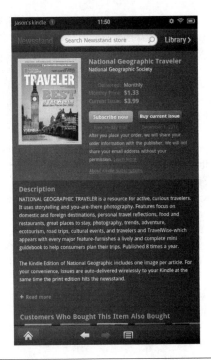

FIGURE 11-9 Every digital publication has its own Description page within the Newsstand section of the online-based Kindle Store.

Description page. The monthly price is what you'd pay per month if you subscribe. This rate is typically much lower than the publication's per-issue rate.

If you sign up for a free trial subscription of a publication, you will not be billed immediately. The free issues will be sent wirelessly, directly to your tablet via Whispernet. Typically, up to seven of the most recent issues of a publication are stored on your tablet. Older issues are automatically deleted to save storage space. However, this varies by publication.

 If you do not manually cancel your free trial subscription before the trial period ends, you will automatically be billed for an annual subscription, and your Kindle Fire will treat the subscription as auto-recurring.

Just below the price of the digital publication, you'll see two command icons, labeled Subscribe Now and Buy Current Issue (shown in Figure 11-10). Tap the Subscribe Now icon if you want to purchase an ongoing subscription to that publication and have new issues automatically downloaded to your Kindle Fire via Amazon's Whispernet service. To purchase just one issue of the publication, tap the Buy Current Issue icon.

FIGURE 11-10   You can either purchase a single issue of a publication or a subscription to it.

 Due to security concerns, in the future, you may be prompted to enter your Amazon.com account password before purchasing a digital publication.

After making a purchase, the issue of the publication will download to your tablet. During this process, a Downloading message will appear on the publication's Description screen in place of the Subscribe Now or Buy Current Issue icons. You can see this in Figure 11-11. The download process will take between one and three minutes per issue.

When the process is done, the Downloading message will be replaced by a green Read Now icon. During the downloading process, if you change your mind and want to cancel the purchase and download, tap the Cancel Order option, which is displayed just below the Downloading message.

FIGURE 11-11   If you change your mind while downloading an issue, you can cancel your purchase.

Tip If the publication is offering a free trial, tap the Subscribe Now icon to subscribe to the publication and begin your free trial. You will not be billed until the trial period expires.

As you scroll your way down within a publication's Description page, you will see a detailed, text-based description of the publication. You'll also see a Customers Who Bought This Item Also Bought section, along with Customer Reviews and a Product Details section.

To exit out of a publication's Description page without purchasing a single issue or subscribing, tap the Back icon that's displayed near the bottom-center area of the screen. To exit out of the Newsstand app altogether and return to the Kindle Fire's Home screen, tap the Home icon.

As you're looking at a publication's Description screen, if you tap the Menu icon, four additional command icons will be displayed near the bottom of the screen. They're labeled Storefront, Magazines, Newspapers, and Kindle Account, shown in Figure 11-12.

Tap the Storefront option to return to the main Newsstand page of the Kindle Store and continue browsing the publications that are offered. Tap the Magazines or Newspapers icon to browse just the magazine or newspaper offerings within Newsstand. Tap the Kindle Account icon to manage your Amazon.com/Kindle account and be transferred to the appropriate Amazon.com website page via the Amazon Silk web browser.

Tip As you're reading a Description page for a publication, tap the blue About Kindle Subscriptions option, which is displayed just below the Subscribe Now and Buy Current Issue icons, to learn more about the terms and conditions related to acquiring, managing, canceling, or reactivating subscriptions.

Storefront icon —
Newspapers icon —
— Magazines icon
— Kindle Account icon

FIGURE 11-12 Depending on when you tap the Menu icon, different command icons and options will be displayed.

Manually Cancel an Auto-recurring Subscription

Once you subscribe to a digital publication, the cost of the annual subscription will automatically be billed to your Amazon.com account and charged to the credit card you have on file with Amazon, unless otherwise noted by the publication. At the end of your subscription period, that subscription will automatically renew. This process will continue indefinitely until you manually cancel a subscription.

To cancel a recurring subscription, visit the Manage Your Kindle Subscriptions page on the Amazon.com website. From the main Amazon.com webpage, click or tap the Subscription Settings option, which is displayed on the left side of the screen, below the Your Kindle Account heading. Next, locate the subscription you wish to modify or cancel, and then click the Cancel Subscription icon. You will be asked to confirm this decision.

As soon as you cancel a subscription, you will no longer receive new issues of the publication as they're published, and you will not be able to access past issues of the publication via the Web. Any issues that are stored on your tablet will remain yours until you manually delete them. If you cancel a subscription partway through the subscription period, a prorated refund will be issued for the unused portion of your subscription.

Reading a Digital Publication on Your Tablet's Screen

When you begin reading the digital editions of various newspapers and magazines on your Kindle Fire's seven-inch, full-color touch screen, you'll discover that the various publishers utilize the on-screen real estate and touch screen capabilities in different ways. As a result, how you navigate your way around a publication will vary.

As you read a national magazine on your tablet, you will have access to a Page View (shown in Figure 11-13) and Text View viewing mode (shown in Figure 11-14), which will be explained shortly. When you read most digital newspapers, such as *The New York Times,* an interactive front page (table of contents) is displayed. From there, you can select which article you want to read. In the upper-left corner of the screen, you'll also discover a Sections icon, which allows you to jump to a specific section within that newspaper.

 Some interactive magazines that have their own proprietary apps will function very differently than the publications that use the Newsstand app when it comes to reading content. The goal of each publication, however, is to offer an intuitive and easy-to-use interface that allows you to read a publication's content in a way that's visually appealing on your tablet's screen. Some publishers have achieved this better than others.

FIGURE 11-13 The Page View mode shows you an overview of the entire page of a newspaper or magazine.

To begin reading a newspaper or magazine that's been downloaded to your Kindle Fire, return to the Library screen of the Newsstand app. To launch a specific publication and begin reading it, tap the publication's cover thumbnail.

When a publication is opened on your tablet's screen, it will typically look very much like its traditionally printed counterpart, shown in Figure 11-15. Using your finger, swipe from right to left to turn the page forward. Or swipe from left to right to move back one page at a time.

Note The concept of digital newspaper and magazine publishing is relatively new. As a result, many publishers are still experimenting in order to discover what works and what does not when it comes to adapting printed newspaper or magazine content to be read on a tablet device.

As you're reading most digital publications using the Page View mode, you can zoom in on text or graphics either by double-tapping an area of the screen where you want to zoom in (and then zoom out by double-tapping again) or using a reverse-pinch finger motion to zoom in and then a pinch motion to zoom out again.

FIGURE 11-14   The Text View mode allows you to view the text of an article in an easy-to-read format that's customizable.

When viewing a digital publication's table of contents, it is often interactive. So, if you tap an article title or page number, you will immediately jump to that page of the publication. To access the table of contents, as well as other menu icons, tap near the bottom of the screen to make the Home, Back, Aa, Table of Contents, and Search icons appear. Tap the Table of Contents icon to display the publication's table of contents. When you do this, thumbnail images of each of the publication's pages will also be displayed in a row near the bottom of the screen. Use your finger to swipe right to left (or left to right) to view all of the thumbnails, or tap any page thumbnail to view that page in Page View mode.

Depending on the publication, you may find it advantageous to hold your tablet sideways in landscape mode. However, most publications are formatted so you can easily view one page at a time while holding your tablet in portrait mode.

Also, depending on the publication you're reading, you may discover that any website addresses that are displayed within the text of articles or within advertisements are active hyperlinks. Thus, if you tap them, the Kindle Fire's Silk web browser will launch, and you'll be directed automatically to the appropriate webpage.

To make reading individual articles easier, when you tap anywhere on the tablet's screen as you're reading a newspaper or magazine, the on-screen command icons will

FIGURE 11-15 Shown here is a sample page from a magazine using the Page View mode of the Newsstand app.

be displayed. Near the upper-right corner of the screen are the Page View and Text View tabs. Tap the Page View tab to view the entire page of the publication in full-screen mode. When you want to read a specific article, tap the Text View tab to view just the text and photos for a specific article, formatted in a way that's easy to read on your Kindle Fire's screen.

When viewing an article in Text View mode, you'll discover the "Aa" icon displayed at the bottom of the screen becomes active when the command icons are visible. Tap this icon to adjust the font style and typeface of the article text, shown in Figure 11-16, allowing you to personalize how it appears on the screen. These controls work the same way as they do when reading an eBook, so refer back to Chapter 10 for details on how to utilize these text customization options.

Also while in Text View mode, you can hold your finger on any word to instantly see the definition of that word, or perform a search for additional occurrences of that word within the publication by tapping the Search tab that appears within the Word Definition window. Within the Word Definition window, a Wikipedia and Google search tab is also displayed. An Internet connection is required to use these features. Keep in mind, the Search option that's displayed as you're reading a publication allows you to quickly search the content of a publication for a keyword or phrase and then jump to where the search word or phrase appears within the publication.

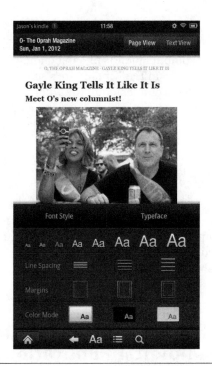

FIGURE 11-16   In Text View mode, you can customize the on-screen text to make it easier for you to read.

If you hold your finger on any photograph or graphic that appears within a digital publication, you'll be able to view that image in full-screen mode on your tablet by tapping the Zoom icon that appears. You can also double-tap the image to view it in full-screen mode.

 As you're viewing a publication in Page View mode, when you tap anywhere on the screen, in addition to the command icons being displayed at the bottom of the screen, the Page View and Text View tabs appear near the upper-right corner of the screen. You'll also see a slider bar displayed just above the command icons. Using your finger, slide the button on this slider to the right or left to quickly navigate your way around a publication as you're viewing the thumbnails of the pages.

To switch from Text View mode back to Page View mode while reading a publication, tap anywhere near the bottom of the screen to make the on-screen command icons reappear. Then, tap the Page View icon or the Back icon. To exit out of a publication and return to the Home screen of the Kindle Fire, tap the Home icon. The cover thumbnail image for the publication you were reading will appear on the Home screen's Carousel. Tap the thumbnail to pick up reading where you left off after the digital publication reopens.

Once you get used to switching between Page View and Text View mode as you're reading a magazine, or you learn how to navigate your way around the table of contents and/or contents menus of a digital newspaper, you'll find that reading most digital publications on the Kindle Fire's screen is both easy and convenient. Plus, when your tablet is connected to the Internet, you have access to an entire newsstand's worth of newspaper and magazine content available for downloading and reading.

Remember, by using the interactive table of contents and/or Search field within a digital publication, you can easily jump to and read only the articles or content that are of direct interest to you and quickly find exactly what you're looking for. This will save you a lot of time.

Because you can store many digital publications on your tablet at once and begin reading them virtually anytime and anywhere, you may discover it's convenient for you to catch up on your reading when you have a few minutes of downtime throughout your day, especially in situations where you would not normally carry around a physical copy of a newspaper or magazine.

Sometimes Special Apps Are Required to Read Digital Publications

In situations where a particular newspaper or magazine requires a publication-specific app to acquire and read that publication's content, you'll be able to download the app for free from within the Newsstand app. However, once the app is installed on your tablet, instead of accessing and reading it from the Newsstand app, you'll need to launch the publication's proprietary app.

So, from Newsstand, for example, you can download the proprietary *People* or *GQ* magazine app. Then, once the app is installed, from your Kindle Fire's Home screen, instead of launching the Newsstand app, tap the Apps icon that's displayed along the Navigation bar. When the Apps screen appears, tap the magazine app icon (shown in the following illustration) to launch it. From within the publication-specific app, you will be given the option to purchase individual issues or subscribe to the publication and then actually read the content you purchase and download.

In some situations, if you're already a paid subscriber of the print edition of a publication (such as *People* or *GQ*), you will be able to access the digital edition using the proprietary app for free, once you enter your subscription account number, name, and address into the app. Your subscription number will be displayed on the printed magazine's mailing label.

Once issues of the publication are loaded into the publication-specific app, how you navigate your way around that app will vary. Some of these apps have special icons overlaid on specific pages of the publication. When you tap one of these icons, you can access multimedia content (such as video, an image slide show, or audio) that's related to what you're reading about. In some cases, you can also make online purchases for products or services you're reading about. The functionality built into publication-specific apps varies as much as the content within those publications.

GQ app icon ————

People app icon ————

12

Download and Listen to Music on Your Kindle Fire

HOW TO...

- Find, purchase, and download music from the Amazon MP3 Music Store from your Kindle Fire using the Music app.
- Listen to music stored on your Kindle Fire using the Music app.
- Transfer digital music from other sources to your Kindle Fire.

So far, you've discovered a handful of tasks that your Kindle Fire was designed for and that it handles exceptionally well. Now, add to this list the fact that your tablet can be used as a full-featured digital music player. As you'd expect, the Music app that comes preinstalled on your Kindle Fire works seamlessly with the Amazon's MP3 Music Store, which is an online-based music store that offers a selection of more than 18 million songs available to purchase and download.

No matter what genre of music you enjoy listening to, you'll find it available from Amazon's MP3 Music Store. This includes current and past chart-topping hits, older music from well-known artists, timeless classics, and music from up-and-coming and even unsigned artists. As you begin browsing the MP3 Music Store, you'll discover that music can be purchased one song at a time, or with a tap on the tablet's screen, you can purchase an entire album.

To introduce you to new music and up-and-coming artists, the MP3 Music Store also offers a new selection of free music each week. Once you purchase a song or download a free song, it becomes a permanent part of your digital music collection, which you can enjoy listening to on your computer(s), smartphone, and/or your Kindle Fire, as well as other digital music players.

Your Kindle Fire's Music app is designed to make it easy for you to purchase, download, and then listen to digital music on your tablet. It's also possible, however, to transfer other digital music you already own that's stored on your computer to your Kindle Fire and listen to that music using the Music app. Or you can purchase and acquire digital music from other online sources (or rip your own music CDs), but this requires a few extra steps, which will be explained later in this chapter.

You Can Shop for Digital Music from Your Tablet or Your Computer

You can browse, purchase, and download music from the Amazon MP3 Music Store directly from your Kindle Fire, or use the web browser on your PC or Mac computer. If you're shopping for music via the Kindle Fire, the Music app is used.

If you're using your computer, visit www.Amazon.com. Click the MP3s & Cloud Player option that's displayed below the Shop All Departments heading on the left side of the screen, and then click the MP3 Music Store option.

As with other types of content purchases from Amazon.com made from a computer, once you make a music purchase from the Amazon MP3 Music Store, the downloadable content you purchase will be added to your Amazon Cloud Drive account. This also includes music offered for free from Amazon's MP3 Music Store.

Your Kindle Fire Is Compatible with Multiple Digital Audio Formats

Beyond purchasing music from the Amazon MP3 store or streaming music directly from the Internet, you can purchase and/or acquire music from other sources, including Apple's iTunes Store. You can also convert (or "rip") your own audio CDs into digital audio files that are compatible with your tablet.

The Music app that comes preinstalled on your Kindle Fire is capable of playing digital music that's saved in a handful of popular formats, including MP3, WAVE, MP4, non-DRM AAC, MIDI, OGG, and VP8. If your digital music is currently saved in another file format, you can use optional software on your computer to convert those files into compatible audio music files (such as MP3s) so they can be stored and played on your Kindle Fire.

Note DRM stands for Digital Rights Management. This is a form of copy protection that prevents certain digital audio files from being illegally copied or transferred between computers or mobile devices.

The open-source (free) Miro software (www.getmiro.com) for PC or Mac can be used to convert existing digital music into audio files that are compatible with your Kindle Fire. Miro version 4.0.4 (or later) offers Kindle Fire support. The software can also be used to manage your existing digital music library, rip audio CDs, and then sync music between your computer and tablet using an optional Micro-B USB–to–USB cable. Keep in mind, in addition to audio and music files, the Miro software can be used to transfer non-DRM video content to your tablet.

Both the Apple iTunes (for PC or Mac) or Microsoft Windows Media Player (PC) software can be used to convert music from audio CDs to MP3 or other popular audio format files. For both PCs and Macs, there are also many other optional software packages that can be used for "ripping" audio CDs and converting them into MP3 files. You'll easily find these software packages using Google, Yahoo!, or any Internet search engine. Use the search phrase "Music Conversion Software."

The Cost of Digital Music from the Amazon MP3 Music Store

As with any type of downloadable content (such as movies, eBooks, or audiobooks), the price of music varies. However, most individual songs available from the Amazon MP3 Music Store are priced between $0.69 and $1.29 each, and full albums are priced between $3.99 and $12.99. Each week, however, the Amazon MP3 Music Store offers a selection of music that you can download and make a permanent part of your digital music collection for free.

For an additional annual fee of $20.00, it's possible to upgrade your free Amazon Cloud Drive account so that it works with your entire digital music collection, not just music purchased from the Amazon MP3 Music Store. This allows you to easily transfer and share all of your digital music between your computers, Kindle Fire, and other devices (including your smartphone) via the Internet.

Use Your Kindle Fire to Browse or Purchase Music from the Amazon MP3 Music Store

To begin building your digital music collection using your Kindle Fire, make sure it's connected to the Internet, and then launch the Music app that comes preinstalled. To launch the Music app, access the tablet's Home screen, and then tap the Music option that's displayed on the Navigation bar near the top of the screen.

Music purchased or acquired from Amazon's MP3 Music Store can be downloaded and played on your Kindle Fire or stored within your online-based Amazon Cloud Drive account and then streamed to your tablet, computer, smartphone, or another device. This is music you paid for (or that was offered for free from Amazon's MP3 Music Store) and that you can listen to whenever and wherever you wish. Using other services, such as Pandora, you can stream music for free from the Internet to listen to on your tablet (when it's connected to the Internet), but this music is never stored on your tablet, nor do you own it.

Upon launching the Music app, the Library screen for this app will be displayed (shown in Figure 12-1). This Library screen lists either the music that's stored on your tablet or music that's saved within your Amazon Cloud Drive account that you own and that's currently accessible from your tablet.

FIGURE 12-1 Among other things, the Library screen offers access to music you own and that's accessible via your Kindle Fire.

To browse the Amazon MP3 Music Store to acquire new music, tap the Store option that's displayed in the upper-right corner of the Music app's Library screen.

 Your Kindle Fire must be connected to the Internet to access the Amazon MP3 Music Store.

When accessed from your Kindle Fire, the Amazon MP3 Music Store's offerings are formatted to be displayed on your tablet's seven-inch screen. The same content is available if you visit the Amazon MP3 Music Store (www.Amazon.com) using your computer's web browser. The layout of the content, however, will be different.

Displayed near the top-center area of the Music app's screen (shown in Figure 12-2) when you access the Amazon MP3 Music Store is the Search Music Store field. Use this search field to quickly find the music you're looking for. Tap the empty Search field to make the tablet's virtual keyboard appear. Then, enter the title of a song; title of an album; an artist, band, or music group's name; or any keyword or search phrase that's associated with the music you're looking for.

When you're done entering your search word(s), tap the Search key that's displayed to the right of the spacebar on the virtual keyboard to initiate your search. Matches to what you're looking for will be displayed on the tablet's screen.

FIGURE 12-2 The Search field makes it easy to quickly find the music you're looking for, no matter how you search for it.

At the top of this Search Results screen will be two tabs, labeled Albums and Songs. Tap the Albums tab to view a listing of full-length albums that relate to your search, or tap the Songs tab to view a listing of individual songs that relate to your search. Tap any search listing to access the Description screen for the related music and purchase it.

How to... **Redeem an Amazon Gift Card or Promotional Code**

If you receive an Amazon.com gift card or promotional code, to redeem it when shopping for music from your Kindle Fire and visiting the MP3 Music Store, tap the Menu icon that's displayed near the bottom-center area of the screen, and then tap the Settings option. Next, tap the Enter A Claim Code option that's displayed at the top of the General Settings screen. Using the virtual keyboard, enter your gift card activation number or promotional code. Tap the Apply icon to submit your request. The value of the gift card or promotional code will be credited to your Amazon.com account.

As you're looking at the main MP3 Music Store screen via the Music app on your Kindle Fire, below the Search Music Store field, a section of the screen is dedicated to displaying the MP3 Daily Deals, which includes the Daily Deal Album, Song of the Day, Featured $0.69 Song, and other featured albums or songs.

Use your finger to swipe from right to left (or left to right) to scroll horizontally through these Daily Deal offerings. If you see something that interests you, tap the album/song graphic thumbnail or title to view more information, or tap the orange price icon to immediately purchase that song or album.

 When you tap the orange price icon that's typically displayed next to or immediately below a music listing, it will change into a green Buy icon. Tap this Buy icon to confirm your purchase decision and acquire that song or album. Due to security concerns, in the future, you may also be prompted to enter your Amazon.com password before making a purchase.

Displayed below the Daily Deal section of the Amazon MP3 Music Store, you'll see four command tabs, labeled Featured, Bestsellers, New Releases, and Genres. Tap any of these tabs to begin browsing the Amazon MP3 Music Store's vast and ever-growing music selection. Once you tap the Featured tab, for example, appropriate music listings are displayed on the tablet's screen. The Featured music listings change constantly.

To see the songs and albums that are currently the most popular on the Amazon MP3 Music Store, tap the Bestsellers icon. When you do this, the Bestsellers screen is displayed (shown in Figure 12-3). By default, the bestselling albums (listed in order of their popularity) are displayed. At the top of the screen, tap the Songs tab to switch from viewing a list of 100 bestselling albums (from all genres) to a list of 100 bestselling songs.

Whether you're looking at the listing of bestselling albums or bestselling songs, on the screen will be a series of individual music listings. Each listing contains a graphic thumbnail of the song or album's cover, its ranking on the Bestsellers list, the album or song's title, the artist's name, its average star-based rating (if you're looking at the Album list), and its price (displayed within an orange price icon). A sample music listing for an album can be seen in Figure 12-4.

Use your finger to scroll downward on the Bestsellers screen to view the entire bestselling albums or bestselling songs listing, which contains the top 100 albums or songs. When viewing an album's listing, by tapping its thumbnail graphic or title, a Description screen for that album is displayed. You will see a list containing each song featured within the album. On this screen, you can tap the orange price icon that's associated with the Buy Entire Album option, or in most cases, select one song at a time to purchase and download (shown in Figure 12-5).

When you view the bestselling songs listing (shown in Figure 12-6), instead of displaying a star-based rating, each music listing will include a Play Sample option. Tap this to stream a 30-second sample of the song and play it on your tablet. You can then tap the orange price icon to purchase and download that song, or tap the Play Sample option again to stop the music from playing before the 30 seconds are up.

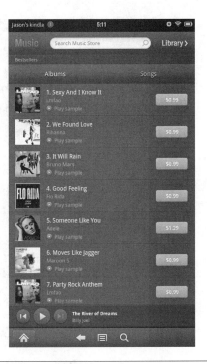

FIGURE 12-3   View 100 of the bestselling albums or songs as separate lists.

By tapping the New Releases tab that's displayed near the top-center area of the main MP3 Music Store screen (just below the Daily Deals), a listing of 100 brand-new albums or songs will be displayed. Tap the Albums or Songs tab that's displayed near the top of the screen to choose between viewing entire albums or individual newly released songs. Then, use your finger to scroll downward on the New Releases screen to see the entire list. The layout of the new releases album or song listings are identical to what you'd see when you tap the Bestsellers option, only the selection of music is different.

To browse through a selection of available music by genre, begin by tapping the Genres tab that is displayed to the right of the Featured, Bestsellers, and New Releases tabs. The Genres screen displays a listing of 22 different music genres, including Alternative Rock, Blues, Broadway & Vocals, Children's Music, Christian & Gospel, Classic Rock, Classical, Country, Dance & DJ, Folk, Hard Rock & Metal, International, Jazz, Latin Music, Miscellaneous, New Age, Opera & Vocal, Pop, R&B, Rap & Hip-Hop, Rock, and Soundtracks. Upon tapping one of these genre categories, a submenu

FIGURE 12-4   A sample music listing for a full-length album

FIGURE 12-5 You can purchase an entire album or just select songs from it.

screen will be displayed, allowing you to narrow down your search. For example, if you tap the Pop option, subcategories include Adult Alternative, Adult Contemporary, Compilations, Easy Listening, and eight other options.

Tap your subcategory selection to then display a listing of music that's appropriate to your genre and category selection. Once again, you will have the option to display albums or songs by tapping the appropriate tab that's displayed near the top of the screen. As you view the Albums listing, for example, when you tap any album cover thumbnail graphic or title, a listing of individual songs from that album is displayed. When you view the Songs listing, part of each song's listing includes a Play Sample option.

FIGURE 12-6 When viewing a listing of bestselling songs or new releases, for example, this is what a song listing looks like. You can listen to a sample of a song before purchasing it.

Regardless of which screen you're looking at when browsing the Amazon MP3 Music Store, to return to the previous screen without making a purchase, tap the Back icon that's displayed near the bottom-center area of the screen. Or, tap the Home icon to exit out of the Music app altogether and return to the Kindle Fire's Home screen.

Continue exploring the Amazon MP3 Music Store until you find and purchase all of the music you're looking to acquire, you want to return to the Music app's Library screen so you can listen to your music, or you want to exit out of the Music app and do something else entirely with your tablet.

Make a Music Purchase from Your Kindle Fire

Any time you tap the orange price icon to purchase a song from your Kindle Fire and then tap the green Buy icon (shown in Figure 12-7) to confirm your decision, the price of that song or album will be immediately charged to the credit card you have on file in conjunction with your Amazon.com account. Within a few seconds, a Purchase Confirmed pop-up window will be displayed on the tablet's screen.

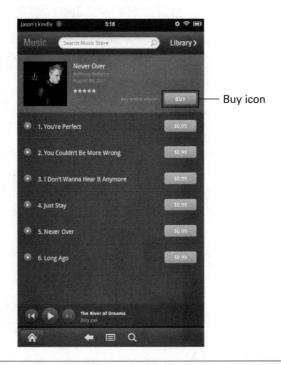

FIGURE 12-7   After tapping an album or song's price icon to purchase it, tap the Buy icon to confirm your decision.

Depending on how you set up the options within the Settings menu of the Music app, this screen may include two command icons, labeled Save To Your Amazon Cloud Drive and Save To This Device. If you select the Save To Your Amazon Cloud Drive option (which is recommended), the digital music file will be stored online, within your cloud-based account, and will immediately become accessible to your tablet, computer(s), and other devices.

However, if you select the Save To This Device option, it will be downloaded to your tablet only. Next, add a check mark to the Terms of Use screen (if it appears) and tap the Continue icon to proceed with the music download. (Remember, you can adjust this option from the Settings menu within the Music app.)

Once music is stored within your Amazon Cloud Drive account, you can return to the Library screen of the Music app, tap the Cloud tab to view that music listing (shown in Figure 12-8), and then tap the Download icon associated with the listing to transfer (download) the song to your Kindle Fire, shown in Figure 12-9. It will then appear within the music listing when you tap the Device tab at the top-center area of the Library screen. You also have the option to stream that music from the cloud to your tablet and skip the download process. To do this, tap the song or album title.

FIGURE 12-8   When looking at the Library screen, tap the Cloud icon to view music stored online within your Amazon Cloud Drive account. Here, the Albums tab has been selected.

FIGURE 12-9   You can download or stream music to your tablet.

If you stream music from the cloud, a constant Internet connection must be maintained. The benefit, however, is that the music does not utilize any of the tablet's 8GB of internal storage space. By downloading the music to your tablet, however, it will be saved within the Kindle Fire's internal storage and can be accessed any time, whether or not an Internet connection is available.

 As a general rule, it's a good idea to store all of your new music purchases within your Amazon Cloud Drive account and then download (or stream) that music from whatever device or computer you want, including your Kindle Fire.

Making a Music Purchase from Your Computer

When you're shopping for music from the Amazon MP3 Music Store via your computer, obviously a lot more content can be displayed on the screen at once. However, the process for previewing and then purchasing music is basically the same as it is when you do your music shopping from your tablet.

 Music purchased from the Amazon MP3 Music Store from your computer is saved automatically to your Amazon Cloud Drive account. You can then stream or download it from the Library screen of the Music app on your Kindle Fire or use the Amazon Cloud Player to listen to it on your PC or Mac. Also, visiting the Amazon MP3 Music Store from your computer allows you to view more expansive music listings.

Listening to Music on Your Kindle Fire

There's a difference between streaming music from a music service, like Pandora Internet Radio, and streaming music that you own from your Amazon Cloud Drive account. When you use the Music app that comes preinstalled on your tablet, in addition to shopping for music from the Amazon MP3 Music Store, you can listen to music that's either stored within your Amazon Cloud Drive account or that's saved within the internal storage of your Kindle Fire. Either way, what's available is music you own.

To listen to music that's stored within your Amazon Cloud Drive account or that's stored within the internal storage area using your Kindle Fire, launch the Music app to access the Library screen. At the top of the Music Library screen, tap the Cloud tab to view music that's stored within your Amazon Cloud Drive account (online) but that's not currently saved on your tablet. When selected, the Cloud tab will turn orange, and a listing of available music will be displayed on the screen. Again, to play this music, your tablet must have access to the Internet.

If you tap the Device tab at the top of the Library screen of the Music app, music that's currently stored on your tablet will be displayed. An Internet connection is not required to access and listen to this music.

Displayed just below the Cloud and Device tabs are four additional tabs that allow you to select the music you want to listen to. These command tabs are labeled Playlists, Artists, Albums, and Songs (shown in Figure 12-10). Here's a summary of what each of these command tabs is used for:

- Tap the **Playlists** tab to create and listen to a playlist that you create. A playlist is a compilation of songs that you own and that you select. The music you add to a playlist can be from any artist or music genre. You determine what songs or albums are added to your playlists and in what order the music is played. How to create and listen to a playlist will be explained shortly.
- Tap the **Artists** tab to view a listing of artists, music groups, or bands whose music you own and have access to using the Music app. Below each artist listing will be a list of the albums and/or songs currently accessible to you based on what you own. From the artists listing, tap the artist of your choice to view a list of albums or songs you own from that artist, and then tap any of the song listings to begin playing the selected song.

FIGURE 12-10 You can sort your music by playlist, artist, album, or songs. The Device and Artists tabs have been selected here.

- Tap the **Albums** tab to view a listing of album titles that you own music from. An album will be listed whether you own one or two songs from that album or the entire album. However, when you tap a specific album's listing, only the songs you currently own will be playable. You will see an on-screen option called Shop This Artist, which you can tap to acquire additional songs from that artist. Tap any of the album listings to view a list of songs you own from that album, and then tap any song listing to begin playing it.
- Tap the **Songs** tab to view a complete listing of songs that are accessible to you. Each song listing includes its album cover thumbnail graphic, the song's title, and the artist, along with its length. Tap any song listing to begin playing it.

When a song begins playing on your Kindle Fire, on-screen control icons appear and the song's album cover thumbnail will be displayed in the center of the Now Playing screen, shown in Figure 12-11.

Just below the album/song cover graphic is a slider. Place your finger on the white dot that appears within this slider to quickly fast-forward or rewind the currently playing song or return to a specific location within the song. To the right and left of the slider are timers. The timer on the left shows how much of the song has already played, while the timer on the right shows the length of the song currently playing.

FIGURE 12-11 The Now Playing screen shows what song is playing and offers on-screen icons for controlling the music.

Below the slider are five on-screen control icons. To the extreme left is the Shuffle button. If you have multiple songs selected to play within your Now Playing queue or you're listening to a playlist, you can randomize the order in which you'll hear the songs by tapping this icon. When activated, it will turn orange. To the right of the Shuffle icon is the Rewind icon. Tap this to immediately return to the beginning of the song you're listening to. (If you tap the Rewind icon a second time, you can return to the beginning of the previous song that was played.) Moving to the right is the Play/Pause icon. Tap the Play icon to begin playing the selected song. Or when music is playing, tap this icon to pause (stop) the music.

To the right of the Play/Pause icon is the Fast Forward icon. Tap it to advance to the next song in your Now Playing queue or playlist. This icon only becomes active when you have multiple songs queued up to play. Finally, to the right of the Fast Forward icon is the Repeat icon. When activated, the currently playing song will play in an endless loop until you tap the Pause icon to stop it; tap the Repeat icon again to turn off this feature.

Displayed just below the five on-screen control icons is the volume slider. Move the white dot within this slider to the right to increase the volume. Or move it to the left to decrease the volume.

To view your Now Playing queue or the songs in the currently playing playlist, tap the Now Playing Queue icon that's displayed near the upper-right corner of the Now Playing screen. To return to the Now Playing screen, tap the tiny album thumbnail graphic that replaces the Now Playing Queue icon near the upper-right corner of the screen.

Tip While music is playing, you can tap the Back, Library, Home, or Search icon to exit out of the screen you're looking at and do something else on your tablet. Unless you tap the Play/Pause icon first, the music will continue playing. To stop the music, change playlists, or choose other music playback options, you will need to return to the Music app.

How to... # Relaunch Music from the Home Screen

When you exit out of the Music app and return to the Kindle Fire's Home screen, displayed within the Carousel will be thumbnail images of the album or song cover artwork for the last few songs or albums that were played. Tap any of these thumbnails (representing songs or albums) within the Carousel to play them again. Doing this will automatically relaunch the Music app.

To add that song or album to the Favorites area of your tablet, as you're looking at a thumbnail for an album or song's cover, hold your finger on it for a second to two, and then tap the Add To Favorites tab that appears on the screen.

Create and Listen to Playlists

Playlists are a way for you to group together songs you love and be able to play them back, either in order or randomly. You control what music gets added to your playlists, and you can create as many different playlists as you'd like and store them within the Music app. For example, you can create a special playlist that contains music you enjoy listening to when you drive, work out, meditate, work, clean the house, walk your dog, or that you prefer to hear when you're depressed or happy. The music within your playlist can be composed of albums or songs that you own and that are stored within your tablet (or accessible via your Amazon Cloud Drive account).

To create a customized playlist, from almost anywhere within the Music app, tap the Playlist tab that's displayed near the upper-left corner of the screen. A listing of your available (stored) playlists will be displayed by name. However, if you have not yet created a playlist, you'll see the Create New Playlist option displayed in orange. Tap it and follow these steps:

1. Using the virtual keyboard, enter a name for the playlist when the Create New Playlist pop-up window appears and displays a blank field that says Enter Playlist Name (shown in Figure 12-12). Tap the Save icon to continue. "Driving Music," "Workout Music," or "Meditation Music" are sample playlist names you can create.

FIGURE 12-12 Give each of your playlists a descriptive name so that you'll know what music is included within it. In this example, the title "Sample Playlist" was used.

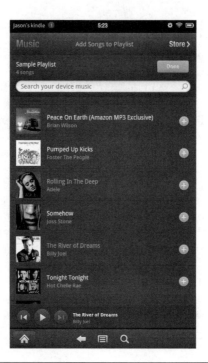

FIGURE 12-13 Tap the plus sign icon associated with a song to add it to your playlist.

2. When the Add Songs To Playlist screen appears, shown in Figure 12-13, a complete listing of all available songs stored on your tablet or that are accessible from your Amazon Cloud Drive account are displayed. Scroll down the listing and tap the orange plus sign icon that's associated with each song you want to add to your playlist. Or, if you have many songs displayed, use the Search field at the top of the screen to quickly find the specific songs you want to add to the playlist.

3. One at a time, add as many songs to your playlist as you desire. Remember, you can mix and match artists, music genres, or albums. Each time you select a song, its listing will turn grey, indicating that it's been selected. Also, near the top-left corner of the screen, just below the playlist's name, the song counter will increase by one.

4. Once you have selected all of the songs to be added to your playlist, tap the orange Done icon that's displayed near the top-right corner of the screen.

5. Your playlist will be displayed on the screen (shown in Figure 12-14), with songs listed in the order they were selected. Tap any song to begin playing the playlist, starting with the selected song.

6. To change the song order of the playlist, to add songs, or to delete songs from it, tap the Edit icon that's displayed near the top-right corner of the screen.

FIGURE 12-14   A sample playlist screen

7. Using the Edit Playlist mode, to move songs around, place your finger on the icon that's displayed to the left of a song listing and drag it upward or downward. This icon looks like a series of eight dots (shown in Figure 12-15). To delete a song from the playlist, tap the minus sign that's displayed to the right of a song's listing. Or to add songs to the playlist, tap the Add icon that's displayed near the top-right corner of the Edit Playlist screen. When you're done making your changes, tap the orange Done icon.

 Once you begin playing a playlist and the Now Playing screen appears, you can tap the Shuffle icon to randomize the order of the songs to be played. You can also exit out of the Music app altogether and do other things on your tablet while the music is playing.

Once a playlist is created, its name will be displayed below the Create New Playlist option whenever you tap the Playlist tab within the Music app. You can now create additional playlists, which will be accessible to you at any time from the Music app. Tap a playlist listing from the Playlist screen to begin playing it.

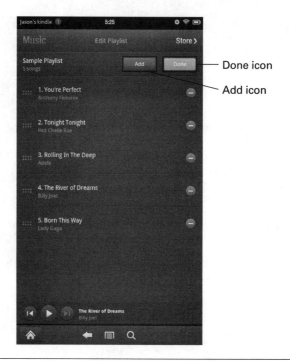

FIGURE 12-15 You can edit your playlist from the Edit Playlist screen.

The Settings Menu Options That Are Available When Music Is Playing

When you tap the Menu icon for any app, a selection of additional menu options is displayed near the bottom-center area of the screen. As music is playing, when you tap the Menu icon, you'll see four command options displayed. They're labeled Downloads, Settings, Now Playing, and Help.

Tap the Downloads option to view the Downloads Queue screen, which includes songs currently in the process of downloading from Amazon.com or your Amazon Cloud Drive account to your tablet. (Each song takes between 15 and 45 seconds to download.)

Tap the Now Playing icon to return to the Now Playing screen. This displays the on-screen icons for controlling the playback of your music and shows what song is currently playing. Tap the Settings option to access the Settings menu that's part of the Music app, or tap the Help icon to view on-screen help for the Music app. The Settings menu of the Music app (shown in Figure 12-16) allows you to determine how certain features within the app function.

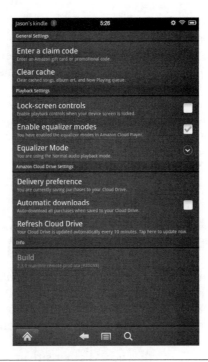

FIGURE 12-16   The Settings menu of the Music app

The Settings menu contains the following eight options:

- **Enter A Claim Code**   Tap this option to redeem an Amazon.com gift card or promotional code as you're shopping for music from the Amazon MP3 Music Store.
- **Clear Cache**   This command will delete the album art, songs, and Now Playing queue information that's taking up storage space within your tablet, but that's no longer needed.
- **Lock-Screen Controls**   Select this option to enable music playback controls even when your tablet is otherwise locked. This allows you to use controls on your optional headphones, for example, to play, pause, fast-forward, rewind, or change songs even when the tablet is in Sleep mode or the Lock screen is visible.
- **Enable Equalizer Modes**   You can control how the music sounds as it's played on your Kindle Fire, based on the mode you select. First, turn on this feature by tapping it to place a check mark within its check box. Then, tap the Equalizer Mode options pull-down menu to choose a specific equalizer mode. Your options include Normal, Classical, Dance, Flat, Folk, Heavy Metal, Hip Hop, Jazz, Pop, or Rock. Experiment with the different modes to determine which one appeals to you, based on the music you're listening to, and whether you're using the tablet's internal speaker, external speakers, or stereo headphones to enjoy the music.

- **Delivery Preference**   Determine if you automatically want to save all of your new music purchases and acquisitions to your Amazon Cloud Drive account, or download the new music just to your tablet when it's purchased from the tablet.
- **Automatic Downloads**   When you activate this option by placing a check mark within its check box, any time you acquire new music and it is stored within your Amazon Cloud Drive account, it will also download automatically to your Kindle Fire, regardless of what device (or computer) it was purchased using.
- **Refresh Cloud Drive**   Every ten minutes, your Kindle Fire checks your Amazon Cloud Drive account for new content to download. Tap this icon to immediately check for new content.

Listen to Music Not Acquired from the Amazon MP3 Store on Your Tablet

For obvious reasons, Amazon, the maker of your Kindle Fire, encourages you to shop for and purchase your digital music from the Amazon MP3 Music Store. Thus, the process for doing that has been fully integrated into the Music app that comes preinstalled on your tablet. However, you have three other options for listening to music on your Kindle Fire.

First, you can stream music from other sources, such as Pandora Internet Radio. How to use this app, as well as access other streaming music sources, are discussed within Chapter 5 and Chapter 9.

Second, you can convert ("rip") your music CDs and transform them into MP3 files on your computer and then transfer those newly created digital music files to your tablet. Third, you can purchase and download music (via your computer) from other online music stores, such as Apple's iTunes Store, and then manually transfer those music purchases to your tablet.

Whether your pursue this second or third choice, once you have .mp3 music files stored on your PC or Mac's hard drive, you can transfer them to your tablet using the directions offered within the next section, as well as within Chapter 13.

Transfer Music Purchased from iTunes to Your Kindle Fire

If you purchase music from Apple's iTunes Store, or if you use Apple's iTunes software to "rip" your music CDs and transform them into digital music files, you can then transfer those files to your Kindle Fire manually. To do this, however, you'll need a Micro-B USB–to–USB cable in order to connect your tablet to your computer via their respective USB ports.

Once you purchase a song from iTunes, using the iTunes software on your computer, tap the Music option that's displayed under the Library heading of the software (near the upper-left corner of the iTunes screen). When all of the music from your iTunes music library is displayed in the main area of the iTunes screen, click the song you want to transfer to your tablet in order to highlight it.

With the song highlighted, select the Create MP3 Version command from the Advanced pull-down menu at the top of the screen. This will reconfigure the digital music file from the iTunes format into an industry-standard .mp3 format.

 If the music files stored on your computer are already in AAC format (which is Kindle Fire–compatible), there is no need to first convert the file into the MP3 format before transferring it to your tablet.

Next, determine where on your computer's hard drive iTunes stored that newly created .mp3 version of the song. You will need to manually access this folder to select the file and transfer it to your tablet. To find this location quickly, select the Preferences option from the iTunes pull-down menu. When the iTunes Preferences window appears, click the Advanced option. The location of the song file will be listed under the iTunes Media Folder location heading. Within whatever location is listed, a subfolder within the iTunes folder, labeled Music, will be available to you. Open the Music subfolder to find the Artist subfolder for the music you want to transfer. When you open the Artist subfolder, the .mp3 file will be listed.

 From within iTunes, you can also right-click a highlighted song listing and select the Show In Windows Explorer (PC) or Show In Finder (Mac) option to quickly locate and access the highlighted music file, which you can then drag-and-drop or copy to another folder, such as the Music folder within your Kindle Fire, if the tablet is connected to your computer via a Micro-B USB–to–USB cable. (On a Mac, hold down the CONTROL key on the keyboard while clicking the mouse to simulate a right-click.)

Next, connect your Kindle Fire to your primary computer via an optional Micro-B USB–to–USB cable. When the connection is made, drag the appropriate .mp3 music file from your computer to the Kindle's internal storage Music folder using the mouse. This is shown in Figure 12-17. How to do this is explained in Chapter 13.

 When you open the Kindle Fire folder on your PC or Mac's desktop, you will see 12 subfolders listed. Be sure to open the Music folder and transfer the .mp3 music files into this Music folder so that they'll be identified and become playable using the Music app.

Once the .mp3 music files have been manually transferred into the Music folder of your Kindle Fire's internal storage, launch the Music app, and from the Library screen, tap the Device tab. The music you just transferred will be displayed and become playable on your tablet.

 Once a music file is saved in .mp3 format, you can transfer it to your Kindle Fire, regardless of where that music was acquired from. Depending on the source of the music, the album/song cover art may or may not transfer with the song. If the artwork does not transfer, just the song title will be listed within the Music app of your Kindle.

FIGURE 12-17 Drag and drop .mp3 files from a folder within your computer's hard drive to the Kindle Fire's Music folder.

Did You Know?

You Can Make All of Your Music Available via Your Amazon Cloud Drive Account

An alternative way to transfer all of your music to your Kindle Fire, regardless of how or where it was acquired, is to pay for a premium Amazon Cloud Player account (starting at $20.00 per year). This allows you to copy all music stored on your computer to your Amazon Cloud Drive account, which is then accessible wirelessly by your Kindle Fire via the Internet.

Once music is stored within your Amazon Cloud Drive account, when you launch the Music app and tap the Cloud tab (with the Library screen displayed), the music will be listed. Thus, it can be streamed or downloaded to your tablet. Visit the Amazon MP3 Music Store from your PC or Mac to learn more about this premium service and sign up for it.

13

Transfer Data Between Your Kindle Fire and Computer

HOW TO...

- Transfer files and data via a USB cable connection
- Transfer files and data using your Send-To-Kindle e-mail address
- Transfer files from your Amazon Cloud Drive account to your Kindle Fire

Your Kindle Fire is equipped with 8GB of internal storage space, which is used to store apps, files, data, e-mails, documents, and content (music, TV shows, movies, audiobooks, third-party apps, eBooks, photos, etc.). To install new apps on your tablet, you'll purchase or acquire them from the Amazon App Store, which is covered in Chapter 14.

 When viewing the available internal storage space of your tablet, it will always be less than 8GB, based on data files, apps, app-related files, or content stored on the device. Even without adding your own content to the tablet, if you use any of the preinstalled apps, for example, some of this internal storage space will be utilized automatically.

Using the apps that come preinstalled or that you add to your Kindle Fire, you'll most likely create and need access to files, data, and documents that contain your personal information, whether it's a document or e-mail you compose, a database of your contacts, or a collection of your digital photos, for example. You'll also acquire content from other sources, such as Amazon.com, Amazon's MP3 Music Store, or Audible.com.

As a Kindle Fire user, you also have the ability to transfer your own files, data, documents, photos, and content from your computer or other devices to your tablet. This chapter focuses on the three primary ways you can transfer information to your Kindle Fire.

Transfer Files, Documents, and Data from Your Computer Using a USB Cable Connection

One way of transferring documents (such as Microsoft Office files or PDF files), music, photos, and videos from your computer to the Kindle Fire is to use an optional Micro-B USB–to–USB cable. This cable is used to directly connect your Kindle Fire to your PC or Mac computer, via their respective USB ports. The Internet is not required.

 Your Kindle Fire's USB port is really a Micro-B USB port. Thus, you'll need a USB cable with this sized connector on one end. When shopping for an appropriate cable, do not purchase one with a Micro-A USB connector, which is a slightly different size and shape. Even though it looks somewhat similar to a Micro-B USB connector, it will not fit into the Micro-B port of your Kindle Fire.

 If you purchase a Micro-B–to–USB cable from a retail store, it will cost anywhere from $19.99 to $29.99. However, if you shop online from a company like Cables To Go (www.cablestogo.com) or a third-party vendor that sells through Amazon.com or eBay.com, a similar cable will cost under $5.00.

Once you purchase the appropriate cable from Amazon.com, a local computer store, or a consumer electronics store such as Best Buy or Radio Shack, simply plug one end of the cable into the bottom Micro-B USB port of your Kindle Fire and the opposite end of the cable into a standard USB port within your computer (or a USB hub that's connected to your computer).

Your computer can be turned on when the cable is connected. However, it's better if the Kindle Fire is turned off or in Sleep mode when you connect the USB cable. When you turn on (or wake up) the tablet and unlock it, a connection between your computer and the Kindle Fire will automatically be established. The message, "You can now transfer files from your computer to Kindle" will be displayed on the tablet's screen (shown in Figure 13-1).

From your PC or Mac, open the Kindle Fire drive or volume on the computer's desktop. You will notice that from your computer's perspective, it considers the tablet to be just another storage device, such as an external hard drive or thumb drive. By double-clicking the Kindle drive on your computer's desktop (shown in Figure 13-2), you'll see a collection of folders, including folders labeled Documents, Music, Pictures, and Video, shown in Figure 13-3. It's within these folders that you can drag and drop your own documents, content, files, and data.

 Whenever your Kindle Fire is connected to your computer, you cannot use the tablet. From your computer, you can copy files to or from it, however. To regain control over your tablet, tap the Disconnect icon that's displayed near the bottom-center area of its screen. This will sever the Kindle-to-computer connection.

FIGURE 13-1   When your Kindle Fire is connected to your primary computer via an optional Micro-B–to–USB cable, this is what appears on the tablet's screen.

FIGURE 13-2   Once a connection between your tablet and computer is established, the Kindle drive will be displayed on your computer's desktop.

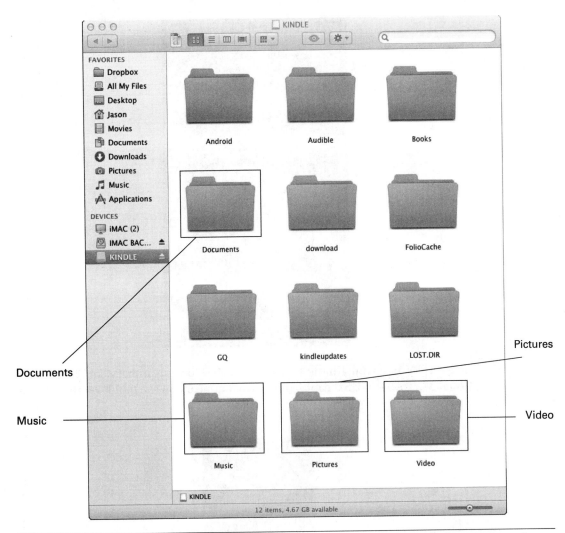

FIGURE 13-3 Double-click the Kindle drive icon on your computer's desktop to reveal a handful of folders.

On your computer's desktop, also open the folder that contains the documents, files, photos, music, or video clips you want to transfer to your tablet. You will now have two windows open on your desktop (shown in Figure 13-4): one displaying content from your computer, and the other representing the internal storage of your Kindle Fire.

Using the computer's mouse, drag and drop the document(s), file(s), music/.mp3 file(s), picture(s), or video clip(s) between these two folders. It's important that you place the transferred content into the appropriate folder(s) on your Kindle Fire so that the tablet will properly identify and be able to access what has been transferred. For example, Microsoft Office text-based documents and PDF files should be placed within the Documents folder on your Kindle Fire. Likewise, digital music (.mp3) files should be placed within the Music folder, digital pictures should be transferred to the Pictures folder, and videos should be copied to the Video folder.

 You can also use this file transfer method to drag-and-drop files from your Kindle Fire's internal storage to your primary computer. Simply drag-and-drop the files in the opposite direction, going from the Kindle subfolder to the appropriate location on your computer's hard drive or external data storage device.

Once the files are transferred into the appropriate folder within your Kindle Fire, tap the Disconnect icon that's displayed on the tablet's screen to sever the connection with your computer. You can then safely disconnect the USB cable and regain full control over your tablet.

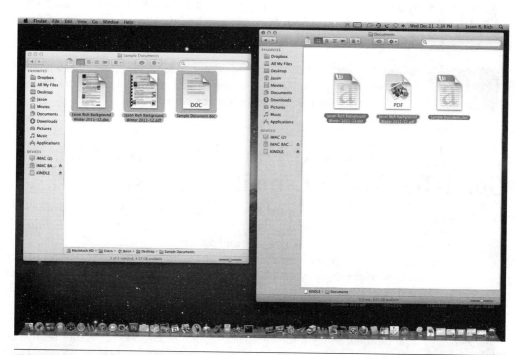

FIGURE 13-4 The Kindle folder on your computer's desktop (shown on the right) and the folder on your computer that contains the content you want to transfer (shown on the left) should both be displayed.

Keep in mind, the files, content, data, or documents you transfer to your tablet's internal storage space will use up some of the device's 8GB of internal storage, and this content will not automatically be copied to your Amazon Cloud Drive account. The data you just transferred into your tablet will need to be accessed by the appropriate app(s) for you to utilize it. For example:

- To open a Microsoft Office file stored within the tablet's Documents folder, use the Quickoffice, Quickoffice Pro, or OfficeSuite Pro app. You can also use the Docs app that comes preinstalled on your tablet and that is accessible from the Home screen's Navigation bar.
- To open a PDF file, you'll need to use the free Adobe PDF Reader app, Quickoffice Pro, OfficeSuite Pro, or another third-party app that's compatible with PDF files. You can also use the Docs app that comes preinstalled on your tablet and that is accessible from the Home screen's Navigation bar.
- To play digital music (.mp3) files, use the Music app or another compatible third-party app.
- To view digital photos, use the Gallery app or another compatible photo viewing/editing app.
- To view video clips, use the Video app or another compatible app.

 By using other third-party apps, your Kindle Fire will become compatible with other types of documents, files, content, and data that you can transfer from your computer to your tablet using this drag-and-drop method.

 To avoid corrupting data on your computer or Kindle Fire, be sure to properly sever the connection by tapping the Disconnect icon on the tablet before detaching the USB cable after the transfer process is completed.

Transfer Files and Data Using Your Send-To-Kindle E-mail Address

When you first set up your Kindle Fire and registered it with Amazon.com, a free Send-To-Kindle e-mail address is set up for you. This is a private e-mail address used by you (and people you authorize) to send documents, pictures, files, data, and other attachments to your tablet wirelessly from any other computer or device using e-mail.

You need to configure your personal Send-To-Kindle e-mail address in order to start using it. Begin by visiting www.Amazon.com/myk. Access the Personal Document Settings option, which is among the Manage Your Kindle options.

 Your personal Send-To-Kindle e-mail address is not used to send or receive e-mail messages via the Email app. It is only used to send your tablet documents, files, or content as attachments via e-mail.

Your Send-To-Kindle E-mail Address Includes Online Storage Space

Your Send-To-Kindle e-mail address includes 5GB of online storage space, which will store incoming e-mails (and their related attachments) until they're retrieved and downloaded by your Kindle Fire. How much of this storage space you're currently utilizing is displayed on the Personal Document Settings screen of Amazon.com.

To prevent just anyone from sending files to your Kindle Fire (and helping to ensure you don't receive spam), from the Amazon.com website, you'll need to set up in advance what e-mail addresses are permitted to send your tablet e-mails that are addressed to your Send-To-Kindle e-mail address (this is in the format username@ Kindle.com). This is done by adding specific e-mail addresses to the Approved Personal Document Email List that's found near the bottom of the Personal Document Settings page on the Amazon.com website.

To edit the Approved Personal Document Email List, visit www.Amazon.com and select the Manage Your Kindle option from the Kindle menu under the Shop All Departments heading on the left side of the screen. You will be required to sign in to your Amazon.com account, if you have not already done so.

Next, from the Manage Your Kindle menu, select the Personal Document Settings option that's displayed on the left side of the screen. This option is listed below the Your Kindle Account heading. Then, from the Personal Document Settings screen (shown in Figure 13-5), click (or tap) the Add A New Approved Email Address option, and enter the appropriate e-mail addresses, one at a time. You can do this from your computer's web browser or using the Amazon Silk web browser on your tablet that's connected to the Internet.

For example, you can set up your Send-To-Kindle e-mail address to only accept e-mails from your primary personal and work-related e-mail accounts. However, you can also allow your work colleagues, friends, or specific family members to send you

You Can Use Your Send-To-Kindle E-mail Address to Send Files to Your Tablet

If you have not already set up your unique Send-To-Kindle e-mail address, you can do this as well, for free, from the Personal Document Settings screen of the Amazon.com website.

Once an e-mail address is listed under the Approved Personal Document Email List heading on the Personal Document Settings page, you can later delete it by clicking the Delete option that's displayed to the right of the e-mail address' listing. This will revoke that e-mail account's ability to directly send your tablet e-mail attachments using the Send-To-Kindle e-mail service.

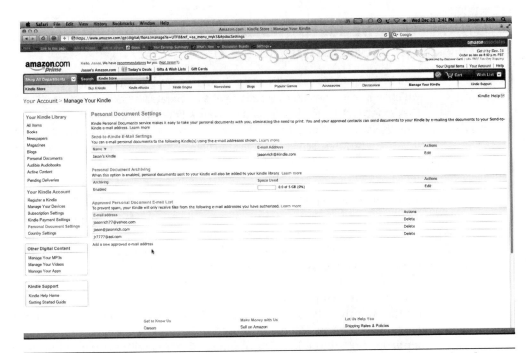

FIGURE 13-5 Customize the Send-To-Kindle e-mail address options so they best meet your needs.

Kindle Fire e-mail attachments addressed to your Send-To-Kindle e-mail address by adding their addresses to the Approved Personal Document Email List.

Tip For the Send-To-Kindle e-mail address to work, you must have preapproved the sender's e-mail address and given the sender your personal Send-To-Kindle e-mail address, and the incoming e-mail attachment must be a supported file type, which will vary, based on which apps you have installed on your tablet.

Once you have set everything up from the Amazon.com website, you can send e-mails containing file attachments to your personal Send-To-Kindle e-mail address (username@kindle.com). When addressing e-mails to this e-mail address, adding a subject to the outgoing e-mail is not necessary. The file attachment within the e-mail cannot be larger than 5GB, and it can be sent from any computer or device, as long as it originates from a preapproved e-mail address.

Currently, the Send-To-Kindle e-mail service is free for Kindle Fire owners. It is compatible with the following file types:

- .bmp
- .gif
- .html or .htm
- .jpeg or .jpg
- Kindle Format (.mobi, .azw)

- Microsoft Word (.doc, .docx)
- .pdf
- .png
- .rtf

Remove Newly Added Content from the Home Screen's Carousel

If you're using the latest version of the Kindle operating system (version 6.2.1 or later), when new content automatically appears on your Home screen's Carousel that was downloaded from your Send-To-Kindle e-mail account, you can add it to the Favorites section of the Home screen, remove that attachment from the Carousel (it will still be accessible from compatible apps), or delete it from your tablet altogether. To do any of these tasks, hold your finger on the document or content's thumbnail for one or two seconds. Then, tap the Add To Favorites, Remove From Carousel, or Remove From Device pop-up menu option that appears.

After an e-mail containing a compatible file or document is sent to your Send-To-Kindle e-mail address, assuming your tablet is connected to the Internet, it will automatically be downloaded to your tablet and become accessible within five minutes or less. For example, if the incoming e-mail contains a document or PDF file, that attachment will appear in your Kindle's Documents folder, as well as on the home page's Carousel, and can be accessed with compatible apps.

A document or PDF file that's sent to your tablet can be opened using the Docs app that comes preinstalled on your Kindle Fire, or you can use another third-party app for this purpose, such as Quickoffice or OfficeSuite Pro.

 To learn more about how to use this Send-To-Kindle e-mail service and the types of files it's compatible with, visit www.amazon.com/kindlepersonaldocuments.

Transfer Files from Your Amazon Cloud Drive Account to Your Kindle Fire

Your Amazon Cloud Drive account is designed to make it easy for you to wirelessly transfer Amazon-purchased content (eBooks, digital publications, TV shows, movies, music, apps, audiobooks, etc.) to your Kindle Fire via the Internet. This is done using Amazon's Whispernet service.

Whenever you make a content purchase or acquire free content from Amazon.com or one of its subsidiaries, that content is automatically stored within your personal Amazon Cloud Drive account. Then, using the appropriate app on your tablet, you can access the account (via the Internet) and download it to your tablet. For example, when you access the Newsstand, Books, Music, Apps, or Video apps from the Navigation bar on your tablet's Home screen, a Cloud command tab is available from within those (and other) apps that allows you to view and access content stored within your

Amazon Cloud Drive account. How to use this feature is explained within the chapters of this book that cover these preinstalled apps.

 From the Settings menu within each appropriate app, you can make it so all newly purchased or acquired content automatically gets downloaded from your Amazon Cloud Drive account to your tablet, whether that content was purchased using your Kindle Fire, your primary computer, a smartphone, or another device that's also linked to your Amazon.com account.

Transfer and Sync App-Specific Data

Depending on what you're using your Kindle Fire for, you may have a personal database of contacts, your schedule, or other information that is created and/ or managed using a specific Kindle Fire app. In some cases, you may be able to synchronize this personal data with your primary computer, smartphone, or other mobile device. This is functionality that's made possible via the third-party apps you're using.

You can set up your tablet to automatically synchronize your eBooks, digital publications, music, TV show episodes, movies, audiobooks, and other content purchased through Amazon.com. By doing this, if you purchase a new song on your smartphone or computer, for example, it will almost immediately also become available on your Kindle Fire. The ability to auto-synchronize Amazon.com-purchased content is set up through the Settings menu of specific apps used for acquiring and accessing this content, such as Newsstand, Books, Music, Audible, and Video.

If you opt to manage your personal schedule using a calendar or scheduling app on your computer, and you want to access that schedule on your Kindle Fire, a third-party app will be required, as will access to the Internet for keeping the scheduling information synced. You'll learn more about third-party apps for scheduling, contact management, and other tasks that may allow you to sync data with your computer or other devices later in this book.

 If you use Microsoft Exchange to manage your corporate e-mail, contacts, calendar, tasks, and notes, you can use the Exchange By TouchDown Key app ($9.99) to synchronize data between your computer(s) and your Kindle Fire. Likewise, if you use the popular Evernote software on your computer, you can synchronize Evernote data with your Kindle Fire using the Evernote app (free).

14

Find and Download Apps to Your Kindle Fire

HOW TO...

- Distinguish between apps based on their pricing structure
- Find, purchase, and download apps from Amazon's App Store

Thus far in this book, much of the focus has been on what the Kindle Fire can do right out of the box, thanks to the apps that come preinstalled on the tablet. However, everything that you've read about so far is just the beginning. Because the Kindle Fire operating system is really an Android-based operating system, a growing number of third-party app developers have created apps capable of dramatically expanding the capabilities of your tablet.

Unlike other Android-based tablets, your Kindle Fire uses a proprietary version of the Android operating system created by Amazon. As a result, the tablet easily allows you to acquire apps from the Amazon App Store, which offers a smaller selection of apps than the Android Market (https://market.android.com/apps), which is the store that offers apps to a wide range of other Android-based tablets and smartphones.

 Apps available from the Amazon App Store have been preapproved and selected by Amazon to be offered to Kindle Fire users. In other words, Amazon determines which Android-based apps you can (or can't) install on your tablet.

There are two ways to access the Amazon App Store in order to purchase apps or acquire free ones for your Kindle Fire. Using your computer's web browser, visit www .Amazon.com. On the left side of the main page of the Amazon.com website, click the Appstore for Android option, which is listed under the Shop All Departments heading. You can also shop for apps online directly from your Kindle Fire.

How to... **Set up an Amazon Account with the 1-Click Buying Feature Activated**

Before you can begin shopping for apps for your Kindle Fire, it's necessary to set up an Amazon.com account and turn on the 1-Click payment method. To create an account, if you have not already done so, visit www.Amazon .com/sign-in, enter your e-mail address, and then select the No, I Am A New Customer option. Follow the on-screen prompts to establish your account.

You will be required to supply a valid credit or debit card number so you can make online purchases on Amazon.com using your tablet, computer, smartphone, or other device. This includes buying and downloading content (music, TV shows, movies, eBooks, audiobooks, apps, and digital publications) for your Kindle Fire.

To set up the 1-Click payment option after your Amazon.com account is established, select the Manage Addresses And 1-Click Settings option, which is listed under the Kindle Payment Settings heading. Be sure this feature is turned on. As its name suggests, the 1-Click option allows you to make online purchases with one tap on the tablet's screen or one click of the mouse on the computer's screen. The credit or debit card you associate with your account will automatically be charged for your online purchases.

 Tip One advantage to shopping for apps using your computer is that you can preview many apps right on your computer screen before purchasing or acquiring them for your tablet. To do this, tap the Test Drive Now icon when looking at an app's Description screen.

When you purchase or acquire a free app from the Amazon App Store via your computer, after clicking the Get Now With 1-Click icon, that app will be sent automatically to your Amazon Cloud Drive account in seconds, and can then be accessed and downloaded directly from your tablet.

What You Should Know About Third-Party Apps

Apps are like optional software programs for your computer. They need to be purchased or acquired, downloaded, and then installed on your tablet. Many third-party developers currently are creating apps for the Kindle Fire. These apps can be purchased or acquired directly from the Amazon App Store.

Some third-party apps are offered for free. Others you'll need to pay for. To fully utilize some apps, additional in-app purchases may be required. Typically, a free app serves as a demo version for a paid app and offers limited functionality. A free app, however, can be a full-featured app, but include in-app advertising that you need to view as you're using it. Or a free app can, in fact, be free, but then may charge you for premium content or in-app purchases as you use it.

A paid app will cost anywhere from $0.99 to $9.99 (or more). Once you purchase an app, you own it, and unlimited updates for that version of the app are included in the price. However, in-app purchases for premium content or extra features may still be necessary.

Any time you purchase an app or acquire a free app from the Amazon App Store, it is saved automatically within your Amazon Cloud Drive account. If you purchase an app directly from your Kindle Fire, it also downloads and installs on your tablet automatically.

Note The only limit to the number of apps you can install and use on your Kindle Fire is the 8GB of internal storage space your tablet has built in. This internal storage is used to store your apps, content, data, and files.

As you're about to discover, the third-party apps available for the Kindle Fire are optional, but they can be used to dramatically expand the capabilities and functionality of your tablet. Keep in mind that some apps require a constant Internet connection to function properly. Also, the library of apps available for the Kindle Fire is expanding daily. Chapter 15 offers an overview of some popular apps you may be interested in.

Tip Download a free demo version of an app (if available) to test it out before purchasing the premium paid version of that app.

Did You Know?

Many Apps May Offer Similar Functionality

When you begin browsing the Amazon App Store, you'll discover many apps from different developers may serve the same or very similar purposes. The trick is to select the app that will offer the features and functionality you want or need. When choosing which app to purchase, don't just look at the price and assume that the highest-priced app is the best.

Also pay careful attention to the app's description, its list of features and functions, its average user rating and user reviews, and the sample screen shots provided as part of the app's description. If two or more apps seem similar, focus on specific features and functions, discover what makes each of them different, and try to determine which offers the most intuitive user interface.

While the app's description is written by the app's developer, and is designed as a sales and marketing tool, the ratings and reviews associated with each app are created by your fellow Kindle Fire users. Thus, if an app contains bugs, is poorly designed, or does not offer the features and functions that are advertised, you can often quickly determine this from the user ratings and reviews. For example, if an app has a dozen or more one- or two-star ratings and just a few or no four- and five-star ratings, there's probably a good reason for this.

Acquiring Apps from the Amazon App Store Using Your Kindle Fire

To begin browsing for apps to purchase or acquire for free using your Kindle Fire, first make sure it's connected to the Internet. Then, from the Home screen, tap the Apps option, which is displayed on the right side of the Navigation bar. The Apps app will launch, and its Library screen will display the collection of third-party apps that are currently installed on your tablet (shown in Figure 14-1) or that are available for download from your Kindle Fire Cloud Drive account.

Displayed in the upper-right corner of the Library screen is the Store option. Tap this to access the online-based Amazon App Store in order to shop for new apps. At the very top of the Amazon App Store screen, shown in Figure 14-2, you'll discover the blank Search In Appstore field. Tap this to quickly locate and acquire an app by entering its name or any keyword associated with the type of app you're looking for.

For example, if you're looking for an app to manage your schedule, enter the keywords **time management**, **schedule**, or **schedule planner** into the Search field, and then tap the Search key on the virtual keyboard. A listing of related apps will be displayed.

FIGURE 14-1 Acquired apps can be accessed from the Library screen. Tap the Device tab to view installed apps.

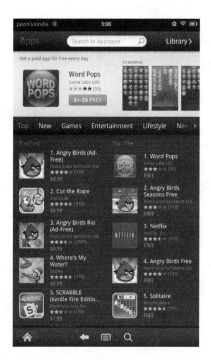

FIGURE 14-2 The main Amazon App Store screen

 To return to the Library screen of the Apps app, tap the Library option, which is displayed in the upper-right corner of the Amazon App Store screen.

Every day, Amazon offers a different app (normally a paid app) for free. This free app is showcased just below the Search field on the main Amazon App Store screen. To view a more detailed description of the featured app, tap its icon or title. To immediately download and install the free app, tap the orange price icon, which will display the word Free.

Just below the Free App Of The Day listing is a horizontal scrolling list of app categories. Use your finger to scroll through the list horizontally and view all of the options. App categories include:

- **Top** View a listing of the 100 bestselling paid and 100 most popular free apps currently available for the Kindle Fire. This listing is displayed in order based on popularity. On the left, you'll see the list of paid apps. On the right is the list of the most popular free apps. These listings are composed of apps from all categories.
- **New** See a listing of the newest apps to be made available from the Amazon App Store. This listing constantly changes, and includes both free and paid apps from all categories.

- **Games** One of the most popular uses of the Kindle Fire is to play games. You'll discover one-player games, multiplayer games, and games you can experience safely with total strangers via the Web. When you tap the Games option, by default, a comprehensive listing of games is displayed.

  To narrow down your options, tap one of the Games subcategories that are displayed along the top of the Games screen, shown in Figure 14-3. These include All, Top, Action, Adventure, Arcade, Board, Cards, Casino, Casual, Educational, Kids, Multiplayer, Music, Puzzles & Trivia, Racing, Role Playing, Sports, Strategy, and Recommended For You.

  You can further narrow down your game options by tapping the Refine icon that's displayed on the right side of the screen, just below the Games subcategory headings. This allows you to sort the games by their relevance, release date, average customer rating, and/or price.

- **Entertainment** Aside from games, there are other apps you can use to entertain yourself using your Kindle Fire. These apps are showcased when you tap the Entertainment option. Once again, after tapping the Entertainment heading, near the top of the screen, you'll see a selection of subcategories, and also a Refine command icon to help you narrow down your search.

Games subcategories —

FIGURE 14-3 A game can fit into one or more game subcategories.

- **Lifestyle**   After tapping the Lifestyle option, displayed at the top of the screen are subcategory headings, including Top, Home & Garden, Self-Improvement, Astrology, Relationships, Hair & Beauty, Celebrity, Quizzes & Games, Advice, Parenting, and Recommended For You.

After you tap any app category heading, one of the subcategories that's always offered is Recommended For You. Based on your past app purchases and searches, the Amazon App Store will recommend apps you may be interested in that fall into the selected category.

- **News & Weather**   Stay up to date on the latest news and weather forecast using specific apps offered by news organizations, news publications, and other sources. Subcategories you can search include Top, World, U.S., Newspapers, Business, Politics, Entertainment, Sports, Science & Tech, Health, Weather, and Recommended For You.
- **Utilities**   There are a wide range of free and low-cost apps that add specific features or functions related to the operation of your Kindle Fire. For example, there are apps to help you find Wi-Fi hotspots, take notes, and manage your apps; apps that serve as an alarm clock; and apps that can be used to manage your tablet's battery life. You'll find these apps listed in the Utilities category. Subcategories include Top, Battery Savers, Alarms & Clocks, Calculators, Calendars, Notes, and Recommended For You.

Displayed just below the subcategory headings within the Amazon App Store is a Refine icon. Use it to further narrow down your search parameters within an app category by sorting apps according to their relevance, release date, average customer rating, and/or price.

- **Social Networking**   If you're active on Facebook, Twitter, LinkedIn, Google+, Tumblr, or one of the other popular online social networking services, in addition to using the Amazon Silk web browser to visit their respective websites and participate in these online communities, you can download and install specific apps to help you utilize the major features of specific online social networking services.
- **All Categories**   In addition to the major app categories, the Amazon App Store allows you to explore third-party app offerings that fit into a wide range of other categories, such as Books & Comics, City Info, Communication, Cooking, Education, Finance, Health & Fitness, Kids, Magazines, Navigation, Novelty, Photography, Podcasts, Productivity, Real Estate, Reference, Shopping, Themes, and Travel. Tap the All Categories option, and then choose one of the listed subcategories to view relevant apps.
- **Recommended For You**   Based on your past app purchases and searches, the Amazon App Store will recommend specific apps you may be interested in. By tapping this main Recommended For You category, a listing of recommended apps from all categories will be displayed.

As you're browsing the Amazon App Store, tap the Back icon that's displayed near the bottom-center area of the screen to return to the previous screen without making a purchase. You can also tap the Library icon to exit the App Store and return to the Library screen so you can use any of the apps you've already purchased. Or tap the Home icon to exit out of the App Store and return to the Kindle Fire's Home screen.

Discover More About an App from Its Description Page

By tapping any of the main headings displayed near the top of the Amazon App Store screen, you'll see a listing of individual apps from third-party developers. Each listing contains an app icon, its title, its sales ranking (if applicable), the developer's name, its average star-based rating, how many individual ratings the average rating is based upon, and the app's price (shown in Figure 14-4). The app's price is displayed within an orange Price icon. If the app is free, the word "Free" will be displayed within the Price icon.

 Tap any app's listing to view a detailed Description page related to that specific app.

Learn More About an App from Its Product Info

To view a detailed Description screen for a specific app, tap its app icon or listing. At the top of the app's Description screen (shown in Figure 14-5), you'll again see the app's icon, title, developer, star-based rating, and the number of individual ratings the average rating is based upon. However, you'll also discover the three command icons near the top of the screen, including a Price, Save, and Share icon.

Tap the orange Price icon to purchase and download the app. If the app is free, tap the Free icon to download it. By tapping the Save icon, you can add it to a custom list of apps you're interested in but don't want to purchase at the moment.

Your Saved For Later list can be viewed at any time while visiting the Amazon App Store. This makes it easier to later quickly locate a specific app you've already

FIGURE 14-4 A sample app listing from the Amazon App Store displays basic details about an app.

FIGURE 14-5 This is a typical Description screen for a third-party app that's featured within the Amazon App Store.

discovered. The Share icon is used to e-mail information about an app to someone else. When prompted, input their e-mail address into the Compose Message field that appears.

Displayed below the app icon, as well as the Price, Saved, and Share icons, are tabs labeled Product Info, Photos, Reviews, and Recommendations. Tap the Product Info tab (which is displayed by default) to view text-based information relating to the featured app.

Before purchasing an app, you can learn more about it by reading the detailed, text-based description that's included under the Description heading. Part of this description is an Applications Permissions section, which includes a bulleted list of information you may need that pertains to the app in terms of how it will function on your tablet. For example, this section will inform you if the app requires Internet access or access to information from other apps, such as your personal contacts database, to function.

Continue scrolling downward on an app's Description page to view its product details. Here you'll discover the current version number of the app, its ASIN number, and its original release date, along with its developer and file size. A brief description of the app developer is also featured. An app's ASIN number is a unique identifier, similar to a physical product's UPC barcode, that makes it easy to identify by inventory control systems, for example.

Preview Screen Shots That Showcase the App in Action

Tap the Photos heading to view screen shots from the app that have been supplied by the app's developer. Looking at these screen shots will give you a preview of the app's user interface and the quality of the graphics the app offers, among other things. You'll be able to see the actual look and layout of the app from the sample screen shots.

 In some cases, the app developer includes a demonstration movie related to the app. This can be accessed by tapping the Photos heading within an app's Description page. You can also tap individual screen shot thumbnails to view each image in full-screen mode.

Read an App's Reviews

There are two ways Kindle Fire users can provide public feedback about an app. You can add a star-based rating and review the app. A rating can be between one and five stars (with five stars being the highest rating possible). Or, you can write your own text-based review for other Kindle users to read before they purchase or acquire the app.

To see the star-based ratings and read the reviews from other Kindle Fire users that relate to a specific app, tap the Reviews option that's displayed near the top of the app's Description page (shown in Figure 14-6). At the top of the Reviews page, you'll see a chart that shows how many one-, two-, three-, four-, and five-star ratings an app has received, as well as its average star-based rating.

 After you've downloaded and installed the app, you can return to this part of the Description screen, tap the Create Your Own Review icon, and write your own review of the app.

Displayed below the star-based ratings are individual text-based reviews written by your fellow Kindle Fire users. Reading these reviews will help you quickly identify the best and worst aspects of an app. As you're reading an app's description, if you like what you see and want to discover what other apps your fellow Kindle Fire users have also purchased that relate to the app you're reading about, tap the Recommendations heading. A listing of similar or related apps will be displayed, along with the heading Customers Who Viewed This App Ultimately Bought.

Making an App Purchase

To purchase, download, and ultimately install an app on your Kindle Fire, tap its Price icon. The orange Price icon will transform into a green Buy App icon. Tap it to confirm your purchase decision. A "Purchasing..." message, followed by a "Downloading..." message will appear on the screen. The credit card or debit card you have associated with your Amazon.com account will be charged immediately for the purchase.

FIGURE 14-6 You and your fellow Kindle users can rate and/or review any third-party app and publically share this information via the Amazon App Store.

Tip If you have an Amazon gift card or promotional code, this can be used to pay for the app, and your credit card or debit card will not be charged. To use an Amazon gift card or promotional code, tap the Menu icon that's displayed at the bottom of the screen, and then select the Settings menu. Choose the Gift Cards option from the Settings menu.

Depending on the app's file size and the speed of your Internet connection, it will take between a few seconds and several minutes to download an app from the Amazon App Store to your Kindle Fire. When the file has been downloaded, the "Downloading..." message will be replaced by an "Installing..." message, followed by an Open icon.

When the Open icon appears, you can tap it to immediately launch the app and begin using it. Or, you can keep shopping within the Amazon App Store, knowing that the app is installed on your tablet and will be accessible from the Library screen when you tap the Apps option from the Kindle Fire's Home screen.

Note If an app is free, upon tapping the Free icon, a green Get App icon will appear, allowing you to confirm your decision. The app will then download and be installed on your tablet, but you will not be charged for it.

FIGURE 14-7 Depending on where you are within the Amazon App Store, some of these options may not be listed.

Access the Amazon App Store's Menu

As you're exploring the App Store, tap the Menu icon that's displayed near the bottom-center area of the screen to access six additional command icons, labeled Categories, Recommended, My Subscriptions, My Apps, Settings, and More, shown in Figure 14-7.

The following is a brief description of what each command icon, which is accessible from the Menu command icon, is used for:

- **Categories**   Quickly access a master list of more than 28 app categories and see the apps that fit into that category.
- **Recommended**   See a listing of apps that the Amazon App Store recommends for you, based on your past purchases and searches.
- **My Subscriptions**   Manage your app-based subscriptions. If you subscribe to a digital magazine that has its own proprietary app, you can manage your auto-renewing subscription using this option, for example.

 How to... **Update Your Apps**

To determine if all of your apps are up to date, or if newer versions of any apps have been released by their respective developers, while visiting the Amazon App Store, tap the Menu icon, and then tap the My Apps option. Near the top of the screen, tap the Update Available heading. Any apps that require updating will be listed. Next, tap the Update icon for each app, as needed, to download and install the free update. It's a good idea to check for new app updates at least once every week or two, in order to ensure you're using the most current versions of your most frequently used apps.

Having the latest version of all apps installed on your tablet ensures that you have access to all of the latest features and functions of each app. Plus, as bugs or problems with apps are discovered, they're often addressed and fixed in updates. In addition, as the Kindle Fire operating system is updated by Amazon, the third-party app developers may release updates to ensure compatibility. It's a good idea to check for app updates at least twice per month.

- **My Apps**   View a list of apps that are stored within your Amazon Cloud Drive account that you own but that have not yet been downloaded and installed on your tablet. Tap the Install icon associated with an app listing to install it.
- **Settings**   Redeem an Amazon gift card, access parental controls related to the Amazon App Store, and control your in-app purchasing capabilities from the options available on this Settings menu.
- **More**   Access your personalized Saved For Later list of apps, see a listing of apps you've recently viewed within the Amazon App Store, contact Amazon Customer Service, leave feedback for Amazon.com, access online-based help related to the Amazon App Store, or view legal information pertaining to the App Store by tapping one of the options displayed after tapping the More command icon.

Access, Use, or Delete Your Third-Party Apps

Once you've acquired one or more third-party apps, you can begin using it (or any other app that's installed on your Kindle Fire) by returning to the Library screen of the Apps app. To do this, from within the Amazon App Store, tap the Library option that's displayed in the upper-right corner of the screen. Or from the tablet's Home screen, tap the App option that's displayed on the Navigation bar.

 The Library screen displays icons representing apps that you own and/or that can be used on your tablet right away. Tap an app icon to launch it and begin using it, if it's currently installed on your Kindle Fire.

At the top-center area of the Library screen, you'll see the now-familiar Cloud and Device tabs. Tap the Cloud tab to see a listing of apps stored within your Amazon Cloud Drive account. Apps that have a downward-pointing arrow displayed in the lower-right corner of the app icon (shown in Figure 14-8) indicate that the app has not yet been downloaded to your tablet, but that it's an app you own. Tap the Device tab to view a listing of apps that are currently installed on your tablet and that are available to use right away.

 Below the Cloud and Device tabs are tabs labeled By Recent or By Title. This determines the order in which the apps are displayed on the screen.

Another way to quickly access your favorite apps is from the Home screen's Carousel. After you've used an app, its icon will temporarily be displayed within the Carousel. Tap the app icon of your choice to relaunch that app.

Or, as you're looking at an app icon, either on the Carousel or on the Library screen of the Apps app, hold your finger on the icon for between one and three seconds. When the Add To Favorites option appears, tap it to add the app icon to the Favorites area of your Kindle Fire's Home screen, where it will remain prominently displayed until you manually remove it. You'll save time by adding your most frequently used apps to the Favorites area of the Home screen.

Downward-pointing arrows indicate apps that haven't been downloaded yet.

FIGURE 14-8 Identify apps that are stored within your Amazon Cloud Drive account but that are not downloaded to your tablet by a downward-pointing arrow on the app icon.

 How to... Delete Apps from Your Kindle Fire

To delete an app from your Kindle Fire, return to the tablet's Home screen and tap the gear-shaped icon. Next, tap the More icon. About halfway down on the Settings screen, tap the Applications option. Tap the Filter By pull-down menu, and choose the Third-Party Applications option. A listing of apps will be displayed.

Tap any of the apps listed. When the Information screen for that app is displayed, near the top of the screen you'll see an Uninstall icon. Tap it to remove (delete) the app from your tablet. Tap the OK icon that appears within a pop-up window to confirm your decision. You can always reinstall the app, for free, from your Amazon Cloud Drive account. Apps that came preinstalled on your tablet cannot be deleted.

You can also delete an app as you're viewing the Library screen. To do this, hold your finger on the icon for the app you want to delete. Then, tap the Remove From Device option when it appears. Tap the OK icon to confirm your decision.

15

Explore a Sampling of Apps for Your Kindle Fire

HOW TO...

- Discover 24 popular apps for the Kindle Fire that are available from the Amazon App Store
- Learn where else you can shop for apps, besides the Amazon App Store

In the previous chapter, you discovered how to utilize the Amazon App Store to find, purchase (if applicable), download, and install Kindle Fire apps. When you begin exploring the Amazon App Store, you'll discover several thousand third-party free and paid apps, plus new ones being added almost every day.

This chapter offers a brief introduction to 24 popular apps that will help you get started using optional apps on your tablet to handle a variety of additional tasks.

Some Kindle Fire Apps Are Not Sold from Amazon's App Store

Google's Android Market (https://market.android.com) is another online-based app store that offers Android-based apps that are compatible with a wide range of tablets and smartphones, including (in some cases) the Kindle Fire. While you can explore this app store from any web browser, Amazon currently prevents Kindle Fire users from easily downloading apps from it. To get around Amazon's blocks, you can first "root" your tablet, which is a polite term for hacking into it. You'll find step-by-step directions for how to do this on the Web. (For example, see the Tabletorials.com website at http://tabletorials .com/2011/12/how-to-install-the-full-android-market-on-your-kindle-fire/.)

(Continued)

Easier accessibility to the Amazon Market could be made available in the future. From some other third-party app sources, you can download and install individual apps by adjusting your tablet's settings to accept them. To do this, from the Home screen, tap the gear-shaped icon that's displayed in the upper-right corner of the screen, and then tap the More option. From the Settings menu, tap the Device option. Make sure the virtual on/off switch that's associated with the Allow Installation Of Applications option is turned on.

Discover 24 Popular Third-Party Apps for Your Kindle Fire

Listed here, in alphabetical order, are 24 popular apps for the Kindle Fire. In some cases, both a free and more feature-packed paid version of each app is currently available from the Amazon App Store.

To discover the very latest apps that have been released and made available from the Amazon App Store, select Apps from the Home screen's Navigation bar, and then tap the Store option, followed by the New category heading.

Adobe Reader (Free)

Created by Adobe, the company that actually developed the PDF file format, this is one of several PDF file readers available for the Kindle Fire. This app allows you to open, view, and navigate your way around PDF files you receive via e-mail from other people using your Send-To-Kindle e-mail account or that you manually transfer to your tablet from another computer or device.

You cannot edit or annotate PDF files using the Adobe Reader app. To do this, check out the free Skitch app, which also can be used to add text, arrows, and diagrams to photos.

The Adobe Reader app offers a bit more functionality than does the Docs app that comes preinstalled on the Kindle Fire, as well as a free alternative to the premium Quickoffice Pro or OfficeSuite Pro apps that, among other things, can be used for this purpose.

As you're viewing a document, you can zoom in or out. You can also view a multipage document as a continuous (vertically scrolling) document or as single pages. The problem with any PDF reader app for the Kindle Fire is that if the document contains many pages, is a large file, and/or is graphic intensive, the app may become unstable due to the internal memory limitations of the tablet. For viewing PDF files containing mainly text, however, you should experience no problems.

American Airlines (Free)

There are a growing number of travel-related apps available for the Kindle Fire. Some allow you to access popular travel-related websites that can help you book and manage your airline, hotel, and car reservations, plus save you money in the process. Others allow you to access ratings and reviews for hotels, tourist attractions, and restaurants, or serve as an interactive travel guide for a destination. The American Airlines app allows you to make and manage American Airlines reservations, create a mobile boarding pass, track flights, and manage your frequent flier account.

Angry Birds HD (Kindle Fire Edition) ($4.99)

One of the all-time most popular game series available for any smartphone or tablet is Angry Birds. While a free edition of the original Angry Birds game is available from the Amazon App Store, the premium Angry Birds HD edition (shown in Figure 15-1) offers 288 challenging and advertising-free levels that are suitable for anyone over the age of six.

Angry Birds has become a worldwide phenomenon because it's very easy to learn how to play, but as you progress through the levels, each becomes increasingly more challenging. Plus, the game has some addictive elements to it. If you have five minutes or less to take a quick game-play break, you can challenge yourself with Angry Birds. Or you can just as easily spend hours at a time trying to master this game, one level at a time, which requires skill, logic, strategy, and perfect timing.

FIGURE 15-1   Angry Birds HD features more than 288 challenging levels.

The concept behind the game is simple. On one side of the screen is a slingshot from which you catapult the different species of Angry Birds toward the target that's on the opposite end of the screen. Each Angry Bird species can be used as a different type of projectile weapon.

Your targets are a series of structures and fortified castles built by the Angry Birds' enemies—the green pigs (shown in Figure 15-2). In each level, you'll need to smash through virtual boards, stones, walls, crates, ice barriers, and other obstacles in order to ultimately crush the pigs.

The game's characters are quirky and somewhat humorous, but while Angry Birds can be played by kids, it's suitable and challenging enough for even the most intelligent adults.

ColorNote Notepad Notes (Free)

If you typically write down reminders to yourself on scrap papers and sticky notes, and then find your pockets to be filled with papers and your desk cluttered with random notes, consider using the ColorNote Notepad Notes app, shown in Figure 15-3.

This app allows you to create multicolored sticky notes and then organize and display them on your tablet's screen. You can use this app to keep track of lists or phone messages, to brainstorm new ideas, or to organize tidbits of information. Sticky

FIGURE 15-2 Your objective is to destroy castles and structures, and ultimately, squash the green pigs.

FIGURE 15-3   The ColorNote Notepad Notes app serves as an endless supply of multicolored virtual sticky notes.

notes can be created in a checklist or freeform format, edited, saved on your tablet, viewed in a variety of formats, and ultimately shared with others via e-mail or several popular online social networking sites.

ColorNote Notepad Notes does not serve as a full-featured word processor, but it is ideal for creating notes, keeping track of deadlines, and organizing information.

DejaOffice (Free)

You already know about the Quickoffice Pro and OfficeSuite Pro apps and how they make Microsoft Office files and documents easily accessible on your Kindle Fire. DejaOffice is another work-related app that serves as a powerful customer relationship manager and contact database and also works as a feature-packed scheduling program, task list manager, file organizer, and digital notepad.

What's great about DejaOffice is that it's a powerful stand-alone app, but it can also sync data with a wide range of applications on your primary computer, including Microsoft Outlook, Lotus Notes, Sage ACT!, and GoldMine. The catch is that to use the app's data-sync capabilities with your PC-based software, you need to purchase the CompanionLink software for $49.95. Whether or not you choose to sync data with your computer, DejaOffice does allow you to manage contacts and scheduling, and more easily organize your professional relationships.

Evernote (Free)

Evernote is a feature-packed brainstorming and information management tool that allows you to document, organize, share, and process ideas and information in a way that's consistent with your existing work habits. You can create text-based notes from scratch, import content from a webpage, add digital photos, or even associate digital recordings to your personal database.

Notes can be sorted into multiple subject-specific virtual notebooks, so you can easily manage information from multiple projects at once but instantly recall information or quickly display content stored using this app. If you use the Evernote software on your PC or Mac, use the web-based Evernote app, or use the Evernote app on your smartphone, information from your database can easily be synchronized.

 To learn more about Evernote and how it can be used to sync information across multiple devices, visit www.evernote.com.

Exchange By TouchDown Key ($9.99)

You can configure almost any Post Office Protocol (POP) or Internet Message Access Protocol (IMAP) e-mail account to function with the Email app that comes preinstalled on your Kindle Fire. This includes Google Gmail, Yahoo! Mail, AOL Mail, and Microsoft Hotmail accounts. However, if you have an e-mail account through work that's administered through a Microsoft Exchange server, you'll need to utilize this third-party app in order to configure and access those e-mail accounts from your tablet.

Once it's set up, you'll be able to access your Microsoft Exchange e-mail account(s), calendars, task lists, and universal widgets. Before purchasing this app, download and install the free Exchange By TouchDown app (also available from the Amazon App Store). Once you confirm this app functions properly with your work's e-mail server, purchase and install the Exchange By TouchDown Key app to unlock and fully utilize the functionality of the Exchange app. To utilize this app, an Internet connection is required.

Fandango Movies (Free)

If you're an avid movie-goer, this app allows you to stream the latest movie previews on your tablet's screen, access current movie listings for any of more than 16,000 movie theaters nationwide, and buy your movie tickets in advance. You can also quickly figure out which movies are playing where within the next hour, plus read movie reviews from both fans and well-respected movie critics.

You can use the Fandango app (shown in Figure 15-4) for free, but a surcharge applies if you use it to purchase your movie tickets online. The app will store your preferred credit card information and favorite theaters, so movie tickets can be purchased online with a few taps on the screen.

FIGURE 15-4   The Fandango app allows you to learn all about the latest movies, view current movie listings, and prepurchase your movie tickets online, among other things.

gReader Google Reader (Free)

Use this app to follow the Really Simple Syndication (RSS) feeds of your favorite websites, download full articles that are of direct interest to you, and stay up to date on news stories that impact your life. This app makes monitoring multiple websites simultaneously as simple as reading an e-mail message, but it offers the customizability needed to ensure you're provided with only the information you want or need from your favorite websites. It can also be used to monitor online social networking accounts, like Facebook and Twitter.

Note   gReader Google Reader is fully compatible with the free Google Reader service (www.google.com/reader), but is not an official Google app. This app offers similar functionality to the Pulse app (described in Chapter 5), which comes free with your Kindle Fire.

IMO Chat/IMO Instant Messenger (Free)

If you enjoy communicating with your friends, coworkers, or family members using the real-time, text-based chat functionality offered by Skype, Facebook Chat, Google Talk, MSN, ICQ, AIM, Yahoo!, Jabber, or MySpace Chat, you can now keep those online conversations going from your Kindle Fire, as long as it's connected to the Internet.

 When you access this app from the Amazon App Store, it is listed as "IMO Instant Messenger." However, the app title when you look at the app icon and launch the app is "IMO Chat."

This app is compatible with multiple real-time online chat services and allows you to participate in multiple text-based conversations simultaneously—and for free. The app even allows you to save your conversations, so you can refer back to them anytime later or pick up where you left off after a break.

What's nice about this app is that you can make contact with your online "friends" and contacts, regardless of which instant messaging service they subscribe to, as long as you also have an account with that service. Using IMO Chat, you can be logged into multiple services simultaneously.

LinkedIn (Free)

LinkedIn (www.linkedin.com) is a free online social networking service designed specifically for business professionals and entrepreneurs. It can be used for professional networking, to find new customers or contents, to learn about job openings, and to promote yourself or your business. It's also a great reference tool. This official LinkedIn app (shown in Figure 15-5) gives you access to the majority of LinkedIn's most popular features and functions from your Kindle Fire, provided it's connected to the Internet.

MapQuest (Free)

When your Kindle Fire is connected to the Internet, you can display detailed maps, obtain driving directions between two or more points, or find specific addresses using the MapQuest app (shown in Figure 15-6), which offers much of the same functionality as the popular MapQuest.com website.

Unless your vehicle or cell phone is equipped with a mobile Wi-Fi hotspot, the MapQuest app can't be used for navigational purposes, but it can help you preplan a driving route or view a detailed map for any address or location.

Netflix (Free)

If you're a paid Netflix streaming video subscriber ($7.99 per month), you can access this service's vast collection of TV show episodes and movies, and watch them on

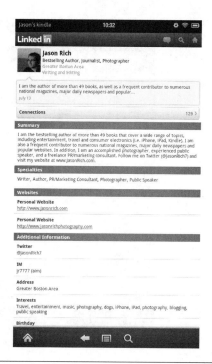

FIGURE 15-5   Access the LinkedIn online social networking service using your Kindle Fire.

an unlimited basis on your Kindle Fire. There are no pay-per-view or rental charges, but since content is streamed from the Internet to your tablet, a constant Internet connection is required.

Any movie or advertising-free TV show episode from the Netflix library can be viewed on demand. You can play, pause, fast-forward, or rewind whatever you're watching. The on-screen controls are intuitive.

 You can learn more about Netflix (www.netflix.com) and other sources for free and paid TV shows and movies you can watch from your Kindle Fire by referring back to Chapter 9.

Official eBay Android App (Free)

If you enjoy finding great deals on eBay.com, participating in online auctions, or selling goods online to earn extra money, this app allows you to shop for and/or sell items on eBay.com with ease, directly from your Kindle Fire, as long as it's connected to the Internet. You can access and manage your existing eBay account, plus access all of the features and functions that the eBay.com website offers. This content is formatted so it's easy to read and navigate through on your tablet's seven-inch screen.

FIGURE 15-6 The MapQuest app allows you to view detailed maps on your tablet's screen.

Pac-Man ($2.99)

Out of all the app categories you'll find within the Amazon App Store, the one that's the most populated and popular is the Games category. You'll discover hundreds of free and paid game apps that faithfully re-create board games, card games, casino experiences, popular video games, or classic arcade games, for example.

Pac-Man from Namco Bandai Games (shown in Figure 15-7) is a near perfect adaptation of the classic coin-op arcade game, complete with the familiar characters, graphics, music, and sound effects. You control the on-screen action using a virtual joystick that's displayed on your Kindle Fire's screen.

 Pac-Man is just one of many classic coin-op arcade games available for the Kindle Fire. At the Amazon App Store, you'll also find games like Frogger, Missile Command, Tetris, Asteroids, Dragon's Lair, and many others.

Read It Later Pro ($2.99)

As you're surfing the Internet, you may often come across articles that you're too busy to read at the moment, but that you'd like to refer back to later. Or, you may discover an article that you want to save and be able to share with colleagues and friends.

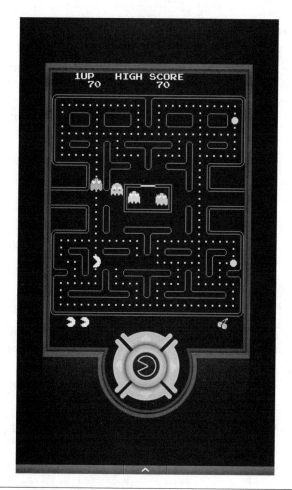

FIGURE 15-7   The classic arcade game, Pac-Man, can be played on your Kindle Fire.

The Read It Later Pro app works in conjunction with the Amazon Silk web browser, and allows you to save webpages, individual articles, photos, videos, and other content for later offline viewing.

Once you set up a Read It Later account, you can view your saved web content on your Kindle Fire, primary computer, or smartphone. The app works with more than 130 software applications and apps. After saving web content, such as an article, for offline viewing, you no longer need an Internet connection to access it because the selected content is stored on your tablet. However, using your tablet's Internet connectivity, you can share your saved web content via e-mail, Facebook, or Twitter.

Scrabble ($1.99)

In addition to adaptations of coin-op arcade games, like Pac-Man, the Amazon App Store offers a vast selection of faithful adaptations of popular and classic board games, like Scrabble, Monopoly, Life, Chess, Checkers, Uno, Backgammon, Othello, and many others. These can be experienced as one-player or multiplayer games.

This Scrabble app (shown in Figure 15-8) is exactly like the board game. However, you can play against friends via the Internet, either in real-time or using a turn-based scenario that can be extended over hours, days, or weeks. The app allows you to participate in up to 50 games at the same time. To prevent cheating, a dictionary is built into the app. Plus, if you want to brush up on your Scrabble playing skills, there's also a Teacher feature.

 If you enjoy word-based games, the Amazon App Store offers a vast selection. For example, there's Words With Friends, Wordoku, Hangman, and a handful of different crossword puzzle and word search apps.

Splashtop Remote Desktop ($0.99)

In Chapter 13, you learned all about how to transfer documents and files between your primary computer and Kindle Fire. However, using this app, there's yet another way

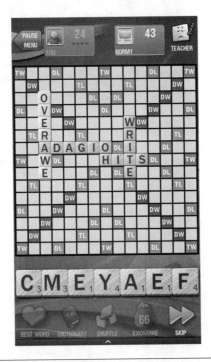

FIGURE 15-8 Play Scrabble as a one-player game against a computer-controlled opponent, or experience it against other human players.

to easily transfer files and documents via the Internet. Splashtop Remote Desktop allows you to actually access your Internet-connected desktop or laptop computer from your Kindle Fire and then access specific files or documents stored on its hard drive. This app works in conjunction with a PC or Mac, and allows you to run software remotely on your computer using your tablet.

For this software to work, the Splashtop Streamer software must be installed and running on your primary computer. This software is available for free from the Splashtop website (www.splashtop.com).

 Tip   Using this Splashtop Remote Desktop app, you can run computer-based software from your tablet without needing any other Kindle Fire apps. This app allows your PC or Mac software to be displayed on your tablet's screen as you control the software remotely.

Text+ Gold ($2.99)

Most people think that text messages and Short Message Service (SMS) messages can only be sent and received via a cell phone that's connected to a cellular network operated by a company like AT&T Wireless, Sprint PCS, or Verizon Wireless. Generally, this is true. However, the Text+ Gold app provides you with a unique texting phone number, and then allows you to send and receive text messages from your Kindle Fire, as long as it's connected to the Internet.

One nice feature of Text+ Gold is that you can send and receive an unlimited number of texts without incurring any fees whatsoever. Once you register with the service, you're provided with a unique phone number to which people can address text messages to you from their cell phone or smartphone (unfortunately, your existing cell phone number cannot be used). The app also allows you to send the same text message to groups of people, or invite three or more people to participate in a group text conversation.

Just like when sending text messages via your smartphone, you can link photos, short audio recordings, or video clips to the outgoing message, or receive and view this type of multimedia content from others.

 Tip   A free, advertiser-supported version of this app is available, but to experience the app without having to view ads, you'll need to purchase the Text+ Gold edition.

TripAdvisor (Free)

Whether you're planning a business trip, family vacation, or a once-in-a-lifetime romantic getaway, the free TripAdvisor app (shown in Figure 15-9) can help you plan your trip and avoid common pitfalls. This app gives you instant access to thousands of hotel, restaurant, and attraction reviews, written by your fellow travelers, covering destinations throughout the world.

Before booking a hotel, for example, you can read reviews to discover if the hotel lives up to its reputation, or if it's poorly maintained, bedbug infested, or simply outdated.

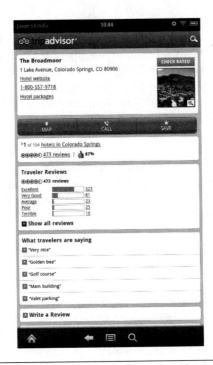

FIGURE 15-9 The TripAdvisor app is a useful research tool when planning any type of trip or vacation.

The reviews offered throughout this service are written by everyday travelers, not professional travel writers, journalists, or the marketing/advertising people who work for a specific hotel, restaurant, or attraction.

 As you'll discover when you begin reading reviews posted on TripAdvisor that have been written by ordinary travelers, the majority of the reviews are negative, since it's often bad experiences that tend to motivate people to share their thoughts. This allows you to learn from other people's experiences or mistakes. Keep in mind that the positive attributes of a hotel, restaurant, or tourist attraction, for example, may not be highlighted.

In addition to shared ratings and reviews, you'll find an abundance of destination-specific travel tips, as well as a forum for asking questions and discovering ways to save money when booking your travel. All of the information offered via this TripAdvisor app is readily available, for free, from the TripAdvisor website (www.tripadvisor.com). However, the app allows you to view the website's content in a format that's best suited for the Kindle Fire's seven-inch touch screen.

Investing just a few minutes in using this app before booking your travel or while planning your itinerary can help you avoid trip-related problems and aggravation, plus save you money. It can also help you select activities to experience, attractions to visit, and places to dine, based on your interests, budget, and time limitations.

TweetCaster Pro for Android ($4.99)

If you actively manage one or more Twitter accounts, you can access Twitter from your Kindle Fire directly via the Twitter website (www.Twitter.com). Or, you can simultaneously manage one or more accounts using the TweetCaster pro app. The paid version of this app is advertising-free, and gives you easy access to the tools you need to read incoming tweets, as well as compose and send tweets right from your tablet, as long as an Internet connection is available.

Urbanspoon (Free)

Whether you're in your home city looking for a new restaurant to experience or you're on a trip and don't know the area or what restaurants are nearby, the free Urbanspoon app offers immediate access to thousands of restaurant reviews and allows you to search for local restaurants based on a wide range of criteria, such as food type, price, location, or average rating.

Finding restaurants using the Urbanspoon app (shown in Figure 15-10) is easy. While your tablet is connected to the Internet, enter your current location. Then, select a type of food you're looking for, a price range, or opt to search for restaurants based on other criteria. Your matching results are displayed in seconds. For some participating restaurants, you can view the entire menu on your tablet's screen and then make and confirm your dining reservation online, directly from the app.

Urbanspoon's restaurant database covers dozens of cities within the United States, Canada, and Australia. One fun feature of this app is its slot machine-like interface.

Words with Friends (Free)

Joining the Angry Birds games as a worldwide phenomenon on cell phones and tablets alike is the extremely popular Words With Friends game. This game allows you to compete against other people online and showcase your vocabulary and gaming skills. This game allows you to compete against up to 20 friends at the same time in separate games. An Internet connection is required to play.

Words with Friends is somewhat similar to Scrabble, but can be played at any pace and with people you know or total strangers. The complexity of the game is determined by who your opponents are. What's nice about Words With Friends is that you can play at your leisure, for just a few minutes at a time, or you can stay entertained and challenged for hours on end.

Yahoo! Mail (Free)

As you know, the Email app comes preinstalled on your tablet and allows you to manage one or more preexisting e-mail accounts. If, however, you utilize a Yahoo! Mail account, this specialized app allows you to manage your Yahoo! Mail account and access all of the Yahoo! Mail features and functions you're already familiar with.

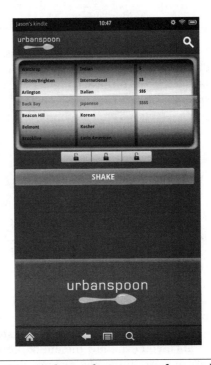

FIGURE 15-10 Find and learn about places to eat that are located within dozens of major cities throughout the United States, Canada, and Australia.

Did You Know?

You Can Perform Mobile Banking from Your Kindle Fire

Using a specialized app from your bank or financial institution, such as Chase, you can manage your checking and/or savings account, pay bills online, monitor your balances, transfer money between accounts, and more. While an Internet connection is required, your online banking transactions are secure.

In addition to online banking, you'll discover a selection of apps that can be used to manage your investments and stock portfolio(s). For example, apps from TD Ameritrade, Charles Schwab, and J.P. Morgan are available.

To find online banking or investment management apps that meet your needs and that work with your preexisting accounts, while visiting the Amazon App Store, perform a search for your bank or financial institution's name, or from the main Amazon App Store screen, tap the All Categories heading, and then select the Finance option from the Categories menu.

In addition to specific apps offered by banks and financial institutions, you'll discover non-company-specific apps for balancing your checkbook, looking up stock quotes, managing a budget, tracking expenses, or calculating costs associated with various types of loans.

A

What to Do If Something Goes Wrong with Your Kindle Fire

Amazon.com has gone to great lengths to create a tablet that's extremely powerful but also easy to use. However, the programming that went into creating the Kindle Fire's operating system, as well as the preinstalled and third-party apps available for this device, is extremely complex. Thus, you may occasionally encounter a bug or problem that is not a result of anything you did when using the tablet.

What to Do If Your Kindle Fire Won't Turn On

If your tablet refuses to power on, the rechargeable battery could be dead. Try plugging the tablet in and allowing its battery to recharge for a few minutes. With the tablet still connected to an external power source, try turning it on again. If the tablet still does not power on, hold down the power button for up to one minute to reset the device. Contact Amazon's Technical Support if these steps fail.

Did You Know?

An Internet Connection May Be Required

If the app you're using requires access to the Internet but your Kindle Fire is not connected to the Internet via a Wi-Fi connection, that app will not function properly.

In this situation, you will most likely receive an error message that says "No Internet Connection. A Wi-Fi network connection is required to complete this task. Please connect to a Wi-Fi network." At this point, find the closest Wi-Fi hotspot or get within the signal radius of a wireless network and connect your tablet to it.

Turn Your Kindle Fire Off and Back On to Solve Many Problems

Should you encounter a problem with your Kindle Fire that's not related to an Internet connection, the first thing to do is power off the device and then turn it back on. More often than not, this will fix the issue. To do this, press and hold down the power button until the "Do You Want To Shut Down Your Kindle?" message appears. Tap the Shut Down icon. Wait a few seconds, and then press the power button again to turn the tablet back on so it reboots itself. Doing this will not erase any content from your tablet, but it may fix your problem.

To reboot the device (but not erase anything), hold the power button down even after the "Do You Want To Shut Down Your Kindle?" message appears. Keep holding down the power button until the screen goes black. Wait about ten seconds, and then press the power button again to turn it back on.

Restore to Factory Defaults

You can use the Restore To Factory Defaults option offered by your Kindle Fire. However, doing this will erase all data, apps, content, documents, files, and personal settings associated with your tablet. If you choose to use this feature, follow these steps:

1. From the Home screen, tap the gear-shaped icon, and then tap the More icon.
2. Tap the Device option from the main Settings menu, and at the very bottom of the Device screen, tap the Reset To Factory Defaults option.
3. Tap the Erase Everything icon that appears to confirm your decision. Everything will default back to the original settings, as if you first purchased your Kindle Fire.
4. You will need to reactivate your Kindle Fire from scratch.

Check to See If Kindle Operating System or App Updates Are Available

If a problem persists, make sure your Kindle Fire is running the most current version of the Kindle operating system and that you're also running the latest versions of the third-party apps that are installed on your device.

Update the Kindle Fire Operating System

In most cases, when an update to the Kindle Fire operating system is made available from Amazon, the tablet will automatically download and install it when it's connected to the Internet. However, to manually check to see if an update is available, and if so, download and install it, follow these steps:

1. From the Home screen, tap the gear-shaped icon in the upper-right corner of the screen, and then tap the More option that appears.
2. From the Settings menu, tap the Device menu option.
3. About halfway down on the Device screen is a System Version setting. If the Update Your Kindle icon is highlighted, tap it to update the operating system of your device. Your tablet will need to be connected to the Internet to do this.

 Updates to the Kindle Fire's preinstalled apps are also done automatically in conjunction with a Kindle Fire operating system update.

Update Your Third-Party Apps

To ensure you're running the most recent versions of your third-party apps, follow these steps:

1. From the Home screen, tap the Apps option from the Navigation bar.
2. Tap the Store option that's displayed in the upper-right corner of the screen.
3. When the Amazon App Store is displayed, tap the Menu icon that appears near the bottom-center area of the screen.
4. Select the My Apps option.
5. Near the top of the My Apps screen, tap the Update Available option. A listing of available apps that require updates will be displayed.
6. Tap the Update icon that is associated with each app to download and install the necessary updates.

Contact Amazon's Technical Support

Amazon offers free technical support for your Kindle Fire by telephone or e-mail. Often, the technical support representative will be able to diagnose the problems and help you fix it in just a few minutes. To contact Amazon's Technical Support department by e-mail or telephone, follow these steps:

1. From your Kindle Fire's Home screen, tap the gear-shaped icon that's displayed near the top-right corner of the screen, and then select the More option.
2. From the Settings menu, tap the Help & Feedback option, which is the first option listed on the Settings menu.
3. Near the top-center area of the Help & Feedback screen, tap the Contact Customer Support tab.
4. Tap the pull-down menu that's associated with the question, "What can we help you with?" Select the type of problem you're experiencing with your Kindle Fire.

5. Tap the pull-down menu that's associated with the Select Issue Details option, and tap the most appropriate option. About halfway down on the Help & Feedback screen, you'll see two command icons associated with the "How would you like to contact us?" prompt. Tap the Email icon to send an e-mail that outlines your problem, or to speak with someone by phone, tap the Phone (Call Us) icon.

If you tap the Call Us icon, you'll be prompted to enter your phone number. Once you've done this, tap the Call Me Now or Call Me In 5 Minutes icon to continue. A technical support specialist from Amazon will call you at the designated phone number and be ready to help you solve your Kindle Fire–related problem.

 Problems related to content you purchase from Amazon.com or any of its subsidiaries should be dealt with by contacting Amazon's Technical Support department. Additional online-based help is available from Amazon.com. From the main website, select the Manage My Kindle option. Then, select the Kindle Help Home menu option that's displayed under the Kindle Support heading.

There's Plenty of Additional Help Online

In addition to Amazon, there are a handful of Kindle Fire online forums, users' groups, and blogs that offer how-to information, tutorials, app reviews, and other information of interest to Kindle Fire users. TabletTutotials.com, for example, offers a handful of highly informative and easy-to-understand step-by-step guides for performing a variety of tasks with your Kindle Fire. The Kindle Fire Forum (www.kfforum.com) and Kindle Fire Wire (www.kindlefirewire.com) are also useful resources that provide free and constantly updated information.

 If you're experiencing a problem with a specific third-party app, you may need to contact that app's developer directly. By tapping the Menu icon when an app is running, most offer a Help or Support option. You can also visit the App Store and view information about a specific app's developer from an app's Description page.

Index